FUNDAMENTALISTS
AND
EXTREMISTS

LIBRARY IN A BOOK

FUNDAMENTALISTS AND EXTREMISTS

Douglas Long

Facts On File, Inc.

Fundamentalists and Extremists

Facts On File, Inc.
132 West 31st Street
New York NY 10001

Library of Congress Cataloging-in-Publication Data
Long, Douglas (Douglas Anthony), 1967–
    Fundamentalists and extremists/Douglas Long.
      p. cm. — (Library in a book)
   ISBN 0-8160-4846-0
    1. Religious fundamentalism—United States. 2. Religion and politics—United States. 3. United States—Religion. 4. Radicalism—United States. 5. Right-wing extremists—United States. 6. United States—Politics and government. I. Title. II. Series.
  BL238 .L66 2002
  306′ .1—dc21   2002001291

CONTENTS

———————————————

PART III
APPENDICES

PART I

OVERVIEW OF THE TOPIC

CHAPTER 1

ISSUES IN FUNDAMENTALISM AND EXTREMISM

INTRODUCTION

Fundamentalism and extremism are closely related phenomena that nevertheless have their own distinct origins and histories. Fundamentalism is a belief in the literal interpretation of holy writings, while extremism is a political philosophy that deviates drastically from mainstream views. Both are characterized by intolerance to opposing points of view, which often leads adherents to exhibit fanatical behavior and use violent means to achieve their ends. These goals usually include challenges to the basic tenets of the secular, liberal, and democratic philosophies upon which North American politics and culture are based. However, a democratic society, by definition, must include provisions for groups and individuals with differing points of view to operate within the system. This struggle to maintain the integrity of mainstream democracy while protecting the rights of those who could undermine democratic authority is an ongoing conflict that has been instrumental in defining the political, legislative, and cultural geographies of the United States.

FUNDAMENTALISM

The term *fundamentalism* originated in the United States during the early decades of the 20th century and referred to a variant of Protestant Christianity that emerged in opposition to the ideas of Charles Darwin, whose theories of evolution were thought to contradict the biblical account of creation detailed in Genesis, and the teachings of the Higher Critics, a group of historians and writers who concluded that the Bible was written by

3

unknown authors and was full of contradictions. Presently *fundamentalism's* use has broadened to refer to antimodernist movements in other religions as well, including Judaism, Hinduism, Buddhism, and Islam.

Fundamentalism is characterized by the search for a purer, simpler, and more authentic form of religion. Fundamentalists are not interested in democracy, pluralism, religious toleration, free speech, or separation of church and state. Rather, they see these tendencies as symptoms of modernity, which is thought to threaten the very survival of religion. Because of this "crisis" mentality, fundamentalists think of themselves as being engaged in a cosmic battle between good (themselves) and evil (secularists). In order to survive, they use holy scripture to create an ideology that provides the faithful with a plan of action, a means to fight back and attempt to resacralize an increasingly atheistic world.[1] In the United States, the general goal of fundamentalists is to recover the "spirit and truth" of the apostolic age of Christianity, a quest firmly rooted in the Protestant Reformation.[2]

THE PROTESTANT REFORMATION

The Protestant Reformation, which occurred in Europe during the 16th century, was a rebellion against the Catholic Church and its religious rituals and practices. On October 31, 1517, theology professor Martin Luther posted his Ninety-Five Theses on the door of the castle church at Wittenberg, in Germany. The document symbolized his attempt to reform the Catholic Church from within by opening a debate on matters of practice and doctrine. Luther's religious creed was based on the principle of accessibility, a "Priesthood of All Believers" in which there was no need for priests to mediate between the individual and God. Contemporaneous translations of the Bible into common language had allowed individuals to read the word of God directly and supply their own interpretation.

At the center of the Reformation's theological doctrine were the *solas: sola scriptura* (the Bible as the sole and infallible source of faith and practice), *solo Christo* (Christ alone as the mediator between God and the individual), and the twin principles of *sola gratia* and *sola fide* (salvation only by the divine initiative of grace as received through God's gift of faith). These ideas, which continue to influence the thought of Protestant theologians, are taken to their extremes by Christian fundamentalists.

The Protestant premise that the Bible was open to interpretation by all individuals resulted in the emergence of a large number of sects with differing points of view. One of these was led by John Calvin, who agreed with Luther on most points but also believed in the doctrine of predestination (which stated that God had already determined who was to be saved), the necessary austerity of the life of the godly, and an emphasis on theocratic government. Calvinism rapidly grew in influence, superseding Lutheranism in some areas of Europe. The Puritans who sailed from England to North America during the early 17th century were also Calvinists, and these doctrines became the basis of religious life in the English-speaking New World.

THE PURITANS

The Puritans were religious separatists who fled to America to escape persecution at the hands of the Anglican Church of England, which believed that the Calvinist doctrine of predestination was not conducive to social stability.

Immigration to New England occurred in stages, the first settlers being the 102 Pilgrims who in 1620 sailed to Plymouth aboard the *Mayflower*. In 1630, a group of Puritans led by John Winthrop founded the Massachusetts Bay Colony, whose religious system remained closely aligned with that of Calvinists who had elected to remain in England. The Puritans, less interested in debating the finer points of theology than in applying their beliefs directly to society in order to build a strong, righteous community, took their Calvinism extremely seriously. There was no tolerance for opposing points of view; dissenters were banished rather than accommodated. One of the primary roles of government was to enforce a rigid moral code by prohibiting such vices as drunkenness, gambling, swearing, and Sabbath breaking. Their model in all regards was the Bible, which they believed represented the definitive word of God.

The Puritans saw themselves as having a covenant with God, the breaking of which would have dire consequences for the community. This belief manifested itself most strikingly in the Puritan allegiance to Providentialism, the idea that God's intentions were communicated through signs and omens. An earthquake would therefore be interpreted as a warning or punishment from God, and the outbreak of war might be preceded by reports of visions of angelic armies in the sky. Rather than being remote, God constantly reached into the human realm to punish the wicked and help the righteous destroy their enemies.

Providentialism helped the settlers deal with harsh conditions by imposing order on the otherwise unfathomable wilderness that surrounded them. It also had its negative consequences, one of which was the Salem witch trials of 1692. Ascribing odd behavior to witchcraft was not unusual at the time, and the publication of Cotton Mather's *Memorable Providences, Relating to Witchcraft and Possessions* just three years before helped raise suspicions that led to the execution of 20 people and two dogs.

Despite this fanaticism, the cultural structures of Massachusetts had begun slipping out of Puritan control by the time of the witch trials.

Calvinist doctrine now shared the pulpit with the cultural imperatives of the Enlightenment that came out of England, leading to a religion of balance and order that downplayed reliance on Providence. Ministers walked a fine line between religion and the new scientific disciplines, which were seen as affirming the order of God's creation even as they offered logical explanations for phenomena previously thought to be supernatural. In 1702, Mather published his history of the Puritans, *Magnalia Christi Americana*, the last important document written in support of the Providential tradition.

THE GREAT AWAKENING

Puritanism lay dormant, as the early 18th century saw the continued decline of religion as a vital force in colonial America, but tense social circumstances in the 1730s set the stage for a spiritual revival. These included the start of a war between Britain and Spain in 1739, a shortage of money in the colonies, and severe outbreaks of disease in New York and New England.

One generation later, public discontent fostered by such tensions would result in the American Revolution, but during the 1730s many colonials turned to religion for salvation. This new spirituality combined the familiar righteous confidence of Puritanism with the tradition of Pietism to give birth to North American evangelicalism.

Pietism was a European-born form of Protestantism that preached rebellion against religious hierarchy and pretensions, while simultaneously emphasizing spiritual discipline and emotion. Although Puritanism and Pietism were allied in their insistence on a personal and introspective form of Christianity, the Great Awakening was characterized by the replacement of Puritanical logic with Pietistic emotion. Religion, as a rebellion against the clerical establishment, was transformed into a theology of the people that urged followers to participate in their salvation through mystical introspection and spiritual rebirth.

One of the Great Awakening's early proponents was Jonathan Edwards, a Northampton, Massachusetts, minister who attempted to revive Puritan idealism decades after it had lost influence to science and secularism. In 1734, he preached his sermon "Justification by Faith Alone," which recalled the 17th-century Calvinism of Puritan ministers and led to a spiritual awakening in Northampton and neighboring towns. Edwards warned listeners that they were sinners destined for eternal damnation unless God granted them rebirth, a state achieved through an emotional, entirely subjective experience. Like Puritans, the converted were exhorted to live a life of austerity; unlike Puritans, they were also expected to display their newfound purity externally rather than merely internally.

The ideas of Edwards and others were brought together to form the Great Awakening by George Whitefield, a Methodist preacher who toured the colonies from 1739 to 1741. Barred from established churches whose ministers felt threatened by his itinerancy and his populist leanings, Whitefield turned to open-air preaching, a tactic that served to divide local churches into evangelical and antievangelical camps and to accelerate the American tendency toward sectarianism.

Dissenters and provincials appreciated Whitefield's unscripted delivery, which emphasized emotions over stilted theology. The minister stressed that God was working to establish his millennial kingdom on earth and judgment of the unconverted was imminent. Only instant repentance and the experience of being "born again" could assure one a place in this heavenly scheme.

After Whitefield returned to England, evangelical pastors who followed his lead concentrated on the rural areas of the colonies. By 1745, however, the Great Awakening had passed its peak. Despite its short life, the Great Awakening had long-lasting effects. Evangelical Christianity has, to this day, retained the movement's emphasis on the born-again experience, the importance of preaching to promote this conversion, the unambiguous distinction between the saved and the unsaved, and emotion over cold intellectualism. It marked the return of an ever present God and sparked an increase in sectarianism, which assured that anyone who had an unorthodox religious vision could split off from their church and form a new one.

ROOTS OF AMERICAN FUNDAMENTALISM

Evangelicalism gained momentum at the beginning of the 19th century with the Second Great Awakening, also known as the Great Revival. Whereas the Great Awakening was rooted in Calvinistic thought, the Great Revival signaled the rise of the Arminian strain of Protestantism. Arminians believed that sinners no longer had to rely on God to initiate salvation, but rather that the individual was capable of making a conscious choice between salvation and damnation. This incorporation of self-determination into religious belief may have been a result of the recent Revolutionary War, during which the colonials had taken their political destiny into their own hands.

With this new sense of freedom, evangelicals instilled their sermons with the language of individualism, equality for all, and optimism. They also keyed to the familiar Puritan rhetoric about a special covenant between God and the United States, a special status that had been reinforced by the success of the Revolution.

By the 1860s, however, the Civil War had dealt this optimism a harsh blow. In the latter half of the 19th century, many Americans also felt threatened by rapid industrialization and urbanization, as well as the influx of non-Protestant immigrants. Meanwhile, evangelicals felt pressure to defend themselves against new intellectual currents inaugurated by Charles Darwin's 1859 *On the Origin of Species*, which questioned the Bible's account of creation and thus the literal truth of the Bible as a whole. Another school of thought from Germany called Higher Criticism questioned the historical validity of the Bible, thereby undermining the basis of evangelical Christian belief.

One response to this pessimism was a shift from postmillennial to dispensational premillennial thought. Postmillennialism hinged on the belief that God was working to improve American society, culminating in 1,000 years of peace and prosperity on earth. After this, Christ would return and begin his eternal reign. Dispensational premillennialism, articulated by England's John Nelson Darby, maintained that the history of the world could be divided into seven dispensations, or historical epochs, and that humans had reached "the age of the church." This particular dispensation immediately preceded the Rapture (during which all Christians would instantly be taken up to heaven), the Tribulation (a seven-year period during which the Antichrist would make life miserable for those left behind), and the thousand-year reign of God. In other words, the United States was hopelessly corrupt and sliding toward judgment day. Dispensational premillennialism caused many evangelicals to distance themselves from the corrupt society they saw all around them, fostering an "us-versus-them" mentality.

In the early 20th century, the widespread use of the term *fundamentalism* resulted from the appearance of a series of pamphlets between 1910 and 1915 called *The Fundamentals; or, Testimony to the Truth*. These pamphlets marked a radical reaction by conservative Christians against the tide of cultural pluralism, modernism, and liberal theology. They attempted to revive a purer, simpler version of Christianity that drew from the theological traditions of the Reformation, Puritanism, and the two Great Awakenings.[3] The "fundamentals" of true religion were declared to center on the belief that the Bible is the literal, inerrant word of God, providing a design for a living and historical record that could not be questioned. Miracles were assumed to be real, and the Rapture was an actual future event that could occur at any moment. Fundamentalists declared all contrary belief systems—religious, scientific, or otherwise—to be illegitimate.

The pamphlets had little impact until the horror of World War I confirmed the premillennialists' convictions that the world was sliding toward apocalypse. Despite their pessimistic worldview, many fundamentalists reacted by becoming involved in social issues. In 1920, Curtis Lee Laws defined fundamentalists as those ready "to do battle royal for the fundamentals of the faith." William Jennings Bryan launched a crusade against teaching Darwinism in school that pushed evolution to the forefront of the fundamentalist agenda. Antievolution laws were subsequently introduced in the state legislatures of Florida, Mississippi, Louisiana, Arkansas, and Tennessee.

THE SCOPES TRIAL

Tennessee's law prohibiting the teaching of evolution in public school was challenged by John T. Scopes, a biology teacher who covered Darwin's theories in his classes. The ensuing trial, which occurred July 10 to 21, 1925, pitted two revered lawyers against each other, pushing the case into the national spotlight and transforming it into a battle of Darwin versus the Bible, of modernism versus fundamentalism. William Jennings Bryan volunteered to work as counsel for the attorney general of Tennessee, while Clarence Darrow, a well-known agnostic who had been involved in a number of high-profile cases during his career, volunteered his services to Scopes and the defense.

Despite the fact that the jury ruled against Scopes after just nine minutes of deliberation (he had, after all, broken the law by teaching evolution), Darrow emerged as the hero of clear, rational thought. Bryan, on the other hand, was discredited as incompetent. During the trial, Darrow had forced Bryan to contradict himself on his own fundamentalist beliefs and admit that the Bible could not be taken literally. As a result, public opinion swayed from religion toward scientific reason, and liberals gained control of the major Protestant denominations for years afterward.

RETRENCHING

Fundamentalists responded to their public-image defeat in the Scopes trial by abandoning politics and mainstream culture. Convinced that the emerging modernist worldview signaled the downfall of secular thought and the imminent return of Christ, they concentrated, from the 1930s through the 1960s, on establishing a subculture of independent churches, religious radio and television stations evangelistic youth organizations, and training schools, such as the Dallas Theological Seminary and the Bob Jones University.

In 1941, Carl McIntire founded the American Council of Christian Churches (ACCC) to oversee the independent church movement. The following year, moderate fundamentalists formed the rival National Association of Evangelicals (NAE). Both organizations agreed that the Bible constituted the literal word of God and adhered to the doctrine of dispensational premillennialism, but a divide developed over tactics. While the ACCC represented the separatism and retreat from the secular world, the

NAE began debating social problems and public policies, making occasional forays into conservative politics. Referring to themselves as "evangelicals" rather than "fundamentalists," NAE members saw their primary goal as saving souls, which demanded cooperation with other Christians and interaction with non-Christians. Despite their disagreements, the ACCC and NAE constituted the dual alignment of conservative Protestantism for the next three decades.[4]

During the 1950s, the NAE began passing political resolutions at its national conventions, mostly centered on combating communism. The most well-known evangelist to convey a patriotic, anticommunist message was Billy Graham, who allied himself with political conservatism during the 1950s by visiting President Harry Truman in the White House and serving as the religious consultant for Dwight D. Eisenhower's presidential inauguration ceremony. In 1960, Graham met a group of evangelical leaders in Montreux, Switzerland, to figure out how to defeat John F. Kennedy's bid for president of the United States. Part of the emergent strategy involved advising Kennedy's opponent, Richard M. Nixon, behind the scenes and promoting the impression that Kennedy represented a dangerous intrusion by the Roman Catholic Church into American politics.[5] Graham, however, grew uncomfortable with the growing anti-Catholic rhetoric and eventually backed away from involvement in the political campaign. The evangelist had previously displayed a similar level of conscientiousness when, during the 1950s, he urged Baptist colleges to accept academically qualified black students, desegregated his crusades, and published an articles in *Life* magazine claiming that racism could not be justified from the Bible. At the time, such views were extremely unpopular among conservative Christians.

Many evangelicals supported the ultimately unsuccessful presidential campaign of Republican Barry Goldwater in 1964, primarily because he advocated a constitutional amendment to override the bans on school prayer and Bible reading instituted by the U.S. Supreme Court in 1962 and 1963. The decisions were viewed by critics as a declaration of war against Christianity and were often cited in later years as a major cause of the breakdown of moral values in society.

These forays by evangelicals into politics during the 1950s and 1960s had little impact on the American political landscape, since they lacked the organization and concentrated mobilization that would characterize the rise of the Christian Right during the 1980s. Ironically, on the eve of fundamentalism's return to the political realm, Graham removed himself from his long-standing affiliation with presidents after close friend Richard Nixon became involved in the Watergate scandal.

Graham, along with Oral Roberts, also pioneered the use of television for evangelism during the 1940s and 1950s. The next generation of televangelists, which included Pat Robertson and Jimmy Swaggart, mixed fundamentalism with Pentecostalism, characterized by faith healing and speaking in tongues. Television allowed the conservative Christian movement to eventually emerge as the great national opposition to the forces of change, enabling them to reach more people, more often, at lower costs.[6] During the 1970s and 1980s, religious broadcasting, both on television and radio, became the single most important resource in the mobilization of the Christian Right.

SOCIAL AND POLITICAL ACTIVISM

Fundamentalists, who began to reevaluate their apolitical stance as a result of the Supreme Court's banning of state-sponsored religious practices, completed their turnaround during the mid- to late 1970s in the wake of the Court's 1973 *Roe v. Wade* decision, which made abortion on demand legal. Widespread anger at the ruling returned many fundamentalists to the evangelical point of view that social issues should be confronted.

This new hybrid, christened "born-again" Christianity, consisted of people who believed in dispensational premillennialism and spoke in terms of end-time scenarios, for example, God was angry at the United States for abandoning biblical morality, and AIDS (acquired immunodeficiency syndrome) and terrorism were divine retribution, while extraordinary political events that favored the nation were miracles. This tendency to see world events as the reflection of God's will hearkened back to the Puritanical belief in Providence.

The most radical contingent of the Christian Right is reconstructionism, also called dominion theology. Unlike fundamentalists, reconstructionists are postmillennialists who believe that Christ will not return until his kingdom is established on earth; therefore, they are dedicated to installing a national government based on biblical law instead of democratic principles in which heretics, abortionists, homosexuals, and even disobedient children would be subject to the death penalty. Despite its radicalism, reconstructionism provides fundamentalists with an excuse to get involved in politics. The movement's founder, John Rousas Rushdoony, has appeared on Pat Robertson's *700 Club* television program, and his books have been endorsed by Jerry Falwell.

Issues

During the 1970s, fundamentalist activism began to congeal around the vague notion of "family values," which grew out of Phyllis Schlafly's 10-year fight against the Equal Rights Amendment (ERA). In 1972, Schlafly founded the Eagle Forum to derail the ERA, which she believed would grant legal sanction to homosexual marriages and make it impossible to overturn *Roe v. Wade*. After the ERA was defeated in 1982, the growing pro-family movement continued to focus its attention on the perceived degeneration of social mores. Among the organizations that have promoted a particularly conservative, born-again Christian view of the family is Promise Keepers, founded by University of Colorado football coach Bill McCartney and Fellowship of Christian Athletes director Dave Wardell. The first official Promise Keepers rally in July 1991 attracted 4,200 men. By 1996, at the height of the organization's popularity, stadium rallies in 22 cities across the United States were attended by a total of more than 1 million men. (Women, though allowed to play support roles behind the scenes, are not allowed to attend the rallies.) At these gatherings, men pray and weep while listening to speakers who promote a strongly patriarchal vision of family in which fathers are urged to exercise, in a compassionate manner, the authority over their wives and children that God has ordained for them. The primary role of women, they are told, is to nurture, guide, and care for their offspring.

An equally elastic concept is "secular humanism," which replaced communism as the main ideological enemy of fundamentalists during the 1990s. Secular humanists were accused of abandoning God's absolute standards of right and wrong, replacing them with a human-centered system of "moral relativism" in which the concepts of good and evil were impossible to define. Some fundamentalists even claimed that secular humanism was a conspiracy whose goal was to lure children into immorality and atheism, thereby undermining America's moral and spiritual foundations. Others saw secular humanism as a rival religion that should be banned from public schools in the same manner that Christianity had been.

Just as *family values* became a generic term to encompass anything fundamentalists support, *secular humanism* is used to demonize any idea that fundamentalists oppose. According to conservative Christians, among the more heinous products of secular humanism, thus constituting the greatest threats to family values, are homosexuality, public education, and abortion.

Antigay Agenda   Among early antigay activists was popular singer Anita Bryant, who in 1977 led a successful campaign to overturn the inclusion of homosexuals in local antidiscrimination laws in Miami–Dade County, Florida. During the 1980s and 1990s, it became common practice for the Christian Right to fight progay laws at the local level, often portraying efforts to secure equal rights for gays as a bid for "special rights" that would have given them privileges other Americans did not have. In 1988, Colorado voters approved Amendment 2, which sought to ban gay rights legislation in the state before it was even introduced. The amendment was later ruled unconstitutional.[7]

Perhaps the most vehement antigay activist presently is Reverend Fred Phelps, pastor of Westboro Baptist Church in Kansas. Phelps and his followers picket the funerals of gay people, carrying signs with such slogans as "Thank God for AIDS."[8] Although Phelps's actions are widely denounced by more mainstream Christian Right groups, several fundamentalist ministers have pointed to the AIDS tragedy as evidence that God is angry with homosexuals. Gay rights activists claim that such accusations heighten antigay sentiment and promote such atrocities as the October 1998 murder of gay college student Matthew Shepard, who was savagely beaten, tied to a fence along a deserted road in Wyoming, and left to die.

In 1996, Christian Right leaders formed the National Pro-Family Forum (NPFF), whose goal was to develop a strategy to combat America's increasing tolerance of homosexuality. The group drafted the Defense of Marriage Act (DOMA), which defined marriage as the union of a man and a woman. President Bill Clinton signed the act into federal law in January 1998. Later that year, the NPFF ran advertisements in national newspapers claiming that homosexuals can walk "out of homosexuality into sexual celibacy or even marriage." This was not a new strategy. Other fundamentalists had previously published material presenting gays as diseased victims ripe for healing by Christian counselors through a process known as "homosexual conversion therapy."[9]

The conversion movement began around 1974 in Anaheim, California, by a group of people who believed that gays could became straight through Christian-based therapy. This practice was criticized by mainstream psychiatrists, and in 1974 the American Psychiatric Association declared that homosexuality was not a disease that could be cured. Many homosexuals reported suffering depression and anxiety after trying to change their sexual orientation, giving rise to an exodus from conversion therapy groups that became known as the "ex-ex gay" movement.[10]

Education Fundamentalists believe that Supreme Court decisions banning prayer in public schools have turned these institutions into bastions of state-sponsored wickedness, which has plunged the United States into national sin. Pat Robertson even blamed the Supreme Court for the 1999 Littleton, Colorado, school massacre during which Eric Harris and Dylan Klebold shot and killed 12 students and a teacher before killing themselves.[11]

Many fundamentalists counsel the wholesale abandonment of public schools, strongly supporting homeschooling and pushing for school voucher plans that would include private sectarian schools. Both would allow parents to insulate their children in a world in which religious beliefs, patriotic sentiments, and conservative behavioral patterns are reinforced rather than challenged.

Fundamentalists and Extremists

Not all fundamentalists favor abandoning public schools. Many advocate Christian-oriented reforms, such as reinstating compulsory state prayer and monitoring school curricula for secular humanism. The concerns that conservative parents have about what their children are taught in school are legitimate, but these conservatives' activism is often extended to include the children of parents who may not share their fundamentalist ideologies.

The precedent for such tactics was set in 1974 in Kanawha County, West Virginia. Local parents and fundamentalist ministers, led by school board member Alice Moore, protested against "moral relativity" in books adopted for the district's language arts program. During the course of the debate, people on both sides of the issue resorted to violence: Schools were dynamited, firebombed, and vandalized; school buses were shot at; and Moore was threatened by anonymous phone calls. One preacher stated, "I am asking Christian people to pray that God will kill the giants [the three board members who voted for the books] who have mocked and made fun of dumb fundamentalists."[12] In the end, all the contested books were approved, but many were never used in schools where opposition was the strongest.

During the early 1990s, the Christian Coalition and other groups used grassroots tactics to get like-minded people elected to local school boards, where they could influence the choice of schoolbooks. Many of those elected were accused of not mentioning any organizational or ideological alliances before or during elections. Once in office, where their fundamentalist agendas were revealed, most were quickly ousted from their positions.

Abortion The strongest immediate opposition to the Supreme Court's 1973 *Roe v. Wade* decision came from Catholic organizations such as the National Conference of Catholic Bishops and the National Right to Life Committee, which backed a constitutional amendment to ban abortion. Protestant fundamentalists did not join in the movement until several years later, when ending abortion on demand became a central point of their agenda.

The most well-known antiabortion direct-action group was Operation Rescue (OR), founded in 1987 by Randall Terry, which sought to limit access to clinics by blocking their doors. Members were required to sign pledges of nonviolence and often compared themselves to civil rights activists. The organization debuted in May 1988 with one week of clinic blockades in New York City. Later that summer, hundreds of OR activists were arrested during protests at the Democratic National Convention in Atlanta, Georgia. In 1991, OR targeted Wichita, Kansas, for a week-long siege of abortion clinics they called Summer of Mercy.

In 1994, OR's tactics were rendered ineffective by a series of court decisions and legal moves. In *Madsen v. Women's Health Center*, the Supreme

14

Court sustained a lower court ruling barring antiabortionists from demonstrating within 36 feet of a clinic. Congress also passed the Freedom of Access to Clinic Entrances Act (FACE), which made obstructing access to clinics a crime punishable by six months in prison and up to $10,000 in fines. Finally, a Texas jury ordered OR to pay more than $1 million in punitive damages to a Houston Planned Parenthood clinic targeted by protesters during the 1992 Republican National Convention.

Antiabortionists typically regard unborn fetuses at any stage of development as a human beings with all the rights of a citizen. Because God creates each child, abortion is murder, and murder is sin. This view has led some fundamentalists to advocate violence as a means to ending abortion. Some 2,000 acts of violence—including bombings, arsons, kidnappings, assaults, and even murders—were carried out by antiabortion groups during the 1980s and 1990s. Seven abortion providers were murdered between 1992 and 2001. In 1993, about two dozen people signed Paul Hill's Defensive Action statement, which declared that killing abortion doctors was justified.[13] In July of the following year, Hill killed an abortion doctor and his bodyguard in Florida.

The American Coalition of Life Activists (ACLA), meanwhile, collected evidence against abortionists to be used in future "crimes against humanity" trials. The Army of God published a manual entitled *When Life Hurts, We Can Help* in the early 1990s that showed how to build bombs and place them at abortion clinics.[14] During the bioterrorism scares that followed the September 11, 2001, terrorist attacks in New York City and Washington, D.C., hundreds of family-planning clinics received packages containing white powder and the threat "This contains anthrax. You're going to die." They were signed by the Army of God. None of the packages, however, tested positive for anthrax or other toxic substances.[15] The primary suspect, fugitive Clayton Lee Waagner, was arrested on December 5, 2001, after eluding the FBI for nearly a year on firearms charges.

In March 2001, an appeals court reversed a jury verdict that had awarded doctors $107 million from antiabortion activists who had posted "wanted" posters listing abortion doctors' names and addresses on the Internet. The court ruled that the site was protected by the First Amendment because it did not threaten direct violence. The web site, which had been shut down following the initial verdict in favor of the doctors, was up and running again within hours of the reversal.[16]

Politics and Elections

The 1976 presidential election marked the Christian Right's first serious attempt to play a role in electoral politics. Fundamentalists initially supported born-again candidate Jimmy Carter, despite his pro-choice position, his belief that homosexuals should not be discriminated against, and his support of the Equal Rights Amendment. Many were scandalized, however, when in an interview with *Playboy* magazine, Carter admitted that he had "looked on a lot of women with lust. I've committed adultery in my heart many times."[17] The few fundamentalists who stuck by Carter later abandoned him when he attempted to deny tax-exempt status to private schools that were still segregated.

The growing fundamentalist opposition to Carter as candidate and as president prompted conservative Christians to begin mobilizing like-minded voters on a massive scale in 1979, eventually resulting in the organizational apparatus that helped elect Ronald Reagan to the presidency.[18]

The Moral Majority and the Reagan Years In 1979, Paul Weyrich, Richard Viguerie, Ed McAteer, and Robert Billings persuaded evangelist Jerry Falwell to use his Thomas Road Baptist Church weekly television broadcast and large network of clergy contacts to influence the 1980 Republican platform in favor of fundamentalism. The resulting organization, the Moral Majority, registered as a nonprofit, non-tax-exempt corporation in order to be eligible to lobby and engage in electoral campaigning.[19] Falwell characterized the organization as "pro-life, pro-family, pro-moral, and pro-American." The Moral Majority's primary enemies were pornography, homosexuality, advocacy of immorality in school textbooks, abortion, divorce, and secular humanism.[20]

The Moral Majority set aside fundamentalist separatism to seek the support of like-minded Catholics, Pentecostals, Mormons, and Jews; however Falwell's radical belief that government policy must be dictated by the Bible ensured that the Moral Majority never gained much support beyond conservative Protestants. It did, nonetheless, form the core of the Christian Right throughout the 1980s, lending its support to Reagan and other conservative Republicans.

In 1980, the Republican Party, recognizing the growing power of fundamentalist Christians, dropped its earlier support of the Equal Rights Amendment and came out in favor of a constitutional amendment to outlaw abortion. In August, presidential candidate Reagan told a room full of Christian Right leaders in Dallas, "You can't endorse me, but I endorse you," sweeping away any doubts fundamentalists may have had about supporting Reagan. Although his huge margin of victory over Carter most likely would have allowed him to win without Christian support, fundamentalists played an important role in the election and convinced many voters to take him seriously.[21]

Reagan followed through on a few of his promises to conservative Christian supporters. In May 1982, he recommended that Congress pass a prayer amendment with the clauses "Nothing in this Constitution shall be construed to prohibit individual or group prayer in public school" and "No person shall be required by the United States to pray." Senate support was 11 votes short of the two-thirds majority needed.[22]

Fundamentalists were also pleased when Reagan appointed Dr. C. Everett Koop, an evangelical antiabortion advocate, to the post of surgeon general. Disappointment followed when Koop not only kept his promise not to use his post to campaign against abortion but also released a report on the AIDS crisis on October 22, 1986, that counseled people determined to have extramarital sex to use condoms and recommended that children should begin sex education as early as third grade. Both strategies were vehemently opposed by members of the Christian Right, many of whom saw AIDS as the wrath of God against homosexuals. Falwell thought that quarantining people with AIDS was no more unreasonable than quarantining diseased cows.[23] At one point he sent out fund-raising letters alleging that homosexuals "have expressed the attitude that they know they are going to die and they are going to take as many people with them as they can."[24]

Disillusionment with Reagan grew when he nominated Sandra Day O'-Connor, a pro-choice judge who had supported the ERA, to the Supreme Court. Fundamentalists looked to ultraconservatives such as Senators Jesse Helms and Orrin Hatch to represent the Christian Right in politics.

Although the Moral Majority played a role in blocking the ERA during the early 1980s, it otherwise failed to change legislation on either the state or federal level.[25] By the end of the 1980s, public opinion polls showed that most people had negative views of the Moral Majority. Much of this resulted from the extremist, antidemocratic agenda of the Christian Right, but part of the blame also lay with Falwell, whose integrity was repeatedly questioned by mainstream politicians and journalists. For example, contrary to Falwell's claims that his Thomas Road Baptist Church had welcomed African Americans during the early to mid-1960s, the first black family to attend his church was not until around 1970; in fact, Falwell had spent most of the 1960s preaching prosegregation sermons and attacking Martin Luther King, Jr. In 1980, Falwell claimed that during a White House breakfast with Carter, the president had admitted that he had homosexuals on his senior staff. When an audiotape revealed that Carter had said nothing of the sort, Falwell attempted to whitewash his lie by characterizing it as a "parable" or an "allegory."[26] With contributions to his television show and university declining, Falwell disbanded the Moral Majority during the summer of 1989.

Pat Robertson's Presidential Campaign   In 1988, televangelist Pat Robertson made a bid for the Republican Party's presidential nomination. He surprised many people with his strong showings in early primaries: In

17

Iowa, he finished second to Bob Dole and defeated both George H. W. Bush and Jack Kemp. He also came in first or second in Hawaii, Nevada, Alaska, Minnesota, and South Dakota.

Robertson's run was derailed just before Super Tuesday (a collection of primary elections held on March 9, 1988, that included key southern states, as well as Oklahoma, Missouri, and Texas) when the story broke that popular televangelist Jimmy Swaggart had been photographed outside a New Orleans, Louisiana, hotel with a prostitute. This followed evangelist Oral Roberts's widely ridiculed claim that God would "call him home" if he did not raise $8 million to save the medical school of Oral Roberts University and televangelist Jim Bakker's confession that he had paid church secretary Jessica Hahn $265,000 to keep quiet about their affair. Bakker, who ran the Praise the Lord (PTL) network and the Heritage USA Christian theme park with his wife, Tammy Faye, later faced an Internal Revenue Service investigation that led to the revocation of the PTL's nonprofit status and a lawsuit for $56 million in back taxes. In 1989, he was convicted on 24 counts of broadcast fraud, mail fraud, and conspiracy. Initially sentenced to 45 years in prison, Bakker had his sentence reduced to eight years on appeal. Tammy Faye divorced him two years after conviction.

How much these scandals affected Robertson's campaign is unclear. In the end, Bush gained the Republican Party's nomination; 80 percent of fundamentalist voters backed him during the election, even though he was never as popular among conservative Christians as Reagan.

The Christian Coalition and the Clinton Years In 1989, Robertson transformed his 1988 campaign apparatus into a new organization called the Christian Coalition. He hired former College Republicans organizer Ralph Reed to act as executive director.

The group took a central role in the Christian Right's efforts to dismantle the National Endowment for the Arts (NEA). Fundamentalists accused the NEA of supporting "taxpayer-funded pornography" that offended their sense of traditional family values. Despite representing a minority of funded works, artist Andres Serrano's "Piss Christ" (a photograph of a crucifix immersed in urine) and Robert Mapplethorpe's homosexually explicit photos were used by the Christian Coalition to force Congress to impose an "indecency" restriction on NEA grant applicants. This was later ruled unconstitutional, but Robertson's organization had succeeded in slashing the art agency's budget.[27]

By the fall of 1991, the Christian Coalition boasted 82,000 members. Reed focused on grassroots political campaigns that allowed Christian Right candidates to take seats on local school boards and city councils. Opponents criticized the candidates' failure to disclose their affiliations before the elections.

Reed characterized his tactics by saying, "I do guerilla warfare. I paint my face and travel at night. You don't know it's over until you're in a body bag. You don't know till election night."[28] The widespread negative reaction caused Reed to later suggest that conservative Christians replace military metaphors with sports jargon in speeches and press releases.

The 1992 Republican National Convention was heavily influenced by the Christian Right. Pat Buchanan spoke, claiming, "There is a religious war going on in this country. . . . This war is for the soul of America. And in that struggle for the soul of America, [Bill] Clinton and [Hilary] Clinton are on the other side, and George Bush is on our side."[29] Fundamentalists may have been pleased by this hard-line approach, but middle-of-the-road voters responded by sending Democrat Bill Clinton to the White House. After the election, Reed published "Casting a Wider Net," an article in which he urged the Christian Right to broaden its base by adding issues related to taxes, college scholarships, and higher wages to its moral agenda.

As part of the conservative backlash against Clinton's election, membership in the Christian Coalition more than doubled in 1993. In 1994, the organization focused on lobbying against Clinton's health care reform legislation and producing 50 million voter guides, which helped bring the Republican Party to power in both houses of Congress.

Despite these successes, the seeds of trouble for the Christian Coalition were sown in 1997. On June 11, Robertson announced his departure as chief executive officer (CEO) of the organization, although he would remain president and retain many of his decision-making powers. He was succeeded by Don Hodel as CEO. On June 16, one-term conservative congressman Randy Tate replaced Reed as executive director. Reed had resigned and started Century Strategies, an Atlanta-based political consulting firm.

In January 1997, a story broke concerning a possible affair between Clinton and White House intern Monica Lewinsky. The Christian Coalition was slow to turn the story into a major issue. Between January 21, when the story first appeared, and August 17, when Clinton admitted his "inappropriate relationship," Christian Coalition literature made no mention of the affair. But after the question of impeachment came up, the organization quickly pushed the scandal to the forefront of its agenda.[30]

Fundamentalists held high hopes that the Clinton-Lewinsky scandal would allow Republicans to pick up as many as 40 congressional seats during the 1998 elections. Instead, the Christian Right was stunned by the voter backlash in the wake of Counsel Kenneth Starr's report to Congress, which caused the Republican Party to suffer its worst showing in 64 years by a party not holding the presidency. The election also led to the resignation of Representative Newt Gingrich from his position as Speaker of the House.

Fundamentalists and Extremists

According to a number of surveys, the turnout of voters identifying with the religious Right dropped 10 to 20 percent from the previous election.[31]

In 1999, the Federal Election Commission determined that the Christian Coalition was acting as an arm of the Republican Party without reporting its spending. The coalition subsequently split into two organizations—one political, the other tax exempt.[32] The same year, Roberta Combs replaced Hodel as CEO after Hodel refused Robertson's request to stop supporting impeachment proceedings against Clinton. Meanwhile, the coalition's annual revenues fell from $26 million in 1996 to $3 million in 2000. On December 5, 2001, Pat Robertson issued a written statement resigning as president of the Christian Coalition so he could focus his attention on ministerial work. The Coalition's board selected Combs to serve as the new president.

Following the 1998 election, some fundamentalists seemed ready to once again retreat from involvement in politics. In February 1999, Paul Weyrich, cofounder of both the Moral Majority and the Christian Coalition, posted a letter on his Free Congress Foundation web site that stated, "I no longer believe there is a moral majority. I do not believe that a majority of Americans actually shares our values. . . . If there really was a moral majority out there, Bill Clinton would have been driven from office months ago."[33] He counseled fundamentalists to "drop out of this culture and find places . . . where we can live godly, religious, and sober lives" and where they could form new institutions that were impervious to "cultural Marxism" (another term for political correctness and secular humanism). Among those who echoed Weyrich's sentiment was syndicated conservative columnist Cal Thomas.

Most Christian Right leaders condemned any thoughts of retreat. Gary Bauer, Pat Robertson, Jerry Falwell, James Dobson, and others reacted to Weyrich's letter with a mix of dismay and disgust.[34]

The 2000 Election and Beyond   Among the early contenders for the Republican Party's presidential nomination in 2000 was Gary Bauer, a former top aide to Reagan and a supporter of the Christian Right. Also in the running was John McCain, who stirred the wrath of fundamentalists when he called Pat Robertson and Jerry Falwell "evil" and "agents of intolerance." Ralph Reed, who had been hired as a senior adviser to George W. Bush's campaign, devised a brutal anti-McCain assault in South Carolina. Bush won the state, building his momentum toward winning the primary.

The Republican National Convention in Philadelphia was characterized by the silence of the religious Right. Jerry Falwell, Pat Robertson, and Gary Bauer attended but were not invited to speak for fear of hampering Bush's appeal to the moderate Republicans. Bush openly referred to himself as born again, but he also kept his distance from fundamentalists. Although he was far from perfect in the eyes of conservative Christians, Falwell said he was the first candidate they felt "energized" about since Reagan.[35]

James Dobson, who founded Focus on the Family radio ministry in 1977, emerged as one of the most influential voices of the Christian Right during the 2000 election. With the Christian Coalition in decline, Dobson filled the role of voicing discontent with the Republican Party. Among other pronouncements, he warned Bush not to pick a pro-choice running mate, and in that regard, Bush did not disappoint fundamentalists. His cabinet picks also demonstrated a rightward shift, particularly in the case of former Missouri senator John Ashcroft, a leader of the Christian Right who was named head of the Justice Department.

Bush gained immediate kudos from fundamentalists when, on March 28, 2001, he barred U.S. foreign aid to family-planning groups involved in abortion. Less than two months later, however, the House International Relations Committee rejected the policy and voted to overturn it.

Less popular among some conservative Christians was Bush's faith-based initiative, a proposal to give government contracts to religious-based organizations that provide social services. Both Falwell and Robertson opposed the plan over worries that non-Christian "cult" groups would receive money and that Christian organizations would be forced to compromise their beliefs to be eligible for the program. The initiative was passed by the House in July but stalled for months in the Senate. In November, Bush introduced a more moderate version of the bill, claiming that the program was urgently needed because charities not involved in efforts to help victims of the September 11, 2001, terrorist attacks were struggling to find funding.[36]

Bush received mixed reviews in August 2001 when he approved limited federal funding for stem cell research (the use of tissue from human embryos for biomedical research, such as cloning for the purpose of creating organs for transplants). Some Christian groups, such as the National Right to Life Committee, declared the decision a reasonable compromise, but others called Bush's approval morally unacceptable because government should not benefit from even the past destruction of embryos, which they considered tantamount to murder. On the other hand, many researchers complained that the ruling was too restrictive.[37]

ISLAMIC FUNDAMENTALISM IN THE UNITED STATES

On September 11, 2001, the United States suffered the worst terrorist attack in its history when Islamic fundamentalists hijacked four commercial airliners and flew two of them into the towers of New York City's World Trade Center and a third into the Pentagon in Washington, D.C. Further destruction was averted when passengers on the fourth plane, notified about the other attacks, tried to wrest control from the hijackers. The airliner crashed into a field in western Pennsylvania.

Bush called the attacks "acts of war" and quickly moved to form a global antiterrorism coalition, while federal investigators identified the 19 hijackers and linked them to Saudi fugitive Osama bin Laden, believed to be running a terrorist network from Afghanistan. The Taliban, Afghanistan's ruling party, refused to hand over bin Laden to the United States, resulting in a military campaign against the extremely poor, war-ravaged nation.

This was not the first time Islamic terrorists had struck on American soil. In 1993, fundamentalists had bombed the very same World Trade Center. In December 1999, Algerian national Ahmed Ressam was arrested as he tried to cross into the United States from Canada with explosives in the trunk of his car, and in April 2001, a federal jury in Los Angeles convicted Ressam of conspiracy to commit acts of international terrorism. During the trial, he was linked to groups trained by bin Laden in Afghanistan.[38]

It is important to note that most Muslims are not fundamentalists and that the vast majority of fundamentalists are not terrorists. Fundamentalists in the Middle East, like those in North America, look to an older model of religion as a defense against modernity. Islamic fundamentalists call for a return to the core texts of Islam, particularly the Koran (word of God), Hadith (sayings of the prophet), and the Shari'ah (the corpus of Muslim law). Militant fundamentalists also adhere to a narrow definition of the dual concept of jihad (struggle), rejecting the idea of *jihad al nafs* (the internal struggle for one's soul against one's own base instincts) in favor of *jihad bi al saif* (holy war by means of the sword). Fundamentalists repeatedly invoke passages from the Koran that ordain warfare as a means for faithful Muslims to rid the world of heretics. Reacting against European colonization and the 1948 establishment of the Jewish state of Israel, activists during the 1950s began specifically defining *jihad* as a revolutionary struggle to seize power for the good of humanity, claiming this to be a central tenet of Islam. The emerging fundamentalist movement turned the prophet Muhammad's life into a simplified ideology declaring that Muslims must work via jihad toward rejecting Western influence, establishing an Islamic state, and rejuvenating the religion.[39] Western Christianity, communism, secularism, and Zionism were declared enemies of Islam. Democracy was denounced as an ideology in which people rebel against God and usurp his rule.

The United States was made aware of the determination of Islamic fundamentalists during the 1970s, when Islamic religious leader Ayatollah Khomeini overthrew the shah of Iran and took power in that country.

President Carter's support of the shah, a brutal dictator who repeatedly ordered the massacre of students attending funerals of those who had been killed by government forces, cast the United States in the role of an enemy of Iran.

After the revolution, liberal and Western-educated Iranians were shocked by the religious extremism of Khomeini's regime. Freedom of the press and political expression were suppressed if they contradicted Khomeini's version of Islam. On November 9, 1979, Iranian students took 90 hostages at the U.S. embassy in Tehran. Women and black marine guards were later released, but the remaining 52 were kept hostage for 444 days. The event illustrated a new determination by Islamic radicals to stand up against perceived injustice and secularism forced upon them by Western nations.[40]

More than 20 years later, American religious reactions to the September 11, 2001, attacks varied. General church attendance rose, as did sales of Bibles and apocalyptic fiction books. On September 13, Jerry Falwell went on Pat Robertson's *700 Club* and declared that the attacks were "probably what we deserve" because of efforts by homosexuals, abortionists, and liberals to secularize America. He added, "I point the finger in their face and say, 'You helped this happen.'" Robertson nodded in agreement. Falwell was immediately rebuked by the White House and faced widespread criticism for his comments. On September 19, Falwell issued a public apology. Robertson called Falwell's remarks "totally inappropriate," despite the fact that he had agreed with Falwell on the air. A Robertson spokesman said he was confused and "didn't really realize what" Falwell was saying at the time.[41]

The federal government, meanwhile, rushed to pass new antiterrorism legislation that shifted the focus of investigations from responding to crimes to trying to prevent them. Part of the package involved expanding law enforcement's ability to obtain search warrants, monitor e-mail, and detain suspects. Civil libertarians complained that the bill was drafted and signed into law with undue haste and sacrificed freedom without enhancing security.[42] Vermont senator Patrick Leahy, head of the Judiciary Committee, said, "This idea that somehow if you just throw our Constitution overboard, then we're safe, that doesn't work."[43]

EXTREMISM

Extremism has been defined by British philosopher Roger Scruton as "taking a political idea to its limits, regardless of unfortunate repercussions, impracticalities, arguments, and feelings to the contrary, and with the intention not only to confront, but to eliminate opposition."[44] Among the characteristics shared by most extremists are intolerance toward other points of view and adoption of means to political ends that show disregard for the life, liberty, and human rights of others. Tactics include name calling, sweeping generalizations based on little or no evidence, a tendency to view critics and opponents (including moderates) as extremist and evil, advocacy of censorship of opponents, assumption of moral superiority over others, apocalyptic thinking, and belief in far-reaching conspiracy theories.[45]

Conspiracy forms the basis of much extremist thought. Most prevalent is the idea that the United States or the world is controlled by a hidden ruling elite and that all world events are the product of their will. Such beliefs remove the element of chance from the world, allowing extremists to fit complex situations more easily into a narrow ideological model.

Far left extremism consists mostly of those who believe in some form of Marxism-Leninism (communism) but also includes some anarchists. Leftism fell out of favor in the 1980s and was considered by many to be obsolete following the breakup of the Soviet Union in 1991; however, Marxist ideologies experienced an upsurge in popularity during the anti–World Trade Organization (WTO) protests that rose in the late 1990s.

Far right extremism values individualism, capitalism, religiosity, and nationalism. Proponents tend to be anticommunist. Many right-wing organizations focus on ethnic bias as a basis for ideology, but others, such as the John Birch Society and many militia groups, have denounced racism and anti-Semitism.

THE AMERICAN REVOLUTION

The history of the United States is rife with extremist activity. The colonial protesters who challenged England's right to tax them without their consent would, if they used similar tactics and rhetoric today, be described as terrorists.[46] Modern militias justify their own existence by pointing to the important role that minutemen militia units played in the American Revolution. April 19, 1775, when minutemen first engaged in combat with British troops and started the Revolutionary War, remains an important date to many right-wing extremists.

By the 1770s, it was a common belief among North American radicals that Britain's Parliament had devised a conspiratorial plot to rob colonists of their liberty. Legislation such as the Stamp Act, Townshend Acts, and Intolerable Acts were held up as proof of incremental efforts to establish tyranny. The colonial revolutionaries, therefore, sought to replace the remote, centralized power of the British monarchy with a decentralized system of governance that would limit the possibility of corruption. This concern came to the forefront during the drafting of the Articles of Confederation, which played itself out as a debate between those revolutionaries who wanted state sovereignty (anti-Federalists) and those who wanted greater centralization (Federalists). The Articles of Confederation, which granted the majority of power to the states, were approved in March 1781 but were later replaced by the Constitution, which sought a balance of power between the states and a centralized national government. The debate has not been completely settled, as extremists on both the left and right continue to argue for decentralization.

THE 19TH CENTURY

The populist movement of the 1890s became the source of many beliefs on both the left and the right. Based largely in the rural Midwest, proponents demanded government action that would benefit struggling farmers, and small businesses: the abolition of national banks (later a hallmark of the right), government ownership of all means of transportation and communication (left), election of senators by direct vote (achieved by the Seventeenth Amendment), restrictions of land ownership by foreigners (right), and an eight-hour workday (left). They also demanded that more political power be given to the average citizen.[47] In 1892, the populist People's Party was formed and managed to elect a number of U.S. House members, senators, governors, legislators, and other officials. By the end of the 1890s, however, its viability as a third party had ended.

The 19th century also saw the birth of the Ku Klux Klan, which designed the blueprint for the vast majority of later right-wing extremist organizations. Socialism and anarchism also grew during the century, laying the foundation for far left activity through the 20th century and beyond.

Ku Klux Klan

The Ku Klux Klan was formed in Pulaski, Tennessee, in December 1865. The six founding members originally intended only to play pranks by wearing disguises, riding horses around at night, and claiming they were the ghosts of dead Confederates.[48] However, the club was organized in the midst of post–Civil War Reconstruction, when the federal government sent troops to the South to enforce acts of Congress giving blacks equal political and civil rights. The Ku Klux Klan quickly changed its focus to intimidating blacks and overthrowing black political rule imposed by the federal government. Former slaves, as well as whites who aided them, were considered fair game for branding, flogging, physical beating, mutilation, and murder.

In April 1867, Klan representatives drew up a constitution that identified the group as a self-appointed police organization.[49] Most white Southerners concurred in viewing the Klan as a law-and-order organization. Despite the constitution and additional attempts to organize, the Klan remained a chaotic organization whose membership and methods varied from one locality to the next.[50]

By 1869, Imperial Wizard Nathan Bedford Forrest determined that the Klan had gotten out of hand and that its use of violence was beginning to garner unfavorable public opinion, even among white southerners. In January, he ordered the Ku Klux Klan to disband and burn all its records. Most Klan groups complied, but a few kept up the violence until 1872, when the Federal Force Act, martial law, mass arrests, and conviction brought the activity to an end.[51]

Socialism and Anarchism

The first significant socialist party in the United States, the Workingman's Party, was formed in 1877. Later known as the Socialist Labor Party in 1890, the group's membership consisted mostly of European immigrants, particularly Germans. Socialism, developed from the ideas of German philosopher Karl Marx, argued that workers who produced industrial wealth should also be its owners. The Soviet Union later corrupted this idea by nationalizing productive property, a view that became dominant among communist parties worldwide during the 20th century.

The summer of 1877 also brought the first widespread protest against post–Civil War industrialization when railroad workers in 17 states walked off the job for two weeks. The resulting transportation nightmare prompted many major newspapers to call for ruthless suppression of the strikes. Police and state militias complied, intervening on the side of employers with unscrupulous use of violence. In Baltimore, Maryland, militiamen fired into a crowd and killed 12 people. More than 20 workers were massacred in Pittsburgh, Pennsylvania, before an angry mob chased the militia away. Chicago suffered through two days of violence that resulted in 25 to 50 deaths, about 200 serious injuries, and 300 to 400 arrests.

German radical Johann Most immigrated to the United States in the early 1880s and established the New York–based *Freiheit*, the most influential anarchist paper in the world.[52] Anarchists contended that power should reside with the individual or a small community, but theorists differed on how this should be accomplished. Most 19th century anarchists subscribed to Russian geographer Peter Kropotkin's ideals of altruism, solidarity, mutual aid, and peaceful change. Johann Most, however, supported Russian writer Mikhail Bakunin's ideas about the necessity of outright revolt, violent destruction of government institutions, and attacks on political leaders. Most is believed to have pioneered the concept of letter bombs, and he wrote a book on revolutionary warfare that later inspired the *Anarchist Cookbook*, widely used by leftists during the 1960s. Most, however, was not a practicing terrorist, and police did not suppress his writings.[53]

Although their ideologies differed, anarchists and socialists in the United States joined forces to struggle for establishing an eight-hour workday. The movement gained momentum during the upsurge in radical labor activity that resulted from the depression of 1883 to 1886.

On May 1, 1886, more than 30,000 workers in 13,000 companies across the nation went on strike. On May 3, police in Chicago fired into a crowd of skirmishing workers and scabs, killing two, injuring many others, and prompting a call for a labor meeting in Haymarket Square on May 4. Toward the end of the meeting, police arrived to disperse the crowd. At that moment, an unidentified person threw a bomb, its explosion prompting police to fire into crowd. The melee that followed ended with seven dead police officers (one by the bomb, six by police gunfire), 60 injured police officers, and an unknown but far greater number of dead civilians.

The Haymarket incident inaugurated the first major Red Scare (widespread fear that communist agents were planning to overthrow the U.S. government) in American history, triggering intense suppression of subversion, demands for reprisals, and a rise in nativism. Although the identity of the bomber was never known, seven men, some of whom were not even present at the time of the explosion, were sentenced to death. Two of the death sentences were commuted to imprisonment on appeal, four defendants were hanged on November 11, 1887, and another killed himself with dynamite in his jail cell the day before. In 1893, Illinois governor John Peter Altgeld pardoned the jailed men, claiming that the presiding judge had conducted the trial with "malicious ferocity" and turned it into a farce. He also exonerated the executed men.

After Haymarket, anarchism was forever linked with terrorism. Efforts were made to pass legislation to remove "dangerous aliens" from the country, but none succeeded until after the assassination of President William McKinley in 1901 by American anarchist Leon F. Czolgosz. In 1903, Congress enacted immigration laws allowing the federal government to deport anarchists.

Haymarket did little to curtail labor struggles. Rapid industrialization during the 1890s led to increased conflict and violence between workers and law enforcement. In 1892, steelworkers in Homestead, Pennsylvania, took over the entire town when magnate Andrew Carnegie tried to eliminate their union. The governor sent the state militia to establish martial

27

law and remove union members from local office. The 1894 Pullman strike tied up the nation's railways until President Grover Cleveland sent in federal troops to end the conflict. These strikes and others prefaced a wave of violent labor conflicts that occurred during the early years of the 20th century.

WORLD WAR I AND THE GREAT DEPRESSION

Concepts of the left wing (liberalism, secularism, internationalism, collectivism, and egalitarianism) and the right wing (conservatism, religiosity, patriotism, nationalism, and racism) began to be more clearly defined during the early 20th century.[54] Leftists claimed to be internationalists, champions of the exploited both at home and abroad, while rightists put their own country and race above all.[55]

World War I inaugurated the second Red Scare era, which lasted through the 1920s. Both the Left and Right were active, and the federal government took sweeping, questionable steps to combat extremism on both ends of the spectrum. Among these was passage of the Espionage and Sedition Acts (enacted in 1917 and 1918, respectively, to punish those who used the spoken or written word to interfere with U.S. involvement in World War I or to cause contempt for the government), the constitutionality of which was repeatedly challenged in court for many years.

Left-Wing Extremism

In 1901, Victor L. Berger, Job Harriman, Morris Hilquit, and Eugene V. Debs founded the Socialist Party, which espoused nonviolence and nonconfrontational policies. In 1910, Berger became the first socialist elected to Congress; Debs won 1 million votes in his quest for the presidency in 1912. In 1920, while serving jail time for an antiwar speech, Debs managed to attract 901,000 votes for president.

The most confrontational labor organization of the era was the Industrial Workers of the World (IWW), formed in 1905 with the goal of replacing capitalism with a workers' commonwealth. From 1909 to 1918, the IWW waged unrelenting industrial warfare against its capitalist adversaries. In 1917, federal authorities, claiming IWW strikes threatened U.S. war efforts, arrested nearly 200 members. More than 100 of these were found guilty of espionage and sedition.

The Bolshevik Revolution of 1917, during which communists took power in Russia, inspired the formation of communist parties around the world during the 1920s. Communism advocated revolution to overthrow capitalism and create a socialist society based on equality and prosperity. Vladimir Ilyich Lenin, the first leader of the Soviet Union, transformed communism into an authoritarian doctrine of discipline and obedience to the revolutionary party. This new, harsher ideology was named Marxism-Leninism.

In February and March of 1919, Senator Lee Overman led hearings on the extent of Bolshevik influence in the United States, which set the pattern for future anticommunist hunts. The scare reached its peak several months later, when Attorney General R. Mitchell Palmer ordered the arrest of more than 4,000 "subversives," most without warrants.[56] Many of those arrested were deported to Soviet Russia.

In May 1938, the House Committee on Un-American Activities (HUAC) was created to investigate subversive activities in the United States. Led by Texas congressman Martin Dies, the committee pioneered many of the tactics later used by Senator Joseph McCarthy for HUAC investigations during the cold war of the 1950s: guilt by association, purporting to seek out communists while harassing those whose views only differed from the committee, use of ex-communists as witnesses, and pretending to have reliable evidence when none existed.[57]

Right-Wing Extremism

The Ku Klux Klan revival was inspired by D. W. Griffith's 1915 film *The Birth of a Nation*, based on Thomas Dixon's 1905 novel *The Clansman*, in which the concept of cross burning was introduced.[58] The novel portrayed blacks as brutes and Reconstruction as a tragedy.[59] Shortly after the film's release, Colonel William Joseph Simmons led 19 followers to Stone Mountain near Atlanta, Georgia, where they imitated the novel's cross burning. The Klan soon had nearly 100 followers who were attracted to Simmons's emphasis on 100 percent "Americanism" and supremacy of the Caucasian race.[60] The new Klan was legally incorporated in Fulton County, Georgia, on July 1, 1916.

During the early 1920s, Simmons added Jews and Catholics to the Klan's list of enemies, and Klan groups appeared across the United States. As membership grew, so did the organization's use of violence. The Klan also gained political power, helping elect governors in Georgia, Alabama, California, and Oregon in 1922. Internal struggles led to the replacement of Simmons by Hiram W. Evans as imperial wizard in 1923. Evans immediately moved the Klan office from Atlanta to Washington, D.C.

Klan membership peaked the following year, with estimates ranging from 2 to 5 million members. Although the Klan failed to nominate William Gibbs McAdoo as the Democrats' presidential candidate in 1924, many Klan favorites won Senate and governor races.[61]

Klan fortunes took a downturn on March 15, 1925, when Indiana grand dragon David C. Stephenson raped and murdered a woman named Madge Oberholzer. Stephenson's conviction broke the Klan's power in Indiana and turned public opinion against the entire movement. To raise morale and attract new members, the organization held a massive parade in Washington, D.C., in August. The rally's failure to stem the ebbing tide of support was illustrated by the fact that the second national parade the following year attracted only half the numbers of the first.

The Klan maintained a low profile throughout the 1930s, shifting its focus to communism and the labor movement and developing relationships with the pro-Hitler German-American Bund and William Dudley Pelley's Silver Shirts. In 1939, Evans was replaced by James A. Colescott as imperial wizard. Due to negative publicity, the Klan broke its connections with Nazi groups and reduced its activity during World War II.[62] In 1944, the U.S. Bureau of Internal Revenue filed a lien for back taxes of $685,000 on profits earned by the Klan during the 1920s. The Klan was forced to sell its assets, hand over the proceeds to the government, and go out of business again.[63]

Among the other extreme-right groups active during the Depression era was the Black Legion, an Ohio-based fascist group that spoke against aliens, blacks, communists, Catholics, Jews, and trade unions. The German-American Bund was formed in Chicago in 1930 by German immigrants sympathetic to Hitler, but it was rendered ineffective by massive government infiltration.

Among the personalities of the era were William Dudley Pelley, a Hollywood writer who converted to fascism after a mystical experience and founded the pro-Nazi Silver Shirt Legion in Los Angeles in 1933. He was arrested in 1942 for subversion, convicted, and sentenced to 15 years in prison. After his release in 1950, he focused on writing metaphysical books.

During the 1930s, Gerald B. Winrod promoted the "Protocols of the Elders of Zion," which purported to be an exposé of a Jewish conspiracy to control the world, and founded the anti-Semitic Defenders of the Christian Faith.

Finally, a Roman Catholic priest, Father Charles Coughlin, a former supporter of President Franklin Roosevelt's New Deal policies, began preaching anti-Semitism and supporting Italian fascism during the 1930s. In 1938, he formed the fascist Christian Front, but the U.S. Post Office banned his materials. His archbishop warned him to stop all "public pronouncements" or leave the church. Coughlin opted for the priesthood, remaining silent about politics until his death in 1979.

In 1944, Winrod and Pelley (who was already in jail), along with 28 others, were charged by a U.S. grand jury with conspiring to bring about insubordination in the armed forces as part of a Nazi plot. Known as the Great Sedition Trial of 1944 (*U.S. v. McWilliams*), the proceedings brought up a number of civil liberties and free speech issues, because the defendants were charged not with overt acts of sabotage but rather with promoting values, beliefs, and opinions. The case ended in a mistrial following the death of the judge and was finally dismissed in 1947.

COLD WAR ERA: RIGHT-WING EXTREMISM

The cold war was defined by an ideological struggle between capitalism and communism that determined U.S. foreign policy and prompted federal authorities to search for communists from Hollywood to the U.S. Army and everywhere in between.

The most notorious communist hunter was Wisconsin senator Joseph McCarthy, who in February 1950 announced that the U.S. State Department was "thoroughly infested with Communists."[64] Goaded on by a media that reported his untruths and undocumented accusations as fact, McCarthy, whose accusations ruined many careers, quickly became one of the most feared men in America. And it was not until 1954, when he began investigating the U.S. Army, that other senators began condemning him. Radio and television broadcaster Edward R. Murrow, during a documentary on McCarthy, said, "The line between investigating and persecuting is a very fine one, and the junior senator from Wisconsin has stepped over it repeatedly. . . . We must not confuse dissent with disloyalty."[65] The broadcast helped sway public opinion against McCarthy, who soon lost his influence in Washington, D.C.

Other strident anticommunists of the era included Reverend Billy James Hargis, who formed the Christian Crusade in 1948 to save America from communism and mainstream Protestant churches. From 1953 to 1957, Hargis chaired the Bible Balloon Project, which used helium balloons to float thousands of Bible passages into Iron Curtain nations from Western Europe.

In December 1958, businessman Robert Welch founded the John Birch Society to combat a supposed communist conspiracy bent on establishing a totalitarian regime in the United States. Welch insisted that President Dwight Eisenhower was a "dedicated, conscious agent" of the communist conspiracy, an accusation that led mainstream conservatives to blame Welch for harming the anticommunist cause. Though sometimes associated with anti-Semitism, the John Birch Society made efforts to distance itself from such ideologies.

Neo-Nazis and Early Militias

In 1957, Willis Carto's Liberty Lobby began publishing the racist and anti-Semitic *Liberty Letter* (replaced in 1975 by the *Spotlight*), which gained a wide readership among right-wing extremists. The support he garnered allowed him to found the neo-Nazi National Youth Alliance in 1969, with which William Pierce (future founder of National Alliance) became associated. During the 1970s, the Anti-Defamation League (ADL) waged a successful campaign to remove Carto's radio program from the airwaves. Carto was not down for long, however: In 1984, he set up the Populist Party, whose 1988 presidential candidate, David Duke, received 47,047 votes nationwide.

George Lincoln Rockwell founded the openly racist and anti-Semitic American Nazi Party (ANP) in 1959. More of a cartoon fascist than a serious threat, Rockwell wore Nazi regalia during speeches. In 1965, he gathered a few thousand votes during a run for governor of Virginia. In August 1967, Rockwell was assassinated by disgruntled Nazi John Patler. The ANP continued as the National Socialist White People's Party under the leadership of Matt Koehl. During the early 1970s, many members split off to form their own groups, including the National Alliance.

Modern militia groups have their roots in the Minutemen, organized by Robert Bolivar DePugh in 1961 to stockpile weapons and conduct paramilitary training to prevent a communist takeover. Several members had run-ins with authorities, usually on firearms violations. On October 30, 1966, three Minutemen groups that set out to firebomb pacifist communes in New York, New Jersey, and Connecticut were intercepted by police, who had been tipped off by an FBI informant. A second attempt to attack the Connecticut commune occurred two years later. A shoot-out with police led to six injuries before the Minutemen surrendered.

In the late 1960s, DePugh jumped bond on firearms and explosives violations and eluded the FBI for 17 months. During DePugh's prison time, the Minutemen declined to insignificance.

Ku Klux Klan Resurgence

The third birth of the Ku Klux Klan (KKK) occurred as a result of a backlash against the civil rights movement that strove to gain legal and social equality for African Americans. Particularly irksome to southern racists was the Supreme Court's 1954 *Brown v. Board of Education* decision, which called for an end to segregation in public schools. Desegregation violence erupted across the South. African Americans were shot, stabbed, and murdered, while their homes and churches, as well as integrated schools, were bombed and set on fire.

By this point, the Ku Klux Klan no longer consisted of a coherent unit but a number of independent Klans with their own constitutions and hierarchies. The largest group during the 1950s was the U.S. Klans, led by

Eldon Lee Edwards. Robert Shelton, who was ousted from the U.S. Klans by Edwards, formed the Alabama Knights. In 1961, the Alabama Knights united with another group to form the United Klans of America (UKA), which remained the largest Klan in the United States until the 1980s.

Civil rights–era Klan violence lasted from 1954 until 1968. From January 1, 1956, to June 1963, 138 dynamitings in the South were attributed to the KKK.[66] The most notorious bombing occurred on September 15, 1963, when an explosion at the Sixteenth Street Baptist Church in Birmingham, Alabama, killed four young black girls and wounded about 20 people. The first conviction for the crime did not occur until 1977, when Klansman Robert "Dynamite Bob" Chambliss was sentenced to life in prison for murder. The case was reopened in 2000, resulting in the conviction of and a life sentence for Thomas Blanton, Jr. In July 2001, defendant Bobby Frank Cherry was found mentally incompetent to stand trial due to memory loss from dementia, a ruling that was reversed in January 2002 by Alabama's Jefferson County Circuit Court. Cherry was found guilty of murder in May 2002.

The slow convictions were a result of the difficulty of bringing Klan members to justice during the 1960s. On June 21, 1964, civil rights workers Michael Schwerner, James Chaney, and Andrew Goodman were murdered by Klansmen with the help of police in Mississippi. State officials refused to bring the accused to trial, so the federal government brought charges under the Conspiracy Act of 1870. Six Klansmen and one deputy sheriff were found guilty and sent to prison for a maximum of 10 years. In July 1964, a black Army Reserve officer, Lieutenant Colonel Lumuel Penn, was murdered by two Klansmen, who were tried in state court and acquitted. Again, the defendants were brought to trial by federal authorities and convicted of conspiracy to violate the civil rights of blacks.

Klan violence inspired passage of the Civil Rights Act of 1964, which increased the federal government's ability to force local school districts to desegregate and provided more protection for civil rights activists. Although it made it illegal to discriminate against an individual because of race, color, or sex in public accommodations or employment, it did not guarantee the unrestricted right to vote.

The law did little to curtail racist violence. In 1965, while driving civil rights marchers from Montgomery to Selma in Alabama, Viola Gregg Liuzzo was murdered by four Klansmen. Outraged, President Lyndon B. Johnson vowed to fight the Klan. In August, he signed into law the Voting Rights Act, which abolished discriminatory literacy tests and allowed the federal government to register local African Americans for the vote.

Additional pressure was brought to bear against the Klan by congressional investigations and the FBI's Counterintelligence Program (COINTELPRO), which used subversion and disinformation to undermine activity. By the 1970s, the FBI claimed that one in six Klansmen was a government informant.[67] This federal pressure, along with general anti-Klan sentiment and the increasing willingness of state governments to prosecute racists, caused many Klan groups to disband between 1967 to 1973.

COLD WAR ERA: LEFT-WING EXTREMISM

Since its founding in 1919, the Communist Party USA (CPUSA) has been the largest leftist group in the United States. The organization suffered during the anticommunist hunts of the 1950s and was subject to COINTELPRO harassment beginning in 1956. In an attempt to recover, the CPUSA formed clubs aimed at recruiting college students during 1960s, which helped foment the student anti–Vietnam War movement. Other communist groups active during 1960s and beyond included the Socialist Workers Party, Workers World Party, Progressive Labor Party, and Revolutionary Communist Party. By the end of the 1960s, Marxist theory was also influencing radical new "black power" groups that were disillusioned with the nonviolent tactics of the older civil rights leaders.

Black Panthers

Huey P. Newton and Bobby Seale formed the Black Panther Party in Oakland, California, on October 15, 1966. Among the first neighborhood recruits were David Hilliard and Bobby Hutton. The group created a new post–civil rights, black nationalist agenda intent on changing the fundamental structures of government to better meet the needs of African Americans.

The Black Panthers initially focused on organizing armed patrols of their neighborhood to keep police abuse in check. At the time, California law allowed citizens to carry weapons in public as long as they were not concealed.[68] When legislators threatened to change the laws in 1967, 30 armed Black Panthers led by Seale walked into the capitol building in Sacramento to protest. The Panthers gained wide media attention but were arrested for "the willful disruption of a State of California legislature body assembly." A law prohibiting the carrying of firearms in public, effectively outlawing Black Panther patrols, passed the month after the protest.

The Black Panthers' confrontational tactics, coupled with the FBI's intention to destroy the organization through its COINTELPRO program, led to a series of bloody incidents. On October 28, 1967, Newton was involved in a shoot-out with Oakland policemen John Frey and Herbert Heanes; Frey was killed, while Newton and Heanes were wounded.

34

Newton was tried and jailed for murder, but he was released in August 1970 after the conviction was overturned on appeal. On April 6, 1968, Hutton was killed in a shoot-out with police. In November, Eldridge Cleaver, who had been involved in the April shoot-out, fled the country. In December 1969, a Chicago police raid resulted in the deaths of Panthers Fred Hampton and Mark Clark. Crime scene evidence showed that only one of the 83 shots fired came from the Panthers, contradicting police claims that they were involved in an intense gun battle.

In the face of this pressure, the Black Panthers split into two factions. The Oakland group—led by Newton, Seale, Hilliard, and Elaine Brown— focused on uplifting the community by registering people to vote, starting a free breakfast program for schoolchildren, and opening free health clinics. The New York City and Kansas City groups, led by Cleaver and Donald Cox, wanted to use terrorist tactics to change the government. The party expelled Cleaver in 1971 and closed all chapters except the one in Oakland. Ousted New York members went on to form the revolutionary Black Liberation Army.

In 1973, the Panthers became involved in electoral politics. Seale ran for mayor of Oakland and Elaine Brown ran for a city council seat, both unsuccessfully. However, four party members were elected to the Berkeley Community Development Council.

Seale left the party in 1974, while Cleaver, exiled in Algeria, converted to fundamentalist Christianity. Newton developed a drug habit and was murdered in 1989. During the late 1970s, the party lost interest in community programs, instead involving itself in extortion, robberies, and other illegal activities before disappearing altogether.

Students for a Democratic Society and the Weathermen

Students for a Democratic Society (SDS) was formed in 1962 by University of Michigan students. The group spelled out its ideological stance in the Port Huron Statement, which called for a system of democratic leftism that would allow individuals to "share in those social decisions determining the quality and direction of [one's] life." Although not strictly a communist group, many members were affiliated with Marxism-Leninism.

The SDS found its direction in 1965 when President Johnson dramatically escalated the war in Vietnam. The SDS subsequently became the center of the antiwar movement and promoted student unrest. Among the more dramatic examples of this occurred in March 1968 when SDS members took over five buildings on the campus of Columbia University in New York City. After five days of negotiations, police stormed the campus, arresting 712 students and injuring 148.

Fundamentalists and Extremists

The SDS began to break into factions in 1969. The most notorious splinter group was the Weathermen, which used terrorist activity as a mean to achieve its ends. In October, several hundred members took to the streets of Chicago during "Four Days of Rage," breaking windows and battling with police; 73 cops were injured, and about 300 Weathermen were arrested. In March 1970, three Weathermen died when a bomb they were building in a New York City apartment exploded. Undeterred, members of the Weather Underground, as the group was also known, injured eight people when they bombed New York City police headquarters in June 1970. Thirteen members were later indicted on charges of planning to detonate bombs in Berkeley, Chicago, Detroit, and New York. Other explosives were successfully detonated at the U.S. Capitol, the Pentagon, and elsewhere. A number of Weathermen were arrested, while others went underground, some of whom eluded capture into the 1980s.

Abbie Hoffman and the Youth International Party

Abbie Hoffman began his career as a radical leftist during the early 1960s as a volunteer for the Student Nonviolent Coordinating Committee (SNCC), mobilizing support and raising money for civil rights activists in the South. In 1966 he moved to New York City's Lower East Side, where he became involved in the antiwar movement. Hoffman gained widespread media attention for his ability to infuse protests with a sense of playfulness. In 1967, for example, he and other activists threw handfuls of $1 bills onto the floor of the New York Stock Exchange, prompting stock brokers to scramble for the money. In October of the same year, Hoffman led protesters in an attempt to encircle the Pentagon, perform an exorcism ceremony to rid it of evil, and levitate it 10 feet off the ground.

In 1968 Hoffman; his second wife, Anita; Jerry Rubin; Paul Krassner; and Nancy Kurshan formed the Youth International Party (Yippies) to organize hippies into political activists. The group's immediate aim was to convince protesters to travel to the 1968 National Democratic Convention in Chicago. On August 25, 1968, several thousand Yippies settled into Chicago's Lincoln Park for a Festival of Peace that coincided with the convention and that was intended to protest the Vietnam War. The festival was marred by constant skirmishes between heavily armed police and jeering protesters. Again and again, police swept through the park, clubbing protesters while camera crews from the major television networks recorded images that were later aired on the evening news.

On March 20, 1969, indictments were handed down against eight participants in the Chicago protests: Yippies Hoffman and Jerry Rubin, Students for a Democratic Society cofounders Rennie Davis and Tom Hayden, Black

Panther leader Bobby Seale, prominent pacifist David Dellinger, and anti-war academics Lee Weiner and John Froines. Known as the Chicago 8, the defendants were charged with violating an antiriot law that made it a crime to cross state lines to incite violence.

The Chicago Conspiracy trial began September 26, 1969. Judge Julius Hoffman demonstrated hostility toward the defendants throughout. Seale, who demanded the right to represent himself, was ordered by the judge to be gagged and bound to his chair in the courtroom. Repeatedly manhandled by court attendants as he struggled to free himself, Seale was eventually separated from the trial and convicted on 16 counts of contempt that added up to a four-year sentence. With the Black Panther out of the picture, the Chicago 8 became the Chicago 7.

On February 18, 1970, the jury found the seven defendants not guilty of the primary charge of conspiring to cross state lines to incite riot. Hoffman, Dellinger, Davis, Hayden, and Rubin were found guilty of crossing state lines to incite riot individually, and each received the maximum sentence of five years, plus a $5,000 fine. In addition, each defendant received contempt sentences ranging from two and a half months for Weiner to more than two years for Dellinger, Davis, and Rubin. (Freedom of Information Act files released at the end of the 1970s revealed that Judge Hoffman had planned to hold the defendants guilty on contempt charges before the trial even began.) In November 1972 an appeals court threw out all of the charges due to various errors committed by Judge Hoffman and the prosecuting attorneys. In 1973 appellate court judge Edward Gignoux ended the whole affair by upholding a few of the contempt charges but limiting the sentences to time already served.

In August 1973 Hoffman was arrested with three pounds of cocaine in his possession. Out on bail, he fled to Mexico and spent the next several years eluding the FBI. In 1978, still underground and living under the name Barry Freed, Hoffman founded the organization Save the River to stop a plan by the Army Corps of Engineers to dredge a stretch of the St. Lawrence River to keep it open for navigation during the winter. Hoffman's effort forced the corps to withdraw its plan in the spring of 1980.

On September 4, 1980, a few days after granting an interview to Barbara Walters, Hoffman officially resurfaced and turned himself in to authorities in New York City. Sentenced to three years in prison, he was paroled in March 1982, after which he continued to focus on environmental issues, as well as U.S. foreign policy. Throughout the 1980s, however, Hoffman found it increasingly difficult to deal with the manic depression from which he had suffered for years. He attempted suicide in 1983, and then tried again, this time successfully, on April 12, 1989, overdosing on phenobarbitals.

Fundamentalists and Extremists

Symbionese Liberation Army

The Symbionese Liberation Army, formed in September 1973 by escaped convict Donald DeFreeze, claimed that members were fighting for the rights of the common man against the tyranny of the police state. The group gained notoriety on February 2, 1974, when members kidnapped newspaper heiress Patricia Hearst from her apartment in Berkeley, California. Code-named Tania by the SLA, Hearst helped the group rob several banks before she was arrested by police. After only 21 months in prison, President Carter, who believed Hearst's claim that she had been brainwashed, commuted her sentence and released her into the custody of her parents. President Clinton granted Hearst a full pardon in early 2001 during his final days in office.

In May 1974, six SLA members (including DeFreeze) were killed during a shoot-out with police at a house in the Watts area of Los Angeles. In June, Kathleen Soliah delivered a eulogy at Ho Chi Minh Park in Berkeley, during which she stated that the six SLA members had been "viciously attacked and murdered by 500 pigs."[69]

In September, five SLA members (including Hearst) were arrested in the Bay Area, but Soliah managed to escape and go underground for 25 years. In June 1999, Soliah, now Sara Jane Olson, was arrested in St. Paul, Minnesota, on charges of planting two pipe bombs under Los Angeles Police Department patrol cars in 1975. The FBI also reopened an investigation into whether Olson had participated in a 1975 Carmichael, California, bank robbery that caused the death of bank patron Myrna Opsahl.[70] Olson along with former SLA members Emily Harris, William Harris, and Michael Bortin were arrested on murder charges in the bank slaying on January 16, 2002, two days before Olson was sentenced to 20 years to life in prison for her role in the plot to bomb the police cars.

POST–COLD WAR RIGHT-WING RESURGENCE

The resurgence of right-wing extremism, beginning in the 1980s, has attracted members from college-educated middle classes and has relied on new technologies, such as the Internet, to spread its ideology.

According to the Simon Wiesenthal Center, an international Jewish rights organization, the number of groups promoting white supremacy on the Internet doubled to more than 2,000 between the spring of 1999 and the fall of 2000. Former Klansman Don Black, whose Stormfront site is believed to be the first white supremacist web site, echoed the views of many racists when he said, "The Net has changed everything. We suddenly have a mass audience rather than a small clique of subscribers."[71] Internet access has also promoted the exchange of ideas between extremist groups in different countries, allowing U.S.-based neo-Nazis, for example, to e-mail Nazi materials to Germany, where they are illegal. Although the neo-Nazi movement is fractured, the Internet is facilitating the spread of a more consistent ideology.[72]

White supremacists are also using music as a recruiting tool. According to National Alliance founder William Pierce, intense white-power rock, also known as hatecore, can "give a rationale to the . . . alienation [of supremacist youth] and a direction and purpose to their anger. If they're going to listen to rock, they ought to listen to rock which has the correct ideological content. These kids are gonna grow up, and they're gonna be the leaders of the resistance ten years from now."[73] CDs by bands with names like Angry Aryans, Max Resist, Midtown Bootboys, the Blue Eyed Devils, Brutal Attack, Bound for Glory, and Skrewdriver are widely available on the Internet.

Ku Klux Klan

The Ku Klux Klan, dormant for most of the 1970s, experienced a sudden upsurge in membership at the end of the decade. Along with this came the inevitable rise in the number of cross burnings, rallies, and shootings.[74]

The most recognizable Klansman during this period was David Duke, head of the Knights of the Ku Klux Klan in Louisiana. Duke displayed a media savvy uncommon in white supremacists up to that point. His skill as an orator gained him invitations to speak on college campuses and television, where middle-class America was exposed to his message.

In 1980, Duke turned his Klan over to Don Black and formed the National Association for the Advancement of White People (NAAWP). The message was the same, but the Klan robes were traded for suits and ties. Duke also tried his hand at politics, winning a seat in the Louisiana state legislature as a Republican in 1989. In 1992, Duke ran in the Republican presidential primaries but never won more than 11 percent in any state. After a failed Senate bid in 1996, he was elected chairman of the Republican Executive Committee in St. Tammany Parish. During his 1999 campaign for a congressional seat in Louisiana, Duke claimed he had renounced his white supremacist ties, but in the late 1990s, he had begun appearing at National Alliance events.

Not all had been going so smoothly for the Klan, however. The Klan made news on November 3, 1979, when some 35 members showed up at an anti-Klan rally in Greensboro, North Carolina, organized by the Communist Workers Party (CWP). A gunfight erupted, killing four CWP members. Murder charges were filed against 14 Klansmen, while police were accused of permitting armed racists to drive to the march and of being inexplicably absent when the shootings occurred. All the defendants were acquitted.

In response, as KKK membership dropped yet again during the 1980s, antihate watchdog organizations began racking up court victories. In 1981, Klanwatch won a lawsuit on behalf of Vietnamese fishermen in Texas who had been harassed by Louis Beam and his Klan. A court order prohibited Klansmen from wearing robes within sight of the fishermen. The following year, five black women collected $535,000 in damages in a civil suit against Klansmen who had shot at them. In 1987, a lawsuit brought by Morris Dees of the Southern Poverty Law Center (SPLC) forced the United Klans of America to surrender its headquarters, which was sold to compensate the mother of a murdered black teenager.

But the Klan refused to disappear. In June 1998, African American James Byrd, Jr., was chained behind a pickup truck and dragged several miles to his death near Jasper, Texas. Lawrence Russell Brewer and John William King were sentenced to death for the grisly crime. Shawn Alan Berry was sentenced to life in prison. Prosecutors alleged that the murder was the initiation rite for a Klan group that the defendants were forming. King, tattooed with images of a black man hanging from a tree, a horned baby Jesus, Nazi SS lightning bolts, and the words "Aryan Pride," remained unrepentant after the sentencing.

Skinheads and Neo-Nazis

Skinhead subculture, consisting primarily of white males with shaved heads, originated among disaffected working-class youths in England during the 1970s. Since then, the movement has spread to the United States and other European countries. Many skinheads have come to espouse white supremacist ideals and use violence as a mean to achieve their ends. There are, however, many skinhead groups that subscribe to left-wing philosophies.

The most effective organizer of white supremacist skinheads was Tom Metzger, a former grand dragon in David Duke's Knights of the Ku Klux Klan and founder of the White Aryan Resistance (WAR) in 1980. Metzger used his public-access television show to promote the growth and cohesion of the skinhead movement.

In 1990, a jury ordered Metzger, his son John (who was involved in a famous on-camera brawl that left talk-show host Geraldo Rivera with a broken nose), and two skinheads to pay $12.5 million to the estate of Mulugeta Seraw, an Ethiopian immigrant killed in 1988 by skinheads in Portland, Oregon. The civil lawsuit, filed by the Anti-Defamation League and the Southern Poverty Law Center, alleged the Metzgers had sent WAR agents to Portland to organize skinheads and incite attacks against minorities. The three skinheads directly involved in the attack pleaded guilty and were sentenced to 20 years to life.[75]

In July 1993, the FBI uncovered a plot by white supremacists in Los Angeles to murder the pastor and congregation of the First African Methodist Episcopal Church. Other African-American targets would then be hit, including much-publicized California beating victim Rodney King, New York politician and activist Al Sharpton, and members of the rap group Public Enemy. The purpose was to trigger a bloody race war. The eight skinheads who were arrested were linked to WAR, the World Church of the Creator (WCOTC), and the Fourth Reich Skinheads.[76]

Another group with a sizable skinhead following is the National Alliance, formed in 1974 by William Pierce. Based in a compound near the small town of Hillsboro, West Virginia, the organization is considered one of the most dangerous hate groups today, mostly because of the savvy of its leader.[77] Pierce displayed a willingness to use a variety of methods to recruit new members, from his shortwave radio show to the acquisition of Resistance Records, the primary U.S.-based source for hatecore music. Pierce was also the author of *The Turner Diaries* (1978), a racist novel that has inspired a number of right-wing extremists to act on their ideals. Timothy McVeigh, who orchestrated an explosion that destroyed a federal office building in Oklahoma City, killing 168 and injuring more than 500, was known to be a fan of the book, and one of the novel's early scenes depicts a bombing whose methods are eerily similar to those used by McVeigh. In 1989, Pierce wrote the novel *Hunter*, which advocates solitary acts of subversion against the government.

The World Church of the Creator (WCOTC) is a white supremacist, anti-Semitic, anti-Christian organization that originated in 1973 and was revived in 1996 by Matthew Hale, who set up the group's headquarters in his father's house in East Peoria, Illinois. The church's ideology is based in the concept of Creativity, or white worship, and purports to be an alternative for those who are unable to reconcile their racism with Christianity. Hale reads from the White Man's Bible during services, and the church performs its own marriage, baptism, and memorial services.[78] Because of his racist beliefs, Hale, a law-school graduate, was declared by an Illinois state bar panel to be "morally unfit" to practice law.

The WCOTC gained national attention when 21-year-old university student Benjamin Smith began a three-day, two-state shooting spree on July 2, 1999. Smith killed a black man and a Korean man and injured nine minorities before shooting himself. Afterward, Hale insisted that the church did not embrace violence but refused to express remorse over the killings.[79]

Fundamentalists and Extremists

Christian Identity

Christian Identity is the common ideological link among many fragmented white supremacist groups. The religion has its roots in 19th-century British Israelism, the belief that the British, not the Jews, are God's true chosen people and are lineal descendants of the 10 lost tribes of Israel. The Bible is therefore a recorded history of Aryans. Proponents of Christian Identity believe that different races originated in separate creations by God (polygenesis). Nonwhites, known as "mud people," were created before Adam and Eve and evolved from lower animal species. Adam and Eve, the first white people, were created by God in his likeness and were endowed with special spiritual capacities not shared by nonwhites. The descendants of Adam and Eve, products of divine creation, are God's chosen people. Jews are the offspring of a union between Eve and Satan and thus are the product of the first incident of race mixing, the "original sin" in Eden.[80] Jews, as the literal children of Satan, are believed to be the root of all problems on earth and are therefore subject to death.

Identity shares with fundamentalist Christianity the view that Armageddon is near. Christian Identity, however, rejects the fundamentalists' dispensationalist view that the Rapture will precede the Tribulation. Rather than wishing to be saved, white supremacists look forward to the end times, during which they will fight the forces of evil in an apocalyptic battle.[81]

This rejection of dispensationalism is the root of the survivalist philosophy. Aryans must prepare militarily for Armageddon and the resulting race holy war (RaHoWa) and guard against a conspiracy to exterminate the white race led by the U.S. federal government (referred to as the Zionist Occupation Government, or ZOG) and Jews.

The person most responsible for popularizing Christian Identity was Wesley Swift, who combined British Israelism, anti-Semitism, and political extremism.[82] Swift founded the Church of Jesus Christ Christian in southern California during the 1950s; out of this grew the paramilitary Christian Defense League (CDL), whose first president was Richard Butler. When Swift died in 1970, Butler briefly took over services at the Church of Jesus Christ Christian before moving to Idaho in 1973 to found Aryan Nations.[83]

In Idaho, Butler built a 20-acre compound that included a Christian Identity church and paramilitary training facilities. Beginning in the early 1980s, the compound hosted an annual gathering of white supremacists. The goal of Aryan Nations—which attracted members of the Ku Klux Klan, neo-Nazi groups, and skinhead gangs—was to establish an Aryan nation in the Pacific Northwest. This idea eventually led to trouble: In 1988, federal officials charged 13 right-wing leaders (including Butler) for seditious conspiracy to overthrow the government for the purpose of setting up this racist homeland. The trial, held in Fort Smith, Arkansas, was based on dubious evidence and ended in acquittals for all defendants.

In September 2000, an Idaho jury awarded Victoria Keenan and her son Jason (represented in court by the Southern Poverty Law Center) $6.3 million for an attack they suffered at the hands of Aryan Nations security guards near the compound. A federal judge awarded the title to the compound to the Keenans, forcing Butler into bankruptcy. The land was bought by millionaire Greg Carr (founder of the Internet service Prodigy), who planned to turn the property into an education center for human rights issues. Butler remained defiant, claiming that Aryan Nations was not dead. In 2001, he held the annual Aryan Congress at a state park not far from the site of his former compound.

In 1983, Robert Matthews organized a group called The Order, also known as Bruders Schweigen (Silent Brotherhood). Although not strictly Christian Identity, the group included a large number of Identity followers recruited from Aryan Nations. Basing its organization on *The Turner Diaries*, The Order sought to overthrow ZOG. To raise funds for this coup, The Order counterfeited money and went on a two-year bank robbing spree. A Brinks heist in Ukiah, California, netted $3.8 million, but evidence from the crime scene was traced to Matthews. He was killed on December 8, 1984, on Whidbey Island, Washington, in a dramatic shootout with law enforcement officials. Other Order members were arrested during 1985 and 1986. In November 1987, two members were sentenced to 150 years in prison for killing Jewish radio talk-show host Alan Berg.

Another associate of Aryan Nations was Buford O. Furrow, Jr. In August 1999, Furrow wounded five people, including three children, when he opened fire at a Jewish community center in Los Angeles. A few hours later, he killed Filipino-American postal worker Joseph Santos Ileto. Furrow turned himself in the following day, pleaded guilty to all charges, and was sentenced to five life terms.

Furrow's shooting spree was inspired by his desire to join the Phineas Priesthood, which grants membership to those who kill Jews, homosexuals, and nonwhites. Identity leader Richard Kelly Hoskins's book *The Vigilantes of Christendom*, a copy of which was found in Furrow's van, advocated violent "Phineas actions" to restore authority of God's law. This call to arms was based on a passage in the Bible (Numbers 25) in which a man named Phineas killed an Israeli and his heathen wife with a spear for violating God's prohibition against consorting with non-Israeli women. (To Identity followers, the term *Israeli* denotes a white descendant of Adam and Eve.)

Fundamentalists and Extremists

Militias

Militias are locally based private groups that engage in paramilitary exercises to protect their communities against tyranny, assert the right to bear arms, and defend the ideals of the U.S. Constitution.[84] Like other right-wing extremists, these so-called Patriots are often preoccupied with conspiracies allegedly bent on undermining the freedoms of American citizens.

On September 11, 1990, President George Bush described his vision of a secure post–cold war world as a New World Order. Conspiracy-minded extremists saw this as a slip of the tongue that revealed secret plans to create a one-world government. Patriots believed that a secret organization of wealthy men would implement their plan for world domination through the use of foreign troops under United Nations command, hundreds of thousands of which were already training on U.S. soil. Road signs were thought to contain secret codes to direct these foreign invaders, while agents in black helicopters kept subversives under surveillance. Militia members believed that gun owners and Patriots would eventually be rounded up and incarcerated in concentration camps built by the Federal Emergency Management Agency (FEMA).[85]

Militia antecedents include the Minutemen and the Posse Comitatus, the latter founded by Henry L. Beach and William P. Gale in 1969. Members claimed that the highest level of legal authority was the county sheriff. They refused to pay taxes or get drivers' licenses, and they relied on conspiracy theories for their motivation.[86]

In 1983, Christian Identity and Posse Comitatus member Gordon Kahl shot and killed two federal marshals who attempted to arrest him for failing to pay income tax and violating parole. Kahl fled and was later tracked to Alabama. During the shoot-out that followed, a local sheriff was wounded, and Kahl was killed. He became the first in a line of right-wing martyrs that includes Robert Matthews, Randy Weaver's family, the Branch Davidians, and Timothy McVeigh.

In the summer of 1992, federal agents surrounded Randy Weaver's cabin at Ruby Ridge, Idaho, in an attempt to arrest him on firearms charges. During the initial shoot-out, Weaver's friend Kevin Harris killed U.S. Marshal William Degan, and federal agents killed Weaver's 14-year-old son, Sammy. An 11-day standoff followed, during which FBI snipers wounded Weaver and Harris, then killed Weaver's unarmed wife, Vicky, who was carrying her baby at the time.

After their surrender, Weaver and Harris were charged with murder, conspiracy, and assault. Harris was acquitted, and Weaver was found guilty only of failing to appear in court on the original firearms charges. In 1995, he collected $3.1 million in damages against the government. A

44

U.S. Senate subcommittee concluded that the incident had "helped weaken the bond of trust that must exist between ordinary Americans and our law enforcement agencies" and that the FBI had violated its own rules of engagement and falsified evidence to hide its transgressions. In June 2001, Boundary County prosecutors in Idaho announced they would not pursue charges against FBI sharpshooter Lon T. Horiuchi for killing Weaver's wife.[87]

The Ruby Ridge incident inspired the far Right to take action. Several months before the standoff, white supremacist Louis Beam had called for "leaderless resistance," or "phantom cells" of fighters who would not report to any central authority. This concept would later be adopted by many militia groups.[88] Just days after Weaver's surrender, Vietnam War hero James "Bo" Gritz called for the establishment of civilian militias. On October 23, 1992, Christian Identity pastor Pete Peters hosted a gathering of 160 extremists in Estes Park, Colorado. In reaction to Ruby Ridge, they discussed strategies for what would become the militia movement.

The momentum for the birth of the militia movement increased in February 1993, when Bureau of Alcohol, Tobacco and Firearms (ATF) agents stormed the Branch Davidian compound in Waco, Texas, based on tips that the group was stockpiling weapons. The unsuccessful raid left six Branch Davidians and four ATF agents dead.

On April 19, 1993, the FBI tried to end the standoff by launching tear gas into the compound. Minutes later, the building burst into flames, leaving about 80 Davidians dead. Government officials claimed the fire had been deliberately set by Davidians, while right-wing extremists blamed the FBI. In September, the Treasury Department released a concluding statement that "law-enforcement officials botched virtually every aspect of their plan to capture [Branch Davidian leader] David Koresh . . . and then misled investigators and congress about their mistakes." Right-wing extremists were further incensed in 1993 when President Bill Clinton signed into law the Brady Bill, which imposed a waiting period for handgun purchasers.

The first modern militia, the Militia of Montana (MOM), was formed on January 1, 1994, by John Trochmann. It served as the organizational model for other militia groups, which began appearing across the United States.[89] The Michigan Militia, formed in April 1994, soon grew into the nation's largest Patriot group, boasting 6,000 members.

Despite its rapid spread, the militia movement remained invisible to the mainstream until April 19, 1995, when Gulf War veteran Timothy McVeigh set off an explosion that destroyed the nine-story Alfred P. Murrah Federal Building in Oklahoma City, Oklahoma. The bomb, consisting of 4,800 pounds of fertilizer and fuel oil hidden in a rental truck, killed 168 and injured more than 500.

Although McVeigh was never directly linked to a militia group, he shared many of their values and ideals. The date he chose for the bombing had significance among militia groups for at least two reasons: The battles at Lexington and Concord, Massachusetts, that marked the beginning of the American Revolution occurred on April 19, 1775; and the disaster that killed some 80 Branch Davidians in Waco occurred on April 19, 1993. The bombing was a protest against federal abuses at Ruby Ridge and Waco.

Two days after the explosion, McVeigh, already in jail for license plate and gun violations, was arrested by federal agents who had traced him to the bomb through the rental truck's serial number. In June 1997, he was convicted of killing eight federal agents. Two months later, he was sentenced to death. Meanwhile, Terry Nichols, a friend of McVeigh, was convicted of conspiracy in the bombing and sentenced to life in prison.

McVeigh was originally scheduled to die on May 16, 2001, by chemical injection at a federal penitentiary in Terre Haute, Indiana. This date was postponed when it was discovered that the FBI had failed to turn over more than 4,000 documents linked to the case. McVeigh, in a departure from his earlier refusals to seek appeals, sought a further delay of the execution to "promote the integrity of the criminal justice system."[90] A judge ruled that the new files contained no evidence that would change the verdict. McVeigh was put to death on June 11, 2001, at 7:14 A.M.

Following the Oklahoma bombing, the militia movement began to decline. In May 2001, the Southern Poverty Law Center reported the existence of 194 Patriot groups, down from 858 in 1996. Militia of Montana leader Trochmann claimed that many former members had "gone underground due to harassment and scrutiny from mainstream media." At the same time that militia groups were declining, membership in racist and anti-Semitic groups was reported to be growing.[91]

Despite their decline in numbers, militia groups continued to make the news. In March 1996, the Montana Freemen began an 81-day standoff with police in Montana after its leaders were arrested and charged with fraud. The standoff ended peacefully. A six-day standoff between police and Republic of Texas separatists in 1997 ended in a gun battle that killed a militia member. On November 6, 2001, Arizona militia member William Milton Cooper, author of the conspiracy book *Behold a Pale Horse*, was killed by police after he shot a sheriff's deputy. Timothy McVeigh had been a fan of Cooper's shortwave radio show.[92]

RADICAL ENVIRONMENTALISM

Radical environmentalists feel that human destruction of the earth has reached a critical stage, leaving no time for compromise or to work within the established legal system. The belief that the only way to save the planet is to destroy civilization has prompted the use of extremist tactics. The pattern for direct-action environmentalism was set by Greenpeace, which used nonviolent confrontation to protest whaling, oil drilling, and seal hunting. The group's first action occurred on September 15, 1971, when a boat with 12 people aboard sailed from Vancouver, British Columbia, to the Aleutian Islands to protest U.S. underground nuclear tests. The headlines garnered by the activists prompted the end of the tests five months later.

Greenpeace renounced the destruction of property in 1977, prompting cofounder Paul Watson to split off and form the more radical Sea Shepherd Society. Watson made a project out of harassing ships engaged in whaling, sealing, and drift-net fishing. In 1985, French government agents sank the Greenpeace ship *Rainbow Warrior* in the Pacific Ocean, killing a photographer. Subsequently, Greenpeace's membership grew, peaking around 1991. Interest declined during the rest of the 1990s, but George W. Bush's antienvironmental politics prompted a resurgence in membership following the 2000 election.

Inspired by Edward Abbey's novel *The Monkey Wrench Gang* (1975), Earth First! hit the scene in 1979. Cofounder Dave Foreman had spent the 1970s working as a lobbyist for the Wilderness Society but grew frustrated at the compromises he was forced to make while working within the system. Earth First! members advocated what they called "monkeywrenching": heavy-equipment destruction, tree spiking, tree sitting, logging-road blockades, and survey-stake removal. These actions led to numerous violent confrontations between environmentalists and loggers in the West, but they sometimes halted projects long enough for activists to file lawsuits against developers.

In May 1989, four Earth First!ers were arrested while destroying a power-line tower in Arizona. Foreman, though not present, was arrested on conspiracy charges. He pleaded guilty and received a suspended sentence. Shortly afterward, he left Earth First! and started The Wildlands Project (TWP), a plan to "re-wild" the United States by making 50 percent of the land off-limits to human occupation.[93]

Meanwhile, Earth First! continued without Foreman. In May 1990, a bomb exploded in the car of activists Judi Bari and Darryl Cherney. The FBI claimed it was being transported by Bari and Cherney; Earth First!ers claimed it had been planted by antienvironmentalists. The FBI dropped the case before charges were filed and never attempted to find the bomber.

During the 1990s, a debate broke out between those who wished to "mainstream" Earth First! and those who wanted to continue the use of monkeywrenching. A radical contingent formed the Earth Liberation Front

(ELF) in 1992. The following year, ELF and the Animal Liberation Front (ALF) issued press releases declaring their solidarity of action.

ELF's intention was to inflict as much financial harm as possible on corporations whose policies degraded the environment. A posting on the group's web site declared, "The earth isn't dying. It's being killed. And those who are killing it have names and addresses." ELF's preferred method of destruction was arson. On the night of October 18–19, 1998, activists burned a ski resort in Vail, Colorado, that was scheduled to expand into lynx habitat. The fire caused $12 million in damage, making it the costliest crime of its kind in U.S. history. Although many people were questioned, no one was arrested for the deed. Other arson attacks followed. Targets included U.S. Forest Service equipment, genetic engineering laboratories, and new homes that were under construction.

Environmental extremists who acted in the name of ELF operated independently of each other, exhibiting no hierarchical structure or leadership. This made it difficult for the FBI to infiltrate ELF or stop its activities. Vegan baker Craig Rosebraugh, who acted as the group's mouthpiece, was repeatedly subpoenaed and questioned. (A vegan is a vegetarian who does not eat not only animal food products but also animal-derived food products.) Rosebraugh claimed his knowledge was limited to communiqués he received anonymously and passed on to the media. He refused to answer further questions.[94]

In January 2001, police in Indiana arrested Frank Ambrose in connection with a tree spiking incident for which ELF claimed credit. It was the first arrest in the five-year effort to stop the activists. Ambrose, Midwest coordinator of the American Lands Alliance, denied membership in ELF. The following month, four teenagers were charged with arson and arson conspiracy for burning homes under construction on Long Island, New York. As part of a plea bargain, two of them pleaded guilty as adults and agreed to cooperate in investigations into ELF and ALF.

The Unabomber

The attacks of Greenpeace, Earth First!, and ELF have resulted in the destruction of property, but they have never resulted in death. The tactics of Theodore Kaczynski, who earned the name Unabomber for targeting universities and airlines, are another story. During a 17-year period, from 1978 to 1995, Kaczynski mailed or placed 16 bombs, resulting in three deaths.

Kaczynski, a former math professor at the University of California at Berkeley, waged his deadly campaign of letter bombs from a remote cabin in Montana. For years, federal investigators were unable to determine the source of the explosives. Their break finally came in June 1995, when Kaczynski mailed copies of a manifesto to the *New York Times* and *Washington Post*, along with the claim that the bombings would stop if it was published. It was jointly printed by both newspapers on September 19, 1995.

The manifesto finally revealed the mysterious social agenda of the Unabomber. He claimed that the industrial revolution had been a disaster for the human race and advocated the overthrow of the industrial-technological system. Thus was explained his targeting of the airline and computer industries, as well as faculty members in university science departments.

Theodore's brother David read the manifesto in the newspaper. It aroused suspicions in him by its similarity to an antitechnology essay Theodore had written in 1971: David contacted the FBI in February 1996. Theodore was arrested in early April and sentenced to life in prison.

RADICAL ANTIENVIRONMENTALISM

Like radical environmentalists, members of extremist antienvironmentalist groups have used violence against employees and property of the U.S. Forest Service, seen as representative of a corrupt, centralized federal government. The primary currents of antienvironmentalism have been the Sagebrush Rebellion of the 1970s and the more recent wise-use movement. These land-rights movements, based in the West, have sought to claim state sovereignty over federally owned public lands and to replace the conservationist ethic with a system that would allow private mining, logging, and ranching interests to utilize public land for personal profit. Ranchers, loggers, and farmers fed up with federal laws governing land use, water rights, and endangered species have vandalized offices of the Bureau of Land Management (BLM) and the U.S. Forest Service (USFS). In Nevada, where more than 80 percent of the land is owned by the government, federal employees have been refused service in restaurants and taunted at public gatherings.[95]

Corporations such as Chevron and DuPont have, in the past, funded wise-use groups but later shifted their financial support to think tanks and public relations efforts. As a result, some of the leading wise-use groups have ceased operation, citing declines in funding and membership; however, the land-rights movement received a boost in early 2001 when George W. Bush added wise-use advocates to his cabinet. Interior Secretary Gale Norton's previous employer, Mountain States Legal Foundation, gave free legal advice to such groups, while Agriculture Secretary Ann Veneman represented the Nevada Access and Multiple Use Stewardship Coalition in her law practice. Of the

58 Bush appointees to the Interior Department, more than half were industry lobbyists, executives, and consultants, and 12 were active in the wise-use movement.[96]

POST–COLD WAR LEFTISM

Direct-action leftism was revived in 1999 when 40,000 to 60,000 people representing more than 700 organizations took to the streets of Seattle, Washington, to protest the Third Ministerial of the World Trade Organization (WTO). From November 30 to December 3, protesters—ranging from labor unionists and students to environmental activists and anarchists—attempted to deter WTO delegates from attending meetings. Many were trained in civil disobedience tactics by the Ruckus Society; its cofounder, Mike Roselle, had been involved with Abbie Hoffman's Yippies during the 1960s and Earth First! during the 1980s.

The anti-WTO activity was organized to oppose expansion of corporate-led globalization, which was thought to occur at the expense of important social goals, such as justice, national sovereignty, cultural diversity, and ecological sustainability. Despite this unity of purpose, the protests lacked focus. This was demonstrated most strikingly on November 30, when small bands of Black Bloc anarchists (a collection of anarchists and anarchist affinity groups that organize together for a particular protest action; more a tactic than an established organization, Black Bloc anarchism adheres to no central authority, and participants very their methods of protest from one action to the next) smashed windows while nonviolent protesters begged them to stop. Contrary to most media reports, the anarchists, linked by walkie-talkies and cell phones, were well organized, knew their targets, and had drafted hit lists of businesses whose practices were thought to be particularly destructive to global health.

In response, Seattle police moved in and used tear gas, pepper spray, rubber bullets, and percussion grenades on the demonstrators. When protesters retreated, the police chased them into surrounding neighborhoods and, in some cases, began indiscriminately attacking residents, bystanders, and commuters. The National Guard was called in the following day to restore order.[97] The report of the WTO Accountability Review Committee (ARC)—Seattle's official fact-finding committee—concluded that the city government "failed its citizens through careless and naïve planning, poor communication of its plans and procedures, confused and indecisive police leadership, and imposition of civil emergency measures in questionable ways."[98]

The Battle in Seattle, as it was dubbed by the media, was the first in a series of leftist demonstrations against increasing globalization. In 2000, protesters showed up at the Democratic National Convention in Los Angeles and the Republican National Convention in Philadelphia. Similar demonstrations also occurred in cities around the world. In July 2001, the Group of 8 Summit in Genoa, Italy, drew 100,000 protesters, including 2,000 anarchists. The first death of the movement occurred when 23-year-old protester Carlo Giuliani was shot to death by a police officer. Back in the United States, in early February 2002, an estimated 15,000 protesters marched in New York City against a meeting of the World Economic Forum without any incidents of violence.

---

[1] Karen Armstrong. *The Battle for God.* New York: Ballantine, 2000, p. xiii.

[2] James Davison Hunter. *American Evangelism: Conservative Religion and the Quandary of Modernity.* New Brunswick, N.J.: Rutgers University Press, 1983, p. 9.

[3] Ibid., p. 9.

[4] Ibid., pp. 41–42.

[5] Sara Diamond. *Roads to Dominion: Right-Wing Movements and Political Power in the United States.* New York: Guilford, 1995, p. 105.

[6] Michael D'Antonio. *Fall From Grace: The Failed Crusade of the Christian Right.* New Brunswick, N.J.: Rutgers University Press, 1992, pp. 5–7.

[7] Diamond, *Roads to Dominion*, pp. 171, 253.

[8] Robert Dreyfuss. "The Holy War on Gays." *Rolling Stone*, March 18, 1999, pp. 38–41.

[9] Sara Diamond. *Facing the Wrath: Confronting the Right in Dangerous Times.* Monroe, Me.: Common Courage, 1996, p. 82.

[10] Tatsha Robertson. "Gays Return to the Fold." *Boston Globe*, September 9, 2000, p. B1.

[11] Joseph L. Conn. "Exploiting Tragedy." *Church and State*, vol. 52 (June 1999), pp. 7–8.

[12] William Martin. *With God on Our Side: The Rise of the Religious Right in America.* New York: Broadway Books, 1996, p. 130.

[13] Diamond, *Facing the Wrath*, p. 34.

[14] Walter Laqueur. *The New Terrorism: Fanaticism and the Arms of Mass Destruction.* New York: Oxford University Press, 1999, p. 229.

[15] Megan Garvey. "Anthrax Threats Mass Mailed to Abortion Clinics." *Los Angeles Times*, November 9, 2001, p. A3.

[16] Tanya Albert. "Ruling Favors Anti-Abortion Web Site." *American Medical News*, vol. 44 (April 23–30, 2001), pp. 16ff.

[17] Martin, *With God on Our Side*, p. 157.

[18] Diamond, *Roads to Dominion*, p. 174.

[19] Ibid., pp. 174–75.

[20] Martin, *With God on Our Side*, p. 201.

[21] Ibid., p. 220.

[22] Ibid., p. 233.

23 Ibid., pp. 242–43.

24 Ibid., p. 254.

25 Armstrong, *The Battle for God*, p. 313.

26 Susan Friend Harding. *The Book of Jerry Falwell: Fundamentalist Language and Politics*. Princeton, N.J.: Princeton University Press, 2000, p. 26.

27 Diamond, *Roads to Dominion*, p. 254.

28 Martin, *With God on Our Side*, p. 318.

29 Ibid., p. 325.

30 Justin Watson. *The Christian Coalition: Dreams of Restoration, Demands for Recognition*. New York: St. Martin's Griffin, 1999, p. 193.

31 Tony Carnes. "Republicans, Christian Right Stunned by Voter Rebuke." *Christianity Today*, vol. 42 (December 7, 1998), p. 20.

32 Michael Isikoff. "Taxing Times for Robertson." *Newsweek*, vol. 133 (June 21, 1999), p. 39.

33 Joseph L. Conn. "Rift on the Right." *Church and State*, vol. 52 (April 1999), pp. 4–6.

34 Derek H. Davis. "Thoughts on the Possible Realignment of the Christian Right in Twenty-First Century America." *Journal of Church and State*, vol. 41 (Summer 1999), pp. 433–43.

35 "The Religious Right Silent at GOP Convention." *Christian Century*, vol. 117 (August 16–August 23, 2000), pp. 824–25.

36 Jonathan Peterson. "New Life for Bush's Faith-Based Plan." *Los Angeles Times*, November 9, 2001, p. A35.

37 Aaron Zitner and Edwin Chen. "Bush OKs Limited Stem Cell Funding." *Los Angeles Times*, August 10, 2001, pp. A1ff.

38 Josh Meyer. "Man Convicted of Taking Part in Bomb Plot." *Los Angeles Times*, April 7, 2001, p. B1.

39 Armstrong, *The Battle for God*, p. 239.

40 Ibid., p. 322.

41 Gill Donovan. "Falwell Apologizes for Remarks on Terrorist Attacks." *National Catholic Reporter*, vol. 37 (September 11, 2001), p. 10.

42 "The Battle in Congress: Security v. Liberty." *Economist*, vol. 361 (October 20, 2001), pp. 31–34.

43 Will Dana. "Civil Liberties Under Attack." *Rolling Stone*, November 8, 2001, pp. 54ff.

44 Roger Scruton. *A Dictionary of Political Thought*. New York: Hill and Wang, 1982, p. 164.

45 John George and Laird Wilcox. *American Extremists: Militias, Supremacists, Klansmen, Communists, and Others*. Amherst, New York: Prometheus Books, 1996, pp. 56–61.

46 Ibid., p. 16.

47 Lyman Tower Sargent, ed. *Extremism in America*. New York: New York University Press, 1995, pp. 9–10.

48 David M. Chalmers. *Hooded Americanism: The History of the Ku Klux Klan*. 3rd ed. Durham, N.C.: Duke University Press, 1987, p. 9.

49 Ibid., p. 9

[50] Ibid., p. 15.

[51] Ibid., p. 19.

[52] Laqueur, *The New Terrorism*, p. 13.

[53] Ibid., p. 14.

[54] George and Wilcox, *American Extremists*, p. 23.

[55] Laqueur, *The New Terrorism*, p. 106.

[56] Roberta Strauss Feuerlicht. *Joe McCarthy and McCarthyism: The Hate That Haunts America.* New York: McGraw-Hill, 1972, p. 35.

[57] Ibid., pp. 38–39.

[58] Chester L. Quarles. *The Ku Klux Klan and Related American Racialist and Antisemitic Organizations: A History and Analysis.* Jefferson, N.C.: McFarland, 1999, p. 48.

[59] Chalmers, *Hooded Americanism*, p. 34.

[60] Ibid., p. 30.

[61] Ibid., p. 215.

[62] Ibid., p. 323.

[63] Ibid., pp. 323–24.

[64] Feuerlicht, *Joe McCarthy and McCarthyism*, p. 9.

[65] Ibid., p. 124.

[66] George Thayer. *The Farther Shores of Politics.* New York: Simon and Schuster, 1967, p. 95.

[67] Chalmers, *Hooded Americanism*, p. 399.

[68] Jennifer B. Smith. *An International History of the Black Panther Party.* New York: Garland, 1999, p. 37.

[69] Twila Decker. "Unbroken." *Los Angeles Times Magazine*, August 5, 2001, pp. 16–17ff.

[70] Ann O'Neal and Tracy Thomas. "A Long Legal Saga." *Los Angeles Times*, November 1, 2001, p. A28.

[71] Jared Sandberg. "Spinning a Web of Hate." *Newsweek*, vol. 134 (July 19, 1999), pp. 28–29.

[72] David E. Kaplan, et al. "Nazism's New Global Threat: The Internet Helps Build a Sophisticated Web of Violent, Well-Funded Racists." *U.S. News & World Report*, vol. 129 (September 25, 2000), pp. 34–35.

[73] Will Blythe. "The Guru of White Hate." *Rolling Stone*, June 8, 2000, pp. 98–106.

[74] Chalmers, *Hooded Americanism*, p. 406.

[75] Gordon Dillow. "Supremacist Money Goes to Africa." *Orange County Register*, March 19, 1995, p. A1.

[76] "Today Los Angeles, Tomorrow…" *Time*, vol. 142 (July 26, 1993), p. 49.

[77] Carl Mollins. "At Home with a Racist Guru." *Maclean's*, vol. 108 (May 8, 1995), pp. 42ff.

[78] Jody Veenker. "Church Leader Worships Whites." *Christianity Today*, vol. 43 (October 25, 1999), p. 91.

[79] "United States: Hatred Unexplained." *Economist*, vol. 352 (July 10, 1999), pp. 25–26.

[80] Jerome Walters. *One Aryan Nation Under God: How Religious Extremists Use the Bible to Justify Their Actions.* Naperville, Ill.: Sourcebooks, 2001, p. 11.

[81] Michael Barkun. *Religion and the Racist Right: The Origins of the Christian Identity Movement.* Rev. ed. Chapel Hill, N.C.: University of North Carolina Press, 1997, pp. 103–4.

[82] Ibid., pp. 60–61.

[83] Ibid., p. 70.

[84] Ibid., pp. 271–72.

[85] Barkun, *Religion and the Racist Right*, pp. 258–60.

[86] Walters, *One Aryan Nation Under God*, p. 4.

[87] Julie Cart. "No Trial for FBI Sniper at Ruby Ridge." *Los Angeles Times*, June 15, 2001, p. A1.

[88] Barkun, *Religion and the Racist Right*, p. 281.

[89] Marc Cooper and Lisa Westberg. "Montana's Mother of All Militias." *Nation*, vol. 260 (May 22, 1995), pp. 714ff.

[90] Richard A. Serrano. "McVeigh Asks Judge to Delay His Execution." *Los Angeles Times*, June 1, 2001, p. A1.

[91] Robert L. Jackson. "Militia Movement 'a Shadow' of Its Past, Study Finds." *Los Angeles Times*, May 9, 2001, p. A20.

[92] "Arizona Militia Figure Is Shot to Death." *Los Angeles Times*, November 7, 2001, p. A24.

[93] John Elvin. "Wild-Eyed in the Wilderness." *Insight on the News*, vol. 17 (April 23, 2001), pp. 21–23.

[94] Kim Murphy. "Disruption Is Activists' Business." *Los Angeles Times*, April 25, 2000, pp. A1ff.

[95] Jill Smolowe. "Enemies of the State." *Time*, vol. 145 (May 8, 1995), pp. 58ff.

[96] Jennifer Hattam. "Wise Use Movement, R.I.P.?" *Backpacker*, May/June 2001, pp. 20–21.

[97] Walden Bello. "Lilliputians Rising—2000: The Year of the Global Protest Against Corporate Globalization." *Multinational Monitor*, vol. 22 (January/February 2001), pp. 33–36. Margaret Levi and David Olson. "The Battle in Seattle." *Politics and Society*, vol. 28 (September 2000), pp. 309–29.

[98] David Morse. "Beyond the Myths of Seattle." *Dissent*, vol. 48 (Summer 2001), pp. 39–43.

CHAPTER 2

THE LAW AND
FUNDAMENTALISM
AND EXTREMISM

LAWS AND COURT CASES

Issues relevant to fundamentalism and extremism are covered by both state and federal laws. Each U.S. state, for example, has passed its own specific legislation concerning abortion, but these laws must exist within the framework determined at the federal level, often by legal cases that have been heard by the Supreme Court. Similarly, many states have passed laws against hate crimes, which can also apply to some terrorist acts, but terrorism itself is generally dealt with on the federal level.

DEFUNCT FEDERAL LEGISLATION

During the 20th century, the constitutionality of several federal laws dealing with sedition was challenged. Although no longer on the books, one of these laws—the Smith Act of 1940—is excerpted here because of the pivotal role it played in helping determine the parameters of free speech in such Supreme Court cases as *Dennis v. United States* (1951) and *Yates v. United States* (1957).

THE SMITH ACT OF 1940

Sections 2 and 3 specify:

> *SEC. 2. (a) It shall be unlawful for any person —*
> > *(1) to knowingly or willfully advocate, abet, advise, or teach the duty, necessity, desirability, or propriety of overthrowing or*

destroying any government in the United States by force or violence, or by the assassination of any officer of any such government;

(2) with intent to cause the overthrow or destruction of any government in the United States, to print, publish, edit, issue, circulate, sell, distribute, or publicly display any written or printed matter advocating, advising, or teaching the duty, necessity, desirability, or propriety of overthrowing or destroying any government in the United States by force or violence;

(3) to organize or help to organize any society, group, or assembly of persons who teach, advocate, or encourage the overthrow or destruction of any government in the United States by force or violence; or to be or become a member of, or affiliate with, any such society, group, or assembly of persons, knowing the purposes thereof . . .

(b) For the purposes of this section, the term "government in the United States" means the Government of the United States, the government of any State, Territory, or possession of the United States, the government of the District of Columbia, or the government of any political subdivision of any of them.

SEC. 3. It shall be unlawful for any person to attempt to commit, or to conspire to commit, any of the acts prohibited by the provisions of this title.

CURRENT FEDERAL LEGISLATION

Current federal legislation is found in the United States Code. Several provisions within the U.S. Code give updated definitions of *sedition* and *advocacy of revolution*.

SEDITION

18 U.S.C. Sec. 2384 defines *seditious conspiracy* as follows:

If two or more persons in any State or Territory, or in any place subject to the jurisdiction of the United States, conspire to overthrow, put down, or to destroy by force the Government of the United States, or to levy war against them, or to oppose by force the authority thereof, or by force to prevent, hinder, or delay the execution of any law of the United States, or by force to seize, take, or possess any property of the United States contrary to the authority thereof, they shall each be fined under this title or imprisoned not more than twenty years, or both.

18 U.S.C. Sec. 2385 deals with advocating the overthrow of the government:

Whoever knowingly or willfully advocates, abets, advises, or teaches the duty, necessity, desirability, or propriety of overthrowing or destroying the government of the United States or the government of any State, Territory, District or Possession thereof, or the government of any political subdivision therein, by force or violence, or by the assassination of any officer of any such government; or

Whoever, with intent to cause the overthrow or destruction of any such government, prints, publishes, edits, issues, circulates, sells, distributes, or publicly displays any written or printed matter advocating, advising, or teaching the duty, necessity, desirability, or propriety of overthrowing or destroying any government in the United States by force or violence, or attempts to do so; or

Whoever organizes or helps or attempts to organize any society, group, or assembly of persons who teach, advocate, or encourage the overthrow or destruction of any such government by force or violence; or becomes or is a member of, or affiliates with, any such society, group, or assembly of persons, knowing the purposes thereof—Shall be fined under this title or imprisoned not more than twenty years, or both, and shall be ineligible for employment by the United States or any department or agency thereof, for the five years next following his conviction.

If two or more persons conspire to commit any offense named in this section, each shall be fined under this title or imprisoned not more than twenty years, or both, and shall be ineligible for employment by the United States or any department or agency thereof, for the five years next following his conviction.

As used in this section, the terms "organizes" and "organize," with respect to any society, group, or assembly of persons, include the recruiting of new members, the forming of new units, and the regrouping or expansion of existing clubs, classes, and other units of such society, group, or assembly of persons.

ANTITERRORISM ACT OF 1996

The Antiterrorism and Effective Death Penalty Act of 1996 revised segments of the U.S. Code in response to the Oklahoma City bombing of 1995 and, to a lesser extent, the World Trade Center bombing of 1993.

Many provisions of this body of legislation were updated by the USA PATRIOT Act of 2001.

USA PATRIOT ACT OF 2001

The Uniting and Strengthening America by Providing Appropriate Tools Required to Intercept and Obstruct Terrorism (USA PATRIOT) Act of 2001 was passed in response to the September 11, 2001, terrorist attacks on New York City and Washington, D.C. Among the more controversial aspects of the legislation are sections of Title II (Enhanced Surveillance Procedures) that expand the ability of federal authorities to monitor the activities and communications of suspected terrorists. To safeguard against long-term civil liberties abuses, Title II includes a "sunset clause" that renders many of these laws ineffective after December 31, 2005.

A general outline of the 10 titles of the Patriot Act is provided below; however, each of these titles encompasses several subsections that specify and detail legislation. The complete text of the act (Public Law No. 107-56) can be found on the Internet at http://www.cdt.org/security/010911response.shtml. A section-by-section analysis of the act can be found on the Internet at http://www.fps.crs_reps/tssa1210.pdf. The URL http://uscode.house.gov/tbl107.htm provides a table that directs web browsers to sections of the U.S. Code enacted or changed by passage of the USA PATRIOT Act.

TITLE I: Enhancing Domestic Security Against Terrorism
TITLE II: Enhanced Surveillance Procedures
TITLE III: International Money Laundering Abatement and Anti-Terrorist Financing Act of 2001
TITLE IV: Protecting the Border
TITLE V: Removing Obstacles to Investigating Terrorism
TITLE VI: Providing for Victims of Terrorism, Public Safety Officers, and Their Families
TITLE VII: Increased Information Sharing for Critical Infrastructure Protection
TITLE VIII: Strengthening the Criminal Laws Against Terrorism
TITLE IX: Improved Intelligence
TITLE X: Miscellaneous

CONSTITUTIONAL AMENDMENTS

Several amendments to the United States Constitution form the basis of Supreme Court decisions concerning fundamentalism and extremism. Among them are the following.

AMENDMENT I

In the First Amendment, Americans' basic freedoms are stated:

Congress shall make no law respecting an establishment of religion, or prohibiting the free exercise thereof; or abridging the freedom of speech, or of the press; or the right of the people peaceably to assemble, and to petition the Government for a redress of grievances.

AMENDMENT II

The Second Amendment addresses the right to bear arms and organize militia:

A well regulated Militia, being necessary to the security of a free State, the right of the people to keep and bear Arms, shall not be infringed.

AMENDMENT V

Americans' legal rights are outlined in the Fifth Amendment:

No person shall be held to answer for a capital, or otherwise infamous crime, unless on a presentment or indictment of a Grand Jury, except in cases arising in the land or naval forces, or in the Militia, when in actual service in time of war or public danger; nor shall any person be subject for the same offense to be twice put in jeopardy of life or limb; nor shall be compelled in any criminal case to be a witness against himself, nor be deprived of life, liberty, or property, without due process of law; nor shall private property be taken for public use, without just compensation.

AMENDMENT IX

The Ninth Amendment affirms:

The enumeration of the Constitution, of certain rights, shall not be construed to deny or disparage others retained by the people.

AMENDMENT XIV

Finally, the Fourteenth Amendment enumerates:

1. All persons born or naturalized in the United States, and subject to the jurisdiction thereof, are citizens of the United States and of the State wherein they reside. *No State shall make or enforce any law which shall abridge the privileges or immunities of citizens of the United States; nor shall any State deprive any person of life, liberty, or property, without due process of law; nor deny to any person within its jurisdiction the equal protection of the laws.*

2. *Representatives shall be apportioned among the several States according to their respective numbers, counting the whole number of persons in each State, excluding Indians not taxed. But when the right to vote at any election for the choice of electors for President and Vice-President of the United States, Representatives in Congress, the Executive and Judicial officers of a State, or the members of the Legislature thereof, is denied to any of the male inhabitants of such State, being twenty-one years of age, and citizens of the United States, or in any way abridged, except for participation in rebellion, or other crime, the basis of representation therein shall be reduced in the proportion which the number of such male citizens shall bear to the whole number of male citizens twenty-one years of age in such State.*

3. *No person shall be a Senator or Representative in Congress, or elector of President and Vice-President, or hold any office, civil or military, under the United States, or under any State, who, having previously taken an oath, as a member of Congress, or as an officer of the United States, or as a member of any State legislature, or as an executive or judicial officer of any State, to support the Constitution of the United States, shall have engaged in insurrection or rebellion against the same, or given aid or comfort to the enemies thereof. But Congress may by a vote of two-thirds of each House, remove such disability.*

4. *The validity of the public debt of the United States, authorized by law, including debts incurred for payment of pensions and bounties for services in suppressing insurrection or rebellion, shall not be questioned. But neither the United States nor any State shall assume or pay any debt or obligation incurred in aid of insurrection or rebellion against the United States, or any claim for the loss or emancipation of any slave; but all such debts, obligations and claims shall be held illegal and void.*

5. *The Congress shall have power to enforce, by appropriate legislation, the provisions of this article.*

COURT CASES

The cases described below deal with legal issues involving fundamentalism and extremism. Most of these center on the constitutionality of state laws passed for a variety of reasons, including attempts to curb political subversion, to segregate schools, to place undue burdens on women seeking abortions, and to install religion into public schools.

SCHENCK V. UNITED STATES, 249 U.S. 47 (1919)

Background

On June 15, 1917, Congress passed the Espionage Act to prevent interference with the process of drafting men for the American Expeditionary Force to fight in Europe during World War I. On August 20, 1917, while the Socialist Party was preparing to mail antiwar leaflets that urged young men not to submit to the draft, police raided Socialist Party headquarters in Philadelphia, Pennsylvania, and arrested the organizations's general secretary, Charles T. Schenck. He was indicted, tried, and convicted on three charges under the Espionage Act.

Legal Issues

Schenck appealed on the grounds that the First Amendment granted him an absolute guarantee of free speech, thus rendering the Espionage Act unconstitutional.

Decision

The Court upheld Schenck's conviction by ruling that while the act of conspiring to mail antidraft leaflets may be protected in ordinary times, it presented during a time of war a "clear and present danger" of bringing about serious consequences that Congress has a right to prevent. As the Espionage Act punished conspiracies as well as actual obstruction, the fact that the pamphlets were not actually mailed did not prevent the intent to obstruct the draft from being considered a crime.

Impact

Justice Oliver Wendell Holmes invoked for the first time the famous clear and present danger test to determine the degree to which the First Amendment should protect political speech: "The question in every case is whether the words used are used in such circumstances and are of such a nature to create a clear and present danger that they will bring about substantive evils that Congress has a right to prevent." As this case marked the first time the Supreme Court considered a First Amendment free speech case based on federal law, Holmes's groundbreaking test became, for many years, the standard for similar court cases.

GITLOW V. NEW YORK, 268 U.S. 652 (1925)

Background

Benjamin Gitlow, a member of the Socialist Party, was convicted under the 1902 New York Criminal Anarchy Act of circulating copies of a pamphlet called *Left-wing Manifesto*, which urged workers to struggle toward the establishment of a socialist system through strikes and other forms of revolutionary "class action."

Legal Issues

In the initial New York trial, Gitlow's defense team, which included the famous lawyer Clarence Darrow, framed their argument in terms of free speech. Darrow claimed that the manifesto, rather than advocating revolution, merely presented an abstract socialist doctrine and that the New York statute deprived Gitlow of "liberty" without due process of law. The New York court disagreed. Gitlow's appeal eventually reached the Supreme Court, which used the case to consider whether freedom of expression was a right that the federal government should protect against abuses by state laws.

Decision

The Court ruled that the 1902 act, as applied to Gitlow, did not unduly restrict freedom of speech or press, but the justices did accept the view that the freedoms guaranteed by the First Amendment were safeguarded by the due process clause of the Fourteenth Amendment. Justice Edward T. Sanford, speaking for the majority, wrote that "for present purposes, we may and do assume that freedom of speech and of the press . . . are among the fundamental personal rights and 'liberties' protected by the due process clause of the Fourteenth Amendment from impairment by the States."

Impact

This case marked the first time that the First Amendment was determined to have the power to limit the reach of state laws. Over the next 50 years, the parameters of these limitations were hammered out in a series of court proceedings that led to major changes in laws applying to civil liberties. Most significantly, in these proceedings U.S. citizens were often able to turn to federal law if state laws deprived them of fundamental First Amendment rights. On the specific question of Gitlow's guilt, Justice Louis D. Beam's famous dissent from the majority opinion became, by the 1960s, the view of the majority among Supreme Court justices. Calling for the punishment of action, but not expression, he wrote, "The only difference between the expression of an opinion and incitement in the narrower sense is the speaker's enthusiasm for the result. Eloquence may set fire to reason. But whatever may be thought of the redundant discourse before us, it had no chance of starting a present conflagration."

TENNESSEE V. JOHN T. SCOPES (1925)

Background

In March 1925, the Tennessee legislature passed the Tennessee Anti-Evolution Act, making it illegal to "teach any theory that denies the story of the divine creation of man as taught in the Bible, and to teach instead that man had descended from a lower order of animals." This "monkey law" punished any teacher found guilty with a fine of $100 to $500. John Thomas Scopes, a biology teacher in the small town of Dayton, Tennessee, taught a class on evolutionary theory on April 24, 1925. After his arrest on May 7, the American Civil Liberties Union quickly came to his defense. The trial, dubbed the Scopes Monkey Trial by the media, was held July 10–21, 1925.

Legal Issues

Trumpeted as a showdown between modern science and traditional Christian values, the trial pitted legendary lawyer Clarence Darrow, working for the defense, against prosecutor and former presidential candidate William Jennings Bryan. At issue for the defense was the contention that the Tennessee Anti-Evolution Act violated both the Fourteenth Amendment's promise that no one could be deprived of rights without due process of law and the First Amendment's freedom of religion clause. The prosecution, on the other hand, relied on the straightforward argument that Scopes had taught a class that contradicted the biblical Creation story, thus violating Tennessee law.

Decision

The presiding judge, John T. Ralston, ruled out the admissibility of scientific testimony, clearing the way for the jury, after just nine minutes of deliberation, to return a verdict of guilty of teaching evolution. Ralston imposed a fine of $100. Scopes appealed his conviction to the Supreme Court of Tennessee, which agreed that Scopes had broken the law but overturned the conviction on the technicality that the judge had erroneously imposed a fine that should have been set by the jury.

Impact

Although the guilty verdict had few legislative repercussions, the long-term impact of the trial itself cannot be understated. The most dramatic moment occurred when the defense called Bryan to the stand as an expert on the Bible. For the next 90 minutes, Darrow grilled Bryan on his beliefs, forcing the prosecuting attorney to contradict himself on biblical matters. Most significant, the shaken Bryan admitted that it was unlikely that the earth had been created in six days, a core belief among fundamentalists who insisted that the Bible be taken literally. Bryan's death within a week of the trial's end is perhaps symbolic of the fact that the arguments in the case, which was afforded vast amounts of nationwide media coverage, swayed public opinion away from religion and toward scientific reason, forcing fundamentalists to retreat from their recent attempts to influence legislation. Although the Tennessee Anti-Evolution Act remained on the books until 1967, no further attempt was made to enforce it. The conflicts featured in the *Scopes* trial remained largely dormant until the 1960s, when the Supreme Court ruled that a similar state law was unconstitutional because it violated the First Amendment's demand of separation of church and state (*Epperson v. Arkansas*, 1968). Around the same time, fundamentalist Christians were just beginning to reacquaint themselves with American politics after a long absence. These two opposing trends would set the stage for the full-blown culture war that erupted during the 1970s.

WHITNEY V. CALIFORNIA, 274 U.S. 357 (1927)

Background

Charlotte Anita Whitney was convicted of violating California's Criminal Syndicalism Act of 1919 (originally drafted to curtail the activities of the Industrial Workers of the World activist union) by organizing, assisting in organizing, and being a member of a group advocating unlawful force as a political weapon. Whitney was specifically charged with participating in a convention of the Communist Labor Party (CLP) of California, which was affiliated with the Communist International of Moscow. Incidentally, after her proposal that the CLP limit itself to political activity was rejected in favor of a national program advocating strikes and other revolutionary measures, Whitney had resigned from the party.

Legal Issues

The task of the Supreme Court was to determine whether Whitney's short-lived affiliation with the CLP (which she readily admitted) was enough to warrant her conviction under California's Criminal Syndicalism Act.

64

Decision

The Court upheld the original conviction under the California criminal syndicalism law, primarily on the grounds that the state had the right to protect itself from violent criminal action and that a criminal conspiracy was not within the bounds of free speech. This position was echoed by Justice Robert H. Jackson in the *Dennis v. United States* case of 1951.

Impact

Although the decision to uphold the original conviction was unanimous, Justice Louis Brandeis wrote that Whitney's defense team should have invoked the clear and present danger test to determine whether their client's CLP affiliation consisted of dangerous action or mere membership in a political party. Brandeis went on to suggest that the First Amendment, aided in this case by the Fourteenth Amendment's due process clause, guaranteed Whitney's freedom of assembly. This opinion marked another milestone in the Court's adoption of the clear and present danger test in similar cases. *Whitney v. California* itself was eventually overturned by *Brandenburg v. Ohio* in 1969, an era during which First Amendment rights were significantly expanded.

CANTWELL V. CONNECTICUT, 310 U.S. 296 (1940)

Background

On April 26, 1938, three ordained ministers of the Jehovah's Witnesses, Newton Cantwell and his sons, Jesse and Russell, were arrested on a residential street in New Haven, Connecticut, while soliciting contributions and proselytizing. The Cantwells were tried and convicted in a New Haven County court of both soliciting religious contributions without prior municipal approval and inciting others to breach the peace by the nature of their solicitation. (Some residents of the predominantly Catholic street claimed to be so offended by the anti-Catholic nature of the solicitation that they were inspired to threaten violence against the Cantwells.)

Legal Issues

The Cantwells appealed for a reversal of their conviction on the grounds that Connecticut's religious solicitation control law was in violation of the due process clause of the Fourteenth Amendment and denied them First Amendment guarantees of freedom of speech and free exercise of their religion. If this argument of unconstitutionality was accepted, then the conviction for incitement to breach the peace must also fail.

Decision

The Court overturned the Cantwells' conviction. It ruled in the first count that to condition the solicitation of aid for the perpetuation of religious views upon a license, the granting of which rests in the exercise of a determination by state authority as to what is a religious cause, is to lay a forbidden burden upon the exercise of liberty protected by the Constitution. In the second count the Court ruled that the Cantwells' preaching raised no clear and present menace to public peace and order, thus it did not render them liable to conviction.

Impact

This case is considered a milestone because it laid down the application of the "religious clauses" to the states through the Fourteenth Amendment. It was also in this decision that Justice Owen Roberts noted that the free exercise clause "embraces two concepts,—freedom to believe and freedom to act. The first is absolute, but, in the nature of things, the second cannot be."

MINERSVILLE SCHOOL DISTRICT V. GOBITIS, 310 U.S. 586 (1940)

Background

Lillian Gobitis (age 12) and her brother William (age 10), both Jehovah's Witnesses, were expelled from the public schools of Minersville, Pennsylvania, for refusing to salute and pledge allegiance to the United States flag during routine school exercises. Such gestures violated Jehovah's Witness beliefs against worshiping gods other than the Almighty.

Legal Issues

The *Gobitis* case tested the free exercise clause of the First Amendment, which was intended to prevent the persecution of people based on their religious beliefs. Argued on the eve of U.S. entry into World War II, the case took on the added significance of questioning whether national cohesion was more important than religious tolerance under certain circumstances.

Decision

The U.S. Supreme Court upheld the Pennsylvania statute that required all schoolchildren, regardless of religious affiliation, to salute the flag. The Court also upheld the actions of the Pennsylvania school board's expulsion of the Gobitis children for their refusal to salute.

Impact

In an attempt to sway the decision of sole dissenter Justice Harlan F. Stone, Justice Felix Frankfurter wrote a note suggesting that the case should be decided "in the particular setting of our time and circumstances." He continued, "It is relevant to make the adjustment we have to make within the framework of present circumstances and those that are clearly ahead of us." The "circumstances," of course, was the war ravaging Europe and that the United States would enter within half a year.

Despite the lopsided 8-1 vote, the *Gobitis* decision stood for only three years. It was reversed as a result of *West Virginia State Board of Education v. Barnette* (1943), which overturned a similar expulsion as unconstitutional. The dramatic turnaround resulted from both personnel changes (during the interim, Justices Robert H. Jackson and Wiley B. Rutledge had been added to the bench) and a change of viewpoint on the part of Justices Hugo L. Black, William O. Douglas, and Frank Murphy.

EVERSON V. BOARD OF EDUCATION OF EWING TOWNSHIP, 330 U.S. 1 (1947)

Background

The case centered on the constitutionality of a New Jersey law that allowed local boards of education to reimburse the parents of all children attending public and Catholic parochial schools for the cost of bus transportation to and from school.

Legal Issues

The court case was initiated when Arch Everson, a resident and taxpayer in Ewing Township, New Jersey, contended that the state law violated the establishment clause of the First Amendment.

Decision

The Supreme Court upheld the New Jersey statute on the grounds that the religious clauses of the Constitution, while they required the government to maintain neutrality in matters of faith, did not require the government to establish an adversarial relationship with religion. In this case, the New Jersey law, rather than providing monetary assistance directly to parochial schools, merely installed a program that helped get their children to and from school safely, regardless of their religious affiliation. The result was that the Court allowed the state of New Jersey to continue paying the costs of bus transportation of children attending church-affiliated schools and simultaneously set forth the principle that the First Amendment to the Constitution erected a "wall of separation" between church and state.

Impact

The *Everson* case was notable because it represented the first time that a state law was scrutinized under the establishment clause of the First Amendment. In its decision, the Court set the standard by which the religious clauses of the Constitution were later interpreted: It determined that the First Amendment provision denying Congress the power to pass laws respecting establishment of religion was within the scope of the Fourteenth Amendment and was intended to create a "wall of separation" between church and state.

DENNIS V. UNITED STATES, 341 U.S. 494 (1951)

Background

Eugene Dennis, general secretary of the Communist Party USA (CPUSA), and 10 other party leaders were convicted in 1949 of intending to initiate violent revolutionary action. This ruling, coming as it did during a period of growing anticommunist hysteria, was characterized by judicial bias and questionable tactics by both legal teams. Citing violations of their First Amendment rights to free speech, the defendants appealed. The Second Circuit Court of Appeals upheld the convictions based on the clear and present danger test that had been developed by Justice Oliver Wendell Holmes during *Schenck v. United States* (1919).

Legal Issues

The 11 CPUSA members had been convicted under the Smith Act of 1940. The law made it a crime "to knowingly or willfully advocate, abet, advise, or teach the duty, necessity, desirability, or propriety of overthrowing or destroying any government in the United States by force or violence." The Supreme Court agreed to review the case, limiting their consideration to a determination of whether the Smith Act violated the First Amendment and other provisions of the Bill of Rights.

The *Dennis* case posed the tricky question of how far the First Amendment should go to protect the views of antidemocratic dissidents who, if they succeeded in coming to power, would dismantle democratic institutions and processes. Can the government punish subversives for circulating ideas, or must it wait for revolutionaries to act on those ideas before it can take steps to protect itself? In this case, the Court was challenged to determine not whether Congress should have the power to prohibit revolutionary acts intended to overthrow the government, but whether the Smith Act itself was in conflict with the First and Fifth Amendments to the Constitution.

Decision

The Supreme Court, affirming the lower court's ruling, decided that the requisite danger of imminent revolutionary action existed. The fact that the group's activities had never culminated in an actual attempt to overthrow the government was thought to be of no importance in the face of the possibility that members of the CPUSA were standing by to make the attempt when their leaders called upon them to do so. The ruling also took into consideration the current cold war conditions, the fact that communist uprisings had recently occurred in other countries, and the contentious nature of U.S. government relations with countries that CPUSA members ideologically supported.

Chief Justice Fred M. Vinson, in announcing the judgment of the Court, declared, "The basis of the First Amendment is the hypothesis that speech can rebut speech, propaganda will answer propaganda, free debate of ideas will result in the wisest governmental policies." However, the court judged that this was not an unlimited, unqualified right and must sometimes be subordinated to other values and considerations, but only when such speech represented a clear and present danger of attempting or accomplishing the prohibited crime. Vinson continued, "It is the existence of the conspiracy which creates the danger . . . If the ingredients of the reaction are present, we cannot bind the government to wait until the catalyst is added." The purpose of the Smith Act, Vinson contended, was to protect government from change by violence, revolution, or terrorism, and a lack of such laws would lead to anarchy.

Justices Hugo L. Black and William O. Douglas dissented, Douglas arguing that while he agreed that the First Amendment had its limits, "the argument imported much seditious conduct into the record" without evidence that any such activities occurred. He pointed out that the petitioners were not even charged with "conspiracy to overthrow" the government, but rather with conspiracy "to form a party and groups and assemblies of people who teach and advocate the overthrow of our government."

Impact

Despite Justice Vinson's use of the phrase, this decision virtually threw out the 'clear and present danger' test, claiming that while it was applicable in cases involving individuals or small groups, it was inadequate when dealing with speech associated with large-scale conspiracies. Vinson replaced this with his own version of the test, which became known as the "grave and probable danger" rule. It was based on the idea that courts, in each case, "must ask whether the gravity of the 'evil' discounted by its improbability, justifies such invasion of free speech as is necessary to avoid the danger."

The *Dennis* Supreme Court ruling, which exhibited a tremendous amount of judicial tolerance of government attempts to indict and punish anyone thought to be engaged in subversive activities, was the Justice Department's cue to begin an all-out attack on the CPUSA. This assault was stemmed by *Yates v. United States* (1957), although the latter case failed to declare the Smith Act unconstitutional. In addition, although later cases often contradicted the findings of the Dennis case, the Court never repudiated the 'grave and probable danger' rule.

BROWN V. BOARD OF EDUCATION OF TOPEKA, 347 U.S. 483 (1954)

Background

In September 1950, Oliver Brown, an African-American welder living in Topeka, Kansas, tried to enroll his daughter in the local whites-only school, which was closer to his house than the nearest black school. The principal of the white school refused, so Brown sought the help of the local branch of the National Association for the Advancement of Colored People (NAACP). On March 22, 1951, NAACP lawyers representing Brown and several other African-American families in Topeka filed a lawsuit requesting an end to segregation in local schools. The U.S. District Court for the District of Kansas upheld the segregation law, citing the Supreme Court's legitimization of "separate but equal" school systems in *Plessy v. Ferguson* (1896). On appeal, the Supreme Court agreed to hear the case along with several others from across the country that challenged local school segregation policies.

Legal Issues

The lawsuit rested on the question of whether segregation laws were unconstitutional under the Fourteenth Amendment, which promised all citizens of the United States the same legal protections.

Decision

The first hearing in December 1952 ended in a stalemate. Following the second hearing one year later, the Court ruled in 1954 that school segregation was inherently unequal and therefore unconstitutional, and threw out *Plessy v. Ferguson.* Chief Justice Earl Warren stated that "in the field of public education the doctrine of 'separate but equal' has no place."

Impact

In a second *Brown v. Board of Education* decision in 1955, the Court ordered all American school systems to desegregate "with all deliberate speed," but resistance in the South made it necessary to bring many local schools into court one by one. It took until the early 1970s to fully implement the Court's decision. During that 20-year period, the question of desegregation was one of the focal points of both the civil rights movement, which favored desegregation, and the revitalized Ku Klux Klan, which opposed it. Clashes between these polarized interests often led to mass demonstrations and bloody violence that was only quelled by federal intervention.

YATES V. UNITED STATES, 354 U.S. 298 (1957)

Background

In 1951, 14 members of the Communist Party in California were convicted under the conspiracy provisions of the Smith Act, the same charges that had been faced by the 11 defendants in *Dennis v. United States.*

Legal Issues

The Court was again asked to examine the scope of the Smith Act. In the *Dennis* case, it had determined that speech advocating revolutionary action aimed at overthrowing the government was not protected by the First Amendment. Yates, one of the 14 Communist Party members, argued, however, that rather than advocating direct revolutionary action against the government, he had merely expressed his vision of the future based on abstract political doctrine.

Decision

In overturning Yates's conviction, the Court ruled that to violate the Smith Act, a person had to advocate concrete revolutionary action, not just express an abstract opinion.

Impact

The decision, which took a stricter view of the proof necessary to convict members of subversive organizations than the *Dennis* case had, meant that the government now had to prove imminent revolutionary intent in order to sustain a conviction under the Smith Act. This distinction between opinion and advocacy, as well as between indefinite advocacy and immediate advocacy, marked a significant step in the broadening of First Amendment rights.

NATIONAL ASSOCIATION FOR THE ADVANCEMENT OF COLORED PEOPLE V. ALABAMA, 357 U.S. 449 (1958)

Background

The case arose from the efforts of Alabama to oust the National Association for the Advancement of Colored People (NAACP) from its state for conducting activities that allegedly caused irreparable injury to the state's citizens. Among these activities were organizing bus boycotts and providing aid to students seeking to desegregate public universities. Toward this end, Alabama claimed that the NAACP did not qualify to do business within the state because it had not complied with state corporate filing laws. The state circuit court advised the NAACP to stop doing business in the state until the organization produced required documents. After some delay, the NAACP produced all requested documents except a list of the names and addresses of its Alabama members, which the organization claimed the state could not constitutionally compel them to turn over. Publicizing such a list, the NAACP claimed, would threaten the organization's integrity by exposing its members to employment reprisals, harassment, violence, and other activities intended to curtail their freedoms of association and expression. A trial judge held the NAACP in contempt and imposed a fine of $100,000. The Supreme Court of Alabama refused to hear two separate petitions to dismiss the contempt judgment.

Legal Issues

The Court was enjoined to decide whether Alabama's demand that the NAACP reveal the names and addresses of all its Alabama members was rendered unconstitutional by the due process clause of the Fourteenth Amendment.

Decision

The Court reversed the state circuit court's decision and fine, claiming that the NAACP's refusal to turn over the list of names was within its members' Fourteenth Amendment rights. In its ruling, the Court added that publication of the list would significantly curtail the NAACP's activities and would therefore act as an undue burden on the organization's First Amendment right to freedom of association.

Impact

This case established that all the rights of the First Amendment were absorbed into the due process clause of the Fourteenth Amendment and therefore received protection in federal courts against abusive actions by states or the federal government. The decision also expanded the coverage of the First Amendment by recognizing that free expression is a vital component in democratic politics.

SCALES V. UNITED STATES, 367 U.S. 203 (1961)

Background

The defendant, a member of the Communist Party, was convicted under the membership clause of the Smith Act, "which makes a felony the acquisition or holding of membership in any organization which advocates the overthrow of the Government of the United States by force or violence, knowing the purposes thereof."

Legal Issues

In *Dennis v. United States* and *Yates v. United States*, the Supreme Court had considered the constitutionality of the conspiracy provisions of the Smith Act. In *Scales*, as well as in *Noto v. United States* (1961), the Court was asked to rule on the parameters of the Smith Act's membership clause. Scales argued that the Internal Security Act of 1950, which stated in part that "the holding of office nor membership in any Communist organization by any person shall constitute *per se* a violation of that or any other criminal statute," superseded the membership clause of the Smith Act. Therefore, Scales could not be convicted simply for being a member of the Communist Party. Scales also contended that the Smith Act as a whole was unconstitutional on the grounds that it violated both the First Amendment's guarantee of free speech and Fifth Amendment's guarantee of due process.

Decision

The Court upheld the conviction, claiming that Scales had met the Smith Act's requirement of "not only knowing membership, but active and purposive membership, purposive that is as to the organization's criminal ends." The decision therefore held that the act's membership clause was not in violation of the First or Fifth Amendments, and that members of the Communist Party, considered to be an organization that engaged in criminal activity, were open to prosecution as long as they actively and knowingly contributed to the success of these criminal activities.

Impact

This interpretation of the First Amendment, considerably narrower than those handed down during *Yates v. United States* (1957) and *National Association for the Advancement of Colored People v. Alabama* (1958), served to protect "free association" only in cases in which that association was minimal and involved no actual participation in the organization.

NOTO V. UNITED STATES, 367 U.S. 290 (1961)

Background

Like Scales, Noto was convicted of illegal membership in the Communist Party, an organization that advocated the violent overthrow of the United States government.

Legal Issues

Considered a companion case to *Scales v. United States* (1961), the *Noto* case again asked whether the membership clause of the Smith Act was constitutional. However, this case focused more closely on whether the Communist Party actually advocated the overthrow of the U.S. government in a direct way that could be furthered by action, rather than just as an abstract principle.

Decision

Unlike *Scales*, the *Noto* case resulted in a unanimous reversal of the defendant's conviction. Five of the justices decided that the evidence was not "sufficiently strong and sufficiently persuasive" to prove that the Communist Party was engaged in concrete, definitive action intended to overthrow the government "now or in the future." Justice William Brennan and Chief Justice Earl Warren recommended dismissal of the indictment on the ground that the Internal Security Act of 1950, as Scales had unsuccessfully argued in his case, granted immunity from prosecution under the Smith Act's membership clause. Justices Hugo Black and William O. Douglas, meanwhile, stated that Noto's conviction had violated his First Amendment rights.

Impact

Taken together, *Scales* and *Noto* provided a narrow interpretation of the type of advocacy that could be prohibited. In cases where organizations were shown to advocate concrete, revolutionary action, however, membership would be broadly interpreted as illegal. Later First Amendment rulings, as evidenced in *Brandenburg v. Ohio* (1969), were considerably broader.

ENGEL V. VITALE, 370 U.S. 421 (1962)

Background

The Court was asked to consider whether the recitation of a short prayer during opening exercises of school each day in New York's public schools violated the "wall of separation" between church and state.

Legal Issues

The case garnered significant amounts of support among special interest groups. The advocates of separation—backed by the American Civil Liberties Union (ACLU), the American Ethical Union, the American Jewish Committee, and the Synagogue Council of America—argued that state support of religion violated the Constitution. On the other side of the argument were attorney Porter R. Chandler (closely associated with the Archdiocese of New York), the Board of Regents of the State of New York, and 20 state attorneys general, all of whom claimed that prayer fell within the values of free exercise of religion, did not involve coercion, did not involve public money, and therefore created no establishment clause problems.

Decision

The Court invalidated the New York statute and thus banned institutionally sponsored prayer in schools, declaring the practice "wholly inconsistent with the Establishment Clause." Citing no legal precedent for the decision, Justice Hugo L. Black relied heavily on British and American history to support the decision.

Impact

Justice Black, in addressing whether the decision indicated "hostility toward religion or toward prayer," stated that "nothing, of course, could be more wrong. The history of man is inseparable from the history of religion." Advocates of prayer strongly disagreed, and the ruling led to intensely hostile criticism by churches, members of Congress, and the press. As a result, 150 constitutional amendments aimed at reversing the ruling were presented by 111 different members of Congress. The amendment offered by Representative Frank Becker, who had called the *Engel* decision "the most tragic [ruling] in the history of the United States," eventually came to a vote but lost in the House of Representatives.

75

Fundamentalists and Extremists

ABINGTON TOWNSHIP SCHOOL DISTRICT V. SCHEMPP, 374 U.S. 203 (1963)

Background

The Schempps, at the urging of the American Civil Liberties Union, protested a Pennsylvania law requiring the reading of 10 verses of the Bible at the beginning of each public school day. The *Schempp* decision also decided the case of *Murray v. Curkett* (1963), a suit brought by atheists Madalyn and William Murray against a Baltimore statute allowing for the "reading, without comment, of a chapter in the Holy Bible and/or the use of the Lords Prayer" in the city's public schools.

Legal Issues

As in *Engel v. Vitale* (1962), the Court considered whether the establishment clause of the First Amendment forbids prayer, Bible reading, and similar religious observations in public schools.

Decision

Despite widespread opposition to the recent *Engel* case, the Court emphatically reiterated its decision to ban prayer from public school. Toward articulating a test to determine whether legislation was able "to withstand the strictures of the Establishment Clause," Justice Thomas C. Clark stated that laws must have "a secular legislative purpose and a primary effect that neither advances nor prohibits religion." Since the Constitution forbids the establishment of religion by the state and since prayer is a religious exercise, prayer in public schools must be considered unconstitutional.

Impact

Justice Potter Stewart's lone dissent articulated the discontent among those opposed to the ruling. As he had in the *Engel* case, Stewart claimed that the Court had demonstrated hostility, rather than neutrality, toward religion, and that the establishment clause had originally been intended to prevent the government from establishing an official state church. The *Engel* and *Schempp* cases would, in the years to come, be repeatedly cited by fundamentalists as a primary causes for the decline of Christian morality in the United States.

GRISWOLD V. CONNECTICUT, 381 U.S. 479 (1965)

Background

On November 1, 1961, Estelle T. Griswold, executive director of the Planned Parenthood League of Connecticut, and Dr. C. Led Buxton, chairman of Yale University's obstetrics department, opened a birth-control clinic in New Haven, Connecticut. On November 10, state authorities closed the clinic and arrested Griswold and Buxton on charges of violating Connecticut's 1879 anticontraceptive statute by giving information, instruction, and advice to married people as a means of preventing conception. Convicted, they were each fined $100. The Appellate Division of the Sixth Connecticut Circuit Court and the Supreme Court of Errors of Connecticut affirmed the convictions. The defendants appealed to the Supreme Court.

Legal Issues

Attorneys for Griswold and Buxton argued that the anticontraceptive law violated the First Amendment right to free speech, the Fourteenth Amendment's guarantee that the right to liberty cannot be abridged without "due process of law," and the right to privacy guaranteed by the Ninth Amendment.

Decision

The Court, in a 7-2 decision, declared the 1879 law invalid on the grounds that it violated the constitutional "right to privacy." Justice William O. Douglas, in the majority opinion, cited the First, Third, Fourth, Fifth, Ninth, and Fourteenth Amendments. However, the ruling extended privacy protections for contraceptive use only to married couples.

Impact

Before *Griswold*, the Ninth Amendment had been interpreted as reserving to the state government any right not specifically granted to the federal government. Justice Douglas, interpreting the amendment literally, expanded the coverage of such rights "to the people." This view allowed state reproduction laws to be challenged in *Eisenstadt v. Baird* (1972), which extended the legal use of contraceptives to single people, and the controversial *Roe v. Wade* (1973) decision, expanding the right to privacy to include a woman's decision to terminate her pregnancy.

77

Fundamentalists and Extremists

EPPERSON V. ARKANSAS, 393 U.S. 97 (1968)

Background

In 1928, Arkansas passed a law making it illegal, under penalty of fines and dismissal, to teach Charles Darwin's theory that humans evolved from apes. In September 1965, the Little Rock, Arkansas, school system adopted a high school biology text that included evolution, thereby putting biology teachers in an impossible situation: The state of Arkansas would dismiss them for teaching evolution, while the Little Rock school system would dismiss them for refusing to use the new textbook. Susan Epperson, a 10th-grade biology teacher, asked the Arkansas courts to declare the antievolution statute void and to prevent officials of the state and the school system from dismissing teachers for violating the statute's provisions.

Legal Issues

The Chancellery Court determined that the antievolution statute was in violation of the Fourteenth Amendment, which encompasses the promise of protection from state interference with freedom of speech contained within the First Amendment. On appeal, the Supreme Court of Arkansas reversed the lower court. Epperson then appealed to the U.S. Supreme Court.

Decision

The U.S. Supreme Court overturned the decision of the Supreme Court of Arkansas. It agreed with the Chancellery Court's contention that the antievolution statute was in conflict with the constitutional prohibition of state laws respecting the establishment of religion or prohibiting the free exercise thereof. The Court's opinion stated that it was clear that Arkansas had sought to prevent its teachers from discussing the theory of evolution because it is contrary to the belief of some that the Book of Genesis must be the exclusive source of doctrine concerning the origin of humans. The Court also stated that, because the law's reason for existence was clearly fundamentalist sectarian conviction, the Arkansas law could not be defended as an act of religious neutrality.

Impact

This case revived issues similar to those debated during the 1925 trial of John T. Scopes, but in a decidedly less dramatic fashion. The impact of each case was also very different. The *Scopes* trial upheld the antievolution law but forced the retreat of fundamentalists from politics for decades. *Epperson*, on the other hand, decided once and for all that antievolution laws were unconstitutional because they violated the separation of church and state called for by the First Amendment. Rather than retreat from the public spotlight, however, fundamentalist Christians remained on the threshold of reentering the arena of American politics.

BRANDENBURG V. OHIO, 395 U.S. 444 (1969)

Background

Klansman Clarence Brandenburg invited a reporter to film a Ku Klux Klan rally in Hamilton County, Ohio. Portions of the film—which showed 12 hooded figures (some of whom carried firearms) burning a cross and included a speech that called for the possibility of "revengeance" if federal officials continued to "suppress the white, Caucasian race"—were later broadcast on network television news. Based on the evidence contained in the footage, the Klansman was convicted under Ohio's 1919 Criminal Syndicalism Statute of advocating "the duty, necessity, or propriety of crime, sabotage, violence, or unlawful methods of terrorism as a means of accomplishing industrial or political reform" and of assembling with a group whose purpose was to "teach or advocate the doctrines of criminal syndicalism." He was fined $1,000 and sentenced to one to 10 years in prison. The intermediate appellate court of Ohio affirmed the conviction, while the Supreme Court of Ohio dismissed the appeal "for the reason that no substantial constitutional question exists therein."

Legal Issues

Brandenburg appealed his conviction on the grounds that Ohio's Criminal Syndicalism Statute was unconstitutional under the First and Fourteenth Amendments and therefore denied his rights to free speech and press. A similar statute had previously been upheld by *Whitney v. California* (1927).

Decision

The U.S. Supreme Court overturned the conviction on the grounds that "the constitutional guarantees of free speech and free press do not permit a State to forbid or proscribe the advocacy of the use of force or of law violation except where such advocacy is directed to inciting or producing imminent lawless action and is likely to incite or produce such action." This new test was more protective of dangerous speech than the previous clear and present danger test employed in such cases as *Schenck v. United States* (1919) and *Dennis v. United States* (1951). As such, this decision also marked the reversal of the *Whitney v. California* case.

Impact

The *Brandenburg* case was decided in the context of the expansion of First Amendment rights during the 1960s. It marked the final step in the Supreme Court's 50-year development of a constitutional test for speech advocating illegal action and became the foundation of the contemporary understanding of free speech, which seeks to protect political speech in all its forms and to distinguish speech from action. The new test was more objective than the old clear and present danger test and also required an empirical finding of imminent danger, thus protecting the advocacy of lawlessness except in unusually harmful circumstances.

LEMON V. KURTZMAN, 403 U.S. 602 (1971)

Background

Rhode Island's Salary Supplement Act of 1969 and Pennsylvania's Non-Public Elementary and Secondary Education Act of 1969 allowed the states to pay a 15 percent salary supplement to teachers who taught secular subjects in parochial schools.

Legal Issues

The Court was asked to consider whether these two laws violated the First Amendment's religion clauses prohibiting laws that "respect" the establishment of religion or limit its free exercise.

Decision

The Court, in declaring both laws unconstitutional, expressed fear that the practice of paying salary supplements to Roman Catholic schools would "advance" the Catholic religion. Furthermore, the Court worried that efforts by state employees to ensure that teachers aided by the program did not inject religious content would, ironically, lead to "excessive entanglement with religion" by the state. Despite the ruling, Chief Justice Warren Burger readily admitted that "the line of separation . . . is a blurred, indistinct, and variable barrier."

Impact

The excessive entanglement test was added to the two tests devised in the 1963 *Abington Township School District v. Schempp* (that any law must have "a secular legislative purpose and a primary effect that neither advances nor prohibits religion") to create the three-pronged Lemon test. This became the standard measure of establishment. Any law that failed one of these tests was to be considered unconstitutional.

ROE V. WADE, 410 U.S. 113 (1973)

Background

Norma McCorvey (known as Jane Roe during court proceedings), an unmarried pregnant woman who wanted to terminate her pregnancy by abortion, initiated legal action in the U.S. District Court for the Northern District of Texas, seeking a judgment that the 1859 Texas criminal abortion statutes prohibiting abortion except in special medical or life-threatening circumstances were unconstitutional. A separate action was filed by a married childless couple, who stated that they wanted to have the right to terminate pregnancy by abortion if the wife became pregnant at a future date. The two actions were heard together by a three-judge district court, which held that the "Texas abortion laws must be declared unconstitutional because they deprive single women and married couples of their right, secured by the Ninth Amendment, to choose whether to have children." The Fifth Circuit, however, did not issue an order for Texas to stop enforcing the law, entitling McCorvey's attorneys to appeal to the U.S. Supreme Court, which they did.

Legal Issues

The Court was enjoined to decide whether abortion violated the right to privacy guaranteed by the Ninth Amendment.

Decision

The Court upheld the Texas court's decision and acknowledged a constitutional right to abortion. Justice Harry Blackmun, writing for the majority, stated that the right to personal privacy, "whether it be founded in the Fourteenth Amendment's concept of personal liberty and restrictions on state action or in the Ninth Amendment's reservation of rights to the people, is broad enough to encompass a woman's decision to terminate her pregnancy." Rejecting the argument submitted by the state of Texas that states should have the power to infringe women's rights to protect "prenatal life,"

Blackmun said that he had found no evidence that the use of the word *person* in the U.S. Constitution had "any possible prenatal application."

The majority opinion was qualified with the opinion that "the State does have an important and legitimate interest in preserving and protecting the health of the pregnant woman and it has still *another* important and legitimate interest in protecting the potentiality of human life." The decision attempted to balance these competing interests by proscribing increasingly stringent abortion guidelines for each trimester of pregnancy.

Impact

The *Roe* decision, which gave the United States abortion laws that were more lenient than those of any other noncommunist country in the Western world, affected the entire nation, invalidating antiabortion laws in 31 states and forcing the overhaul of abortion legislation in 19 others. The ruling also stirred more passion than perhaps any other judgment in the history of the Supreme Court. The strongest immediate opposition came from Roman Catholics (the abortion issue did not become a linchpin of the fundamentalist Protestant agenda until several years later), which supported a "human rights amendment" that would ban abortion in the United States. This and several other proposed constitutional amendments failed, although some members of Congress have continued attempts, with varying degrees of success, to limit the availability of abortion and to discourage its use.

Ten years after *Roe v. Wade*, six justices refused to overturn and explicitly reaffirmed the 1973 decision in *Akron v. Akron Center for Reproductive Health* (1983). *Webster v. Reproductive Health Services* (1989), however, marked a sharp departure from *Roe*, raising the hopes of fundamentalists that the Court was ready to do away with the 1973 decision.

WALLACE V. JAFFREE, 472 U.S. 38 (1985)

Background

An Alabama statute enacted in 1978 authorized a one-minute period of silence in public schools for "meditation." Additional state laws authorized a period of silence for "meditation or voluntary prayer" (1981) and enabled teachers to lead "willing students" in a specified prayer to "Almighty God . . . the Creator and Supreme Judge of the world" (1982). In 1982, Ishmael Jaffree, whose three children attended public school in Mobile County, challenged the constitutionality of these laws. A federal district court decided that the Supreme Court's *Engel* and *Schempp* rulings had been in error and that states did have the authority to establish religion. A court of appeals reversed this decision.

Legal Issues

The Supreme Court agreed to decide whether the 1981 statute, providing a moment of silence for "meditation or voluntary prayer," violated the First and Fourteenth Amendments.

Decision

Once again ruling against religious exercises in public schools, the Court declared that Alabama's mandated minute of silence was unconstitutional because it was a deliberate effort to encourage religious activity. In his dissenting opinion, Justice William Rehnquist revived Justice Potter Stewart's claim during *Abington Township School District v. Schempp* (1963) that the establishment clause had originally been intended to prevent the government from establishing an official state church, not prevent prayer in public schools.

Impact

Given the changes in political climate since the 1960s, many observers thought the Court might have been ready to use this case to weaken the "wall of separation" between church and state. President Ronald Reagan's administration, along with such fundamentalist organizations as the Moral Majority and the Christian Legal Society, were dedicated to lowering or destroying this wall. In addition, Court decisions during the early 1980s had accommodated direct payment of public funds to religious schools (*Committee for Public Education and Religious Liberty v. Regan*, 1980) and upheld tax credits to parents of children attending both public and private schools (*Mueller v. Allen*, 1983). However, the *Jaffree* case did not live up to the hopes of Christian fundamentalists, as the Court simply reaffirmed its earlier separationist stance.

WEBSTER V. REPRODUCTIVE HEALTH SERVICES, 492 U.S. 490 (1989)

Background

In 1986, Missouri enacted a series of statutes that placed restrictions on abortions. Reproductive Health Services, representing state-employed health professionals and private nonprofit corporations providing abortion services, challenged the constitutionality of these laws in the district court, which struck down the provisions and prohibited their enforcement. The court of appeals affirmed, ruling that the laws violated the Supreme Court's decisions in *Roe v. Wade* and subsequent cases. The state of Missouri subsequently appealed the decision, and the Supreme Court agreed to hear the case.

Legal Issues

The first of the statutes in question was the preamble, which stated that life begins at conception. The second statute barred the use of state property for abortions, making it illegal for any public hospital in the state to perform an abortion even if the patient paid for it. If interpreted in a broad sense, the law might also have barred private hospitals located on land leased from the state from performing abortions. The third provision at issue required physicians to perform tests to determine the viability of a fetus in cases where the doctor thought that the fetus was 20 or more weeks in gestational age.

Decision

The majority of the Court held that the preamble had no legal standing and therefore did not conflict with the statement in *Roe v. Wade* (1973) that a state may not adopt a particular theory of when human life begins. The majority of the Court also declined to rule on whether the second provision would be constitutional if read broadly, holding that the provision was indistinguishable from a ban on public funding of abortions upheld in *Harris v. McRae* (1980).

Concerning the third provision, the *Roe* decision had established a framework in which 20 weeks of gestational age falls within the second trimester and in which regulation was permissible only to safeguard the health of the woman. Justice Sandra Day O'Connor noted that there was a four-week margin of error in determining gestational age; thus, when a doctor believes a fetus to be 20 weeks old, it might be 24 weeks old, placing the pregnancy in its third trimester. Because under *Roe*, states can regulate third-trimester abortions to protect fetuses if they are viable, O'Connor argued that the medical testing provision was consistent with *Roe*. The plurality opinion (5 to 4) of the Court disagreed, arguing that the provision was a second-trimester regulation and therefore could not be upheld unless *Roe v. Wade* was modified. The opinion acknowledged that a woman's interest in choosing abortion was protected by the due process clause but argued that this interest could be affected if the state had a sufficient countervailing interest. Whereas *Roe* had said that the state's interest in protecting potential life increased in importance as the pregnancy advanced, the Court insisted that the state's interest in protecting potential life was of equal weight throughout the pregnancy. Because the medical test promoted that state's interest, it was constitutional.

Although the Court's opinion did not explicitly overrule *Roe v. Wade*, the legal framework it established appeared to authorize states to adopt any regulations they desired to promote the interest in protecting potential life, including criminal bans on performing or obtaining abortions. The Court, however, did not envision such an outcome, stating that it was confident that state legislatures would not return to the "dark ages" of severe restrictions on the availability of abortions. Justice Antonin Scalia, however, chastised the other justices for failing to overrule *Roe*.

Impact

The Court's decision was interpreted by partisan groups organized around both sides of the abortion issue as a major attack on *Roe v. Wade*. Proponents of increased restriction on abortions used the decision to convince some state legislatures to enact laws that were clearly unconstitutional under *Roe*. Interest groups supporting abortion rights mobilized strong support by presenting the decision as a major threat to the right to choose abortion, claiming that courts could no longer be relied on to block restrictions on the availability of abortions.

PLANNED PARENTHOOD OF SOUTHERN PENNSYLVANIA V. CASEY, 505 U.S. 833 (1992)

Background

Planned Parenthood of Southern Pennsylvania brought suit against the state's Abortion Control Act, which sought to eliminate abortions by placing time-consuming and potentially embarrassing restrictions on the procedure.

Legal Issues

The Court agreed to determine the constitutionality of laws that required women to wait at least 24 hours to have an abortion after a doctor informed them about the nature of the procedure and suggested alternatives, minors to have the consent of at least one parent, and women to notify their husbands that they were having an abortion.

Decision

The Court upheld the 24-hour waiting period and the parental consent provision for minors but struck down the spousal notice requirement. Three centrist justices—Sandra Day O'Connor, Anthony M. Kennedy, and David H. Souter—jointly wrote the opinion for the Court, which retained the "central holding" of *Roe v. Wade* that women had a constitutional right to an abortion before the fetus attained viability at roughly six months into the pregnancy. However, the ruling overturned *Roe*'s trimester framework and imposed a new "undue burden" standard that allowed limited, unburdensome state regulation of abortion. Justices Harry A. Blackmun and John P. Stevens both dissented on certain points, favoring upholding more of *Roe* and striking down all provisions of Pennsylvania's Abortion Control Act. Chief Justice William H. Rehnquist and Justices Byron R. White, Antonin Scalia, and Clarence Thomas dissented, arguing that *Roe* had no constitutional basis and should be overturned.

Impact

This decision represented the closest that *Roe v. Wade* has come to being overturned and has, in fact, replaced *Roe* as the dominant precedent on abortion in the United States. Along with *Webster v. Reproductive Health Services* (1989), it has been seen by antiabortionists as another hopeful step toward eventually declaring abortion illegal.

NATIONAL ORGANIZATION FOR WOMEN V. SCHEIDLER, 510 U.S. 249 (1994)

Background

The National Organization for Women (NOW) brought suit on behalf of abortion clinics nationwide against Joseph Scheidler. NOW charged that Scheidler's antiabortion organization, Pro-Life Action League, and similar groups had conspired to use violence, intimidation, and harassment to shut down the clinics.

Legal Issues

The legal basis of NOW's lawsuit was the Racketeer Influenced and Corrupt Organizations Act (RICO) of 1970, which, among other provisions, called for triple damages and other heavy financial penalties for engaging in a "pattern of racketeering activity." Scheidler insisted that RICO did not apply to antiabortionists, as they were not racketeers but rather legitimate social protesters whose actions were protected by the First Amendment. The Court of Appeals for the Seventh Circuit agreed with Scheidler, throwing out NOW's suit on the grounds that the antiabortionists' actions did not have an economic motive and therefore did not fall under the RICO statute.

Decision

The Court, in a unanimous decision, reversed the Seventh Circuit. Chief Justice William Rehnquist wrote, "Nowhere is there any indication that an economic motive is required." Rather, the Court determined that RICO could be applied to any individual or combination of individuals who engaged in a "pattern of racketeering activity," defined as two or more incidents of criminal activity such as extortion, arson, or kidnapping.

Impact

Reactions to the decision were mixed. Antiabortionists accused the Court of siding with abortionists, while advocates of civil liberties worried that RICO would be used to undermine the First Amendment rights of social protesters of all ideologies. On the other hand, law enforcement officials welcomed the decision as giving them a new tool to use against terrorism.

GOOD NEWS CLUB V. MILFORD CENTRAL SCHOOL (2001)

Background

Milford Central School in New York State enacted a policy authorizing district residents to use its building after school for instruction in education, learning, or the arts, and social, civic, recreational, and entertainment uses pertaining to the community welfare. District residents Stephen and Darleen Fournier, sponsors of the Good News Club (a private evangelical Christian organization for children ages six to 12), submitted a request to hold the club's weekly after-school meetings in the school. Milford denied the request on the ground that religious worship was prohibited by the community use policy.

Legal Issues

The Good News Club filed suit, alleging that the denial of its application violated its free speech rights under the First and Fourteenth Amendments. The District Court found the Good Will Club's subject matter to be religious in nature. Because the school had not allowed other religious groups to use its facilities, the court held that it could deny the club access without engaging in unconstitutional viewpoint discrimination. In affirming the first ruling, the Second Circuit court held that because the club's subject matter was religious and its activities fell outside the bounds of pure moral and character development, Milford's policy was constitutional subject discrimination, not unconstitutional viewpoint discrimination.

Fundamentalists and Extremists

Decision

By a 6-3 vote, the Supreme Court overturned the lower court's ruling on the grounds that the Milford Central School's denial of after-school use of its building to the Good News Club, but not to nonreligious groups, was a form of discrimination on the basis of religious viewpoint. It therefore violated the free speech clause of the First Amendment. Writing for the majority, Justice Clarence Thomas declared that when the state operates a "limited public forum" in which citizens may express their views, "speech discussing otherwise permissible subjects cannot be excluded . . . on the ground that the subject is discussed from a religious viewpoint." The Court also rejected the argument that the club's use of the school would put religious pressure on children, noting that children could not attend the club's meetings unless their parents approved. Justices John Paul Stevens, David H. Souter, and Ruth Bader Ginsburg dissented. "It is beyond question that Good News intends to use the public school premises not for the mere discussion of a subject from a particular, Christian point of view, but for an evangelical service of worship calling children to commit themselves in an act of Christian conversion," Souter wrote.

Impact

The decision had the potential to open school facilities to religious organizations nationwide. Supporters declared the ruling a victory for religious free speech, while critics said it would confuse children about the differences between public school and Sunday school. Some public school officials were concerned that the ruling would give groups with extremist political views, such as neo-Nazis, access to school facilities. In addition, legal scholars predicted that the decision would provide a boost for President George W. Bush by heading off litigation threats and court challenges to his faith-based initiatives. In any case, the ruling continued the Supreme Court's trend of increasingly requiring state governments to offer benefits to secular and religious groups on the same basis.

CHAPTER 3

CHRONOLOGY

This chapter presents a chronology of significant dates in fundamentalist and extremist activity in the United States. It focuses primarily on events that occurred in the 1960s and after, because the 1960s were the decade during which fundamentalist Christians began stepping back into politics after a long absence and because the 1960s were characterized by a significant increase in both left- and right-wing extremist activity.

1630

■ A group of English Puritans led by John Winthrop founds the Massachusetts Bay Colony, introducing Calvinism to the New World.

1739

■ George Whitefield, a Methodist preacher from England, begins a three-year evangelical tour of the American colonies. The fervor of his sermons helps ignite the short-lived but influential Great Awakening.

1775

■ *April 19:* A skirmish erupts between colonial minutemen and British troops in the Massachusetts villages of Lexington and Concord. The battle, whose initial gunfire becomes known as the "shot heard 'round the world," marks the beginning of the American Revolution, through which the American colonies eventually win independence from British taxation and rule. The Battle of Lexington, together with the deaths of some 80 Branch Davidians on the same date in 1993, solidifies April 19 as a virtual holy day for antigovernment militias during the 1990s. (In 1995, Timothy McVeigh chooses April 19 as the day to bomb the Alfred P. Murrah Federal Building in Oklahoma City.)

Fundamentalists and Extremists

1833

- William Lloyd Garrison and others form the American Anti-Slave Society in Philadelphia, Pennsylvania, galvanizing the abolitionist movement and turning it into a potent political force.

1859

- Charles Darwin's *On the Origin of Species* is published, positing a theory of evolution based on natural selection.

1865

- *December 24:* The Ku Klux Klan is founded by six men in Pulaski, Tennessee.

1867

- *April:* Delegates from several states convene in Nashville, Tennessee, to officially create the Invisible Empire of the Ku Klux Klan.

1886

- *May 4:* A bomb explodes during a labor rally in Haymarket Square in Chicago, Illinois, causing police to fire their guns into the crowd. In less than five minutes, seven police officers are fatally wounded (one by the bomb, six by police gunfire), and 60 are injured. An unknown number of civilians are killed, but historians believe their casualties far exceed those of the police. Although the identity of the bomber is never known, four men are executed, and three are jailed for the crime. In 1893, Illinois governor John Peter Altgeld pardons the convicted on the grounds that the judge had conducted the trial with "malicious ferocity."

1895

- The Niagara Bible Conference publishes its list of the five essentials of Christianity: inerrancy of the Bible, the deity and virgin birth of Jesus, the substitutionary atonement, the bodily resurrection of Jesus, and the second coming. This list will become the basis for a series of pamphlets titled *The Fundamentals*, published 20 years later.

1905

- Thomas W. Dixon's novel *The Clansman* reignites interest in the Ku Klux Klan.

Chronology

1910–1915

- A series of 12 pamphlets titled *The Fundamentals: A Testimony to the Truth* is published. Paid for by two wealthy Presbyterians, the booklets are distributed free to ministers, theology students, and Sunday school directors.

1915

- D. W. Griffith's film *The Birth of Nation* boosts the revival of the Ku Klux Klan.

1918

- *June:* Eugene V. Debs, cofounder of the Socialist Party, is arrested for delivering an antiwar speech in Canton, Ohio. He is sentenced to 10 years in federal prison, during which time he receives more than 900,000 votes in the 1920 presidential election. He is pardoned by President Warren Harding in 1921.

1919

- *November:* Attorney General R. Mitchell Palmer begins a series of raids on left-wing organizations in the United States. In December, more than 200 of those arrested are placed on the ship *Buford* and deported to Soviet Russia.

1925

- Tennessee enacts a law making it illegal to teach evolution in public schools. A few months later, Dayton teacher John Thomas Scopes is brought to trial for violating the statute. Although fundamentalists win the case, negative public opinion forces them to retreat from their active movement to pass laws that mandate morality. Fundamentalist lawyer William Jennings Bryan dies within a week after the trial, and the World's Christian Fundamentals Association declines rapidly.

1938

- *July:* Father Charles Coughlin founds the Christian Front.

1940

- Congress passes the Smith Act, making it illegal to advocate the overthrow of the U.S. government.

Fundamentalists and Extremists

1942

- The National Association of Evangelicals is founded.

1944

- *April 17:* The Great Sedition Trial *(U.S. v. McWilliams)* begins, which charges 30 Nazi-affiliated extremists with conspiring to foment insubordination in the armed forces. Among the defendants are Silver Shirt Legion founder William Dudley Pelley, "mother's movement" leader Elizabeth Dilling, and Defenders of the Christian Faith founder Gerald B. Winrod. The case ends in a mistrial when the presiding judge dies. The government eventually drops the charges in 1947.

1950

- *February 9:* Senator Joseph McCarthy announces to the press that he possesses a list of government officials who are subversives, jump-starting the hunt for communists in the United States.
- *July 17:* Julius Rosenberg is arrested and charged with conspiring to supply the Soviets with atomic secrets. Three weeks later, his wife, Ethel, is arrested on the same charges. Both are eventually found guilty and executed.

1953

- Billy James Hargis, who founded the Christian Crusade in 1951, heads the Bible Balloon project, which releases 10,000 gas-filled balloons carrying Bible quotes from West Germany into Eastern European communist countries.

1954

- *May 17: Brown v. Board of Education* is decided, ending racially segregated public schooling. The backlash helps inspire the revival of the Ku Klux Klan.
- *December:* After failing to prove his charge that Methodist bishop G. Bromley Oxnam is a communist, Senator Joseph McCarthy is overwhelmingly condemned by the Senate for using investigative tactics "unbecoming a senator." This effectively ends government hunts for communist officials.

1956

- *September:* Jerry Falwell begins preaching over the radio in Lynchburg, Virginia. Three months later, he expands to television.

Chronology

1957

- *September:* Six members of the Ku Klux Klan of the Confederacy abduct and castrate Judge Aron, an African American. All six are subsequently tried and convicted.

1958

- The John Birch Society is founded by Robert Welch.

1959

- George Lincoln Rockwell founds the American Nazi Party.

1960

- *January 11:* The Christian Broadcasting Network (CBN) is launched by Pat Robertson.
- *August 18:* Evangelical leaders meet with Billy Graham in Montreux, Switzerland, to discuss how to prevent the election of John F. Kennedy to the presidency of the United States.

1962

- *June:* Two years after its founding, Students for a Democratic Society (SDS) releases its Port Huron Statement, which calls for a progressive realignment of the Democratic Party. To this end, the organization suggests a political alliance of African Americans, students, peace activists, and liberal organizations.
- *June 25: Engel v. Vitale* U.S. Supreme Court ruling declares school prayer unconstitutional.

1963

- *June 17: Abington v. Schempp* rules against requiring Bible reading in public schools in Pennsylvania and Maryland. In response, several congressmen and senators unsuccessfully attempt to amend the Constitution.
- *September 15:* A bomb explodes at the 16th Street Baptist Church in Birmingham, Alabama, killing four girls.

1964

- *July:* President Johnson signs the Civil Rights Act into law.
- *July 13–16:* During the Republican National Convention in San Francisco, California, presidential candidate Barry Goldwater famously declares, "I

would remind you that extremism in the defense of liberty is no vice! And let me remind you also that moderation in the pursuit of justice is no virtue!" The statement unnerves moderate voters, and Goldwater is ultimately defeated by Lyndon Johnson.

1965

- *February:* President Johnson dramatically escalates the war in Vietnam by increasing the number of ground troops and ordering the first bombing of North Vietnam. The announcement galvanizes the student antiwar movement.
- *March 25:* In Lowndes County, Alabama, members of the Ku Klux Klan murder Viola Liuzzo, a white civil rights worker from Detroit, Michigan. Three Klansmen are sentenced to 10 years in prison under federal civil rights laws.
- *April:* The first national anti–Vietnam War march, organized by Students for a Democratic Society, draws 15,000 protesters to Washington, D.C.

1966

- *June 30:* The National Organization for Women (NOW) is formed.
- *October 15:* Huey Newton and Bobby Seale form the Black Panthers.
- *October 30:* Three groups of heavily armed Minutemen are arrested by police as they prepare coordinated attacks on leftist communes in New York, New Jersey, and Connecticut. Police, who were waiting for the attacks, had been tipped off by an FBI informant.

1967

- *May 2:* Twenty members of the Black Panther Party enter the California State Assembly carrying unloaded guns to protest a state bill that would make it illegal to carry loaded guns in incorporated areas.
- *August 25:* George Lincoln Rockwell, leader of the American Nazi Party, is shot dead in Arlington, Virginia, by former party member John Patler.

1968

- *March 27:* Members of Students for a Democratic Society lead an uprising at Columbia University and seize control of five buildings. Five days later, the police come in, arresting 712 people and injuring 148.
- *August 25:* The Democratic National Convention in Chicago begins, resulting in five days of violent clashes between student protesters and police.

Chronology

1969

- *October 8–11:* Several hundred members of the Weather Underground battle with riot police and damage property during "Four Days of Rage" in Chicago. About 300 Weathermen are arrested, and 73 police officers are injured.
- *December 4:* Chicago police raid a Black Panther apartment, killing Fred Hampton and Mark Clark and wounding four other Panthers. An investigation finds evidence that contradicts the police officers' claim that they had been fired on without provocation.

1970

- *March 6:* Three members of the Weather Underground die in an explosion while making a bomb in the basement of a townhouse in Greenwich Village, New York City.
- *June 9:* A bomb explodes on the second floor of New York City's police headquarters, injuring eight. The Weather Underground claims responsibility.

1971

- Morris Dees founds the Southern Poverty Law Center.
- *March 1:* The Weather Underground bombs the U.S. Senate office building, causing heavy damage to one wing.

1972

- The Equal Rights Amendment passes both houses of Congress and is allotted seven years to achieve the required ratification by three-fourths of the states.

1973

- *January 22:* The U.S. Supreme Court decision on *Roe v. Wade* declares laws restricting abortion during the first six months of pregnancy unconstitutional. Catholic groups immediately decry the decision, but it will take several years before significant numbers of fundamentalist Protestants join the antiabortion movement.

1974

- *February 24:* Patricia Hearst is kidnapped by the Symbionese Liberation Army (SLA). Reinvented as "Tania," she later helps the organization rob several banks.

- *April:* A group of conservative Christians in Kanawha County, West Virginia, seeks to block the adoption of several books for the local K–12 language-arts curriculum. The debate eventually escalates into a battle that includes boycotts, strikes, harassment, physical assaults, and conspiracy to bomb schools. Although the pro-textbook side wins, many of the contested books are never used in schools that opposed their adoption.
- *May 17:* Los Angeles police attack a house in the Watts neighborhood harboring the SLA. Six members of the group are killed.

1975

- Phyllis Schlafly founds the Eagle Forum to fight ratification of the Equal Rights Amendment, a battle in which she eventually triumphs.

1976

- *May 2:* The New York City headquarters of the Communist Party USA is bombed. Three members of Jewish Armed Resistance, an offshoot of the Jewish Defense League, are arrested for the deed.
- *October:* In an interview for *Playboy* magazine, presidential candidate Jimmy Carter confesses that he has looked at women "with lust in his heart." This comment and others cause disillusionment among evangelicals who had previously supported the born-again candidate.

1977

- *October:* David Duke and Tom Metzger organize Klan members to patrol the California-Mexico border to curb the flow of illegal aliens. The patrols are highly publicized.

1978

- *January:* The Illinois Supreme Court rules that a planned neo-Nazi rally by the Nationalist Socialist Party of America (NSPA) in the predominantly Jewish town of Skokie is protected by the First Amendment. The city of Skokie appeals all the way to the U.S. Supreme Court, which declines to prevent the rally. In the end, the NSPA decides to hold the rally in Chicago rather than Skokie on June 24.
- *May:* Two package bombs injure two people at Northwestern University in Evanston, Illinois. These are the first known attacks by the Unabomber.
- *June 24:* The NSPA marches near the Federal Building in Chicago. The handful of neo-Nazis encounters several thousand counterdemonstrators and is led away by police after trying to speak. On July 9, another NSPA rally in Chicago is disrupted by protesters.

Chronology

1979

- *May:* Jerry Falwell is recruited by Howard Phillips, Ed McAteer, and Paul Weyrich to establish the Moral Majority, whose goal is to defeat Jimmy Carter in the upcoming election and politicize conservative Christians. Despite past pronouncements that politics and religion don't mix, Falwell agrees to head the organization.
- *May 26:* Members of the Ku Klux Klan attack civil rights marchers in Decatur, Alabama, resulting in the deaths of two civil rights workers and two Klansmen.
- *November 3:* During a "Death to the Klan" rally in Greensboro, North Carolina, five members of the Communist Workers Party are killed and nine are wounded when gunfire is exchanged with Klansmen and neo-Nazis. The defendants are tried on state murder charges in 1980 and federal civil rights laws in 1984; both trials end in acquittals.

1980

- David Duke, after stepping down from his leadership position in the Ku Klux Klan, founds the National Association for the Advancement of White People.
- *August 14:* Members of the Communist Workers Party attempt to storm the Democratic National Convention in New York City's Madison Square Garden as Jimmy Carter delivers his acceptance speech. Fifteen activists are arrested.
- *August 21:* At a national affairs briefing sponsored by the Religious Roundtable in Dallas, Texas, Southern Baptist Convention president Bailey Smith offends millions of people when he says, "God Almighty does not hear the prayer of the Jew." At the same conference, presidential candidate Ronald Reagan gains the confidence of evangelicals when he tells them, "I know you can't endorse me, but I endorse you."

1981

- *October 20:* Weather Underground fugitive Kathy Boudin is apprehended by the FBI after an attempted armored car robbery near Nyack, New York. Two policemen and one security guard are killed during the unsuccessful holdup. Boudin is sentenced to 20 years to life in prison.

1982

- *July:* The first International Congress of Aryan Nations is held at the Aryan Nations compound in Hayden Lake, Idaho. It becomes an annual event at which racists from across the United States gather.

■ *November 27:* A small Ku Klux Klan rally in Washington, D.C., is over-run by several thousand leftist counterdemonstrators. The ensuing riot causes property damage and leads to 40 arrests. During the unrest, the police surround the Klansmen and lead them to safety.

1983

■ *February 13:* A shoot-out between members of the Posse Comitatus and police ends in the death of two federal marshals and the wounding of three others. Posse member Gordon Kahl escapes the scene.
■ *April:* The Order, a white supremacist group fashioned after events in William Pierce's book *The Turner Diaries*, begins a nearly two-year crime spree by robbing an adult bookstore in Spokane, Washington.
■ *June:* Gordon Kahl is killed by federal authorities during a shoot-out in Arkansas, making him a hero and martyr to the tax protest movement.
■ *November 6:* The leftist Armed Resistance Unit bombs the Senate wing of the U.S. Capitol building to protest the U.S. invasion of Grenada. Laura Whitehorn, Linda S. Evans, and Marilyn Jean Buck are arrested and plead guilty to a conspiracy to bomb eight sites across the United States.

1984

■ *March 20:* The Senate votes on President Ronald Reagan's proposed school prayer amendment. Although a majority supports the amendment, proponents fail to acquire the required two-thirds majority.
■ *June 18:* Radio talk-show host Alan Berg is gunned down by members of The Order in Denver, Colorado. In November 1987, David Lane and Bruce Pierce are each sentenced to 150 years in prison for the murder.
■ *July 19:* The Order robs an armored car in Ukiah, California, netting $3.6 million. A gun left at the crime scene eventually leads the FBI to Order leader Robert Matthews.
■ *November 17:* The Animal Liberation Front claims to have poisoned Mars brand chocolate bars. The ensuing panic leads to millions of bars being removed from store shelves and destroyed.
■ *December 8:* After a 36-hour shoot-out on Whidbey Island, Washington, Order leader Robert Matthews is killed by the FBI.
■ *December 25:* Antiabortion terrorists bomb three abortion clinics in Pen-sacola, Florida.

1985

■ *April 19:* The FBI approaches the Arkansas compound of the Covenant, the Sword, and the Arm of the Lord with an arrest warrant for the group's leader, James Ellison. After a four-day standoff, the heavily armed group surrenders peacefully.

- *September 6:* Members of the Jewish Defense League attempt to kill Elmars Sprogis with a pipe bomb on Long Island. Sprogis, once accused of being a Nazi, had previously been cleared of involvement in war crimes after a federal investigation.
- *October:* Alex Odeh, spokesman for the Arab-American Anti-Discrimination League, is killed by a bomb in Santa Ana, California. The Jewish Defense League, whose members had previously threatened Odeh's life, is suspected.
- *December 11:* A computer store owner is killed by a package bomb in Sacramento, California, the first fatality attributed to the Unabomber.

1986

- *January:* Jerry Falwell announces that the Moral Majority will be renamed the Liberty Federation.
- *October 22:* Surgeon General C. Everett Koop angers fundamentalists when he releases a report on the AIDS crisis recommending that sexually active people use condoms and that children receive sex education.

1987

- A series of scandals involving televangelists Oral Roberts, Jim Bakker, and Jimmy Swaggart undermines the integrity of the evangelical movement.
- *March 4:* More than 30 textbooks are banned from Alabama public schools on the basis that they illegally promote the "religion of secular humanism." The decision is reversed in August by the 11th U.S. circuit court of appeals.
- *May:* Morris Dees wins a judgment against the United Klans of America, which is found liable for the 1981 murder and lynching of an African-American teenager by six of its members. The organization is forced to sell its headquarters and give the proceeds to the deceased man's mother.
- *September:* Pat Robertson resigns his ordination, dropping the title "reverend" in preparation for his presidential campaign.

1988

- Televangelist Pat Robertson campaigns unsuccessfully for president of the United States.
- *April 7:* After a one-year investigation, a federal grand jury in Fort Smith, Arkansas, acquits nine white supremacists on charges that they conspired "between July 1983 and March 1985, to overthrow the government."

Among those indicted were Louis Beam and Aryan Nations leader Richard Butler.

- *November 12:* Ethiopian Mulageta Seraw is beaten to death by three skinheads in Portland, Oregon. One is found guilty of murder, two of manslaughter. The Southern Poverty Law Center and Anti-Defamation League later win a $10-million settlement against White Aryan Resistance founders John and Tom Metzger, who they claim motivated the Portland skinheads to attack minorities.

1989

- The Christian Coalition is formed.
- *April 3:* Animal Liberation Front members break into a research facility at the University of Arizona and release more than 1,200 animals. They then set fire to the laboratory and a nearby administration building.
- *July 3: Webster v. Reproductive Health Services* upholds Missouri law that states "human life begins at conception" and restricts access to abortions. The U.S. Supreme Court comes within one vote of overturning *Roe v. Wade*.

1990

- *April 23:* President George H. W. Bush signs the Hate Crimes Bill into law, mandating stiffer penalties for crimes found to be motivated by bias against a particular group.
- *May 24:* Two members of Earth First! are injured when a bomb explodes under the front seat of their car. Police claim they were planning to use the bomb to disrupt logging operations, but the activists maintain that it was planted by supporters of the lumber industry. No charges are filed.
- *September 11:* President Bush describes his vision for a post–cold war world as the "New World Order." Conspiracy theorists cite this as evidence that federal authorities are involved in a plan to create a one-world government.
- *November 5:* Meir Kahane, leader of the Jewish Defense League, is assassinated in New York. One year later, Arab terrorist El Sayyid al-Nosair is tried for the murder but is convicted only of assault with a deadly weapon.

1991

- *May:* The U.S. Supreme Court decides in *Rust v. Sullivan* that the federally imposed gag rule prohibiting publicly funded clinics from advising women about abortion does not violate free speech rights of doctors or patients.
- *July:* The Promise Keepers holds its first rally in the Colorado University basketball arena.

Chronology

- *July:* Abortion foes begin a six-week Summer of Mercy rally in Wichita, Kansas, during which they block access to family-planning clinics. Thousands of activists are arrested.

1992

- *August 31:* Randy Weaver surrenders after an 11-day standoff at Ruby Ridge, Idaho, that has left his wife, his son, and a U.S. marshal dead.
- *October 23:* Christian Identity minister Pete Peters convenes a summit of 175 right-wing extremists in Estes Park, Colorado, to discuss their response to the Ruby Ridge shootings. Attendees decree that the Bible "provides precedent for what is today termed vigilante action."

1993

- *January:* President Clinton lifts the gag rule that had been upheld in *Rust v. Sullivan.*
- *February 26:* The World Trade Center in New York City is bombed by followers of Egyptian fundamentalist spiritual leader Sheikh Omar Abdel Rahman. Four terrorists are convicted by a federal jury in March 1994, while two others remain at large.
- *February 28:* Law enforcement officials from the Bureau of Alcohol, Tobacco and Firearms (ATF) storm the Branch Davidian compound in Waco, Texas. Six Branch Davidians and four ATF agents are killed. A 51-day standoff follows.
- *March 10:* Antiabortion activist Michael Griffin murders Dr. David Gunn outside a clinic in Pensacola, Florida.
- *April 19:* The FBI fires tear gas into the Branch Davidian compound in Waco. A subsequent fire kills 80 Branch Davidians. The disaster galvanizes the radical Right.
- *July:* Police in Los Angeles uncover a plot by the Fourth Reich Skinheads to start a race war by murdering the pastor and congregation of an African-American church in the city; other targets on the group's hit list include Reverend Al Sharpton and the rap group Public Enemy.
- *July 8:* Randy Weaver is acquitted of murdering a U.S. marshal during the Ruby Ridge standoff.
- *November:* The Brady Bill, mandating a five-day waiting period for handgun purchase, is signed into law. The legislation further angers radicals of the far Right.

1994

- *January 1:* The Militia of Montana, the first modern militia, is founded by leader John Trochmann.

- *February 26:* Eleven Branch Davidians are acquitted of murder charges. Of these, five are convicted of voluntary manslaughter and two of weapons charges, each receiving the maximum allowable prison sentence. The remaining four are acquitted of all charges.
- *April:* The Michigan Militia, which eventually grows into the nation's largest such organization, is formed.
- *July:* Paul Hill, who had circulated a "justifiable homicide" petition, murders abortion provider Dr. John Britton and bodyguard James Barrett in Florida.

1995

- *March:* Ex-Klansman Don Black posts the first white supremacist hate site on the World Wide Web.
- *April 19:* The Alfred P. Murrah Federal Building in Oklahoma City, Oklahoma, is bombed, resulting in the death of 168 people. It is the worst domestic terrorist attack up to that time. Timothy McVeigh is arrested by federal agents in Perry, Oklahoma, on April 21 on suspicion of the bombing, having already been arrested for license plate and gun violations.
- *August 15:* The U.S. Department of Justice agrees to pay $3.1 million to settle a civil lawsuit brought by Randy Weaver for the wrongful death of his wife and son.
- *September 19:* The *Washington Post* and the *New York Times* publish the Unabomber's 35,000-word antitechnology manifesto.
- *October 10:* Ten Islamic fundamentalist terrorists are convicted in U.S. federal court of conspiring to destroy U.S. public buildings and structures. Spiritual leader Sheikh Omar Abdel Rahman is convicted of directing the conspiracy, as well as conspiring to kill Egyptian president Hosni Mubarek.

1996

- *February 14:* Believing that the Unabomber's manifesto was written by his brother Theodore, David Kaczynski contacts the FBI. Theodore is arrested at his remote Montana cabin on April 3.
- *March 25:* The common-law group Montana Freemen begins an 81-day standoff in response to the arrest of its leaders on fraud charges. The confrontation ends with the group's peaceful surrender.
- *April:* Jerry Falwell holds the Washington for Jesus rally in Washington, D.C., during which he stages a mock trial of the United States for engaging in the sins of persecution of the church, homosexuality, abortion, racism, occultism, addictions, and HIV/AIDS. He rules that America is guilty of "violating God's law."

Chronology

- *July 27:* A bomb explodes at Olympic Stadium in Atlanta, Georgia, during the Summer Olympics. Alleged bomber Eric Robert Rudolph is a follower of Christian Identity and is thought to have targeted the Olympics because they represent equality among nations and races.

1997

- *January 16:* Two bombs explode at an abortion clinic in Atlanta, Georgia, causing property damage and injuring six people. Eric Robert Rudolph, suspect in the Olympic bombing, is believed to be responsible.
- *February 28:* A gay and lesbian bar in Atlanta is bombed, injuring five people. Rudolph is suspected.
- *April 23:* Ralph Reed announces he is stepping down as executive director of the Christian Coalition to begin Century Strategies, an Atlanta-based consulting firm dedicated to helping "pro-family, pro-life, and pro-free enterprise candidates at every level of government."
- *May 3:* A six-day standoff between police and Republic of Texas separatists ends in a gun battle that leaves one person dead.
- *June 2:* Timothy McVeigh is convicted of killing eight federal agents in the Oklahoma City bombing.
- *June 11:* Pat Robertson announces he is selling International Family Entertainment to Rupert Murdoch for $1.9 billion and that he is stepping down as president of the Christian Coalition. Despite the moves, he plans to remain active in both organizations.
- *August 14:* Timothy McVeigh is sentenced to death by federal judge Richard Matsch.
- *December 23:* Terry Nichols is convicted of conspiracy in the Oklahoma City bombing; on January 7, 1998, he is sentenced to life in prison.

1998

- The IRS allows Pat Robertson's Christian Broadcasting Network to retain its tax-exempt status if it pays back taxes for 1986 and 1987, during which it violated federal tax laws with its political activities.
- *January 29:* A bomb goes off at an abortion clinic in Birmingham, Alabama, killing off-duty police officer Robert Sanderson and wounding a nurse.
- *May 4:* Ted Kaczynski is sentenced to four consecutive life terms plus 30 years for his mail bombings.
- *June 7:* James Byrd, Jr., is beaten, chained behind a truck, and dragged three miles to his death near Jasper, Texas. Alleged attackers John William King, Lawrence Russell Brewer, and Shawn Allen Berry are avowed white supremacists.

- *October 19:* The Earth Liberation Front sets fire to a ski resort in Vail, Colorado, causing $12 million in damage.
- *October 23:* Barnett Slepian, an obstetrician-gynecologist who performs abortions, is shot by a sniper and killed in his home in Amherst, New York. Suspected murderer James Kopp, an antiabortion activist, is arrested in France on March 29, 2001, after nearly two years on the FBI's Most Wanted list.

1999

- The Internal Revenue Service denies the Christian Coalition's bid to retain its tax-exempt status. The group reorganizes, creating a for-profit branch to support specific candidates for public office.
- *February:* Jerry Falwell alerts parents that Tinky Winky, a character on the PBS children's television show *Teletubbies*, might be gay.
- *February 16:* In a reversal of long-standing philosophy, Paul Weyrich, credited with coining the term *moral majority*, announces, "I no longer believe that there is a moral majority. I do not believe that a majority of Americans actually share our values." He urges Christians to build a separate, parallel structure of Judeo-Christian schools, media and entertainment outlets, and even private courts.
- *February 25:* White supremacist John William King is sentenced to death in the 1998 dragging murder of James Byrd, Jr., in Jasper, Texas.
- *June:* Former Symbionese Liberation Army member Sara Jane Olson, accused of conspiring to kill two police officers in 1975, is arrested after 24 years as a fugitive.
- *July 2:* World Church of the Creator devotee Benjamin Smith begins a killing spree in Indiana and Illinois, during which he shoots eleven members of minority groups, killing two before shooting himself.
- *August 10:* Buford U. Furrow, Jr., shoots five people (four of them children) at a Jewish day-care center in Los Angeles. After leaving the scene, he shoots and kills a postal worker because he looks "like a minority." On March 26, 2001, he is sentenced to five consecutive life terms.
- *November 29:* Anti–World Trade Organization protests erupt in Seattle, Washington, inaugurating a series of large-scale leftist protests in cities around the world over the following years.
- *December 14:* Algerian national Ahmed Ressam is arrested as he tries to enter Washington State from Canada. He is later convicted of conspiracy to bomb unknown locations in the United States around New Year's Day 2000.
- *December 31:* The Earth Liberation Front sets fire to a genetic research facility partly owned by Monsanto Corporation at Michigan State University, causing $400,000 in damage.

Chronology

2000

- *April 17:* James Dobson and other conservative evangelicals launch the Interfaith Council for Environmental Stewardship, which declares that "humans should take priority over nature" and that environmentalists are misguided by "faulty science."
- *May 21:* The Earth Liberation Front claims responsibility for fires at the University of Washington Center for Urban Horticulture in Seattle and at Jefferson Poplar Farms in Clatskaknie, Oregon.
- *June 5:* The U.S. National Commission on Terrorism—created after the 1998 U.S. embassy bombings in Tanzania and Kenya by Islamic fundamentalists—recommends increased spending, tighter controls on financial transactions, and recruitment of informants who may have "unsavory" backgrounds as tactics to fight terrorism. The recommendations raise concerns in some quarters about potential abuses of civil liberties.
- *July 19:* Neo-Nazi Ryan Wilson is ordered to pay $1.1 million to Bonnie Jouhari, a fair-housing activist whom Ryan had terrorized on the Internet.

2001

- President George W. Bush announces plans for "faith-based initiatives," which would supply federal funding for church-based social programs. Among those who denounce the idea are Jerry Falwell and Pat Robertson, who worry that money will go to non-Christian groups.
- *January 16:* Federal officials set May 16, 2001, as the date of execution of Timothy McVeigh.
- *February 14:* A federal judge awards the title of the Aryan Nations's compound in Hayden Lake, Idaho, to Victoria and Jason Keenan, who won $6.3 million in damages after being assaulted by two Aryan Nations security guards.
- *March 28:* A federal appeals court in San Francisco overturns a $107-million Portland, Oregon, jury verdict that had found that a web site with "wanted" posters depicting abortion providers as "baby butchers" posed a threat to the doctors. The appeals court rules that the web site is protected by the First Amendment. Within hours, the site is back on the Internet.
- *May 2:* Ex-Klansman Thomas E. Blanton, Jr., is sentenced to four terms of life in prison for the September 15, 1963, bombing of the 16th Street Baptist Church in Birmingham, Alabama, in which four girls died.

- *May 11:* Timothy McVeigh's original execution date of May 16 is delayed until June 11 pending an investigation into possible mishandling of evidence by the FBI.
- *June 11:* McVeigh is executed.
- *August 9:* George W. Bush OKs limited federal funding for stem cell research, angering fundamentalists who see the research as immoral because it requires the destruction of human embryos.
- *September 11:* Islamic terrorists destroy the World Trade Center towers in New York City and damage the Pentagon in Washington, D.C., by flying hijacked airplanes into them. A fourth plane crashes into a field in southwestern Pennsylvania, apparently after passengers attempt to wrest control from the hijackers. The attack leads to the formation of a U.S.-led global coalition whose goal is to combat terrorism worldwide. On October 7, U.S. and British forces begin a military campaign against Afghanistan, whose ruling Taliban party is suspected of harboring the terrorists who masterminded the plot.
- *October 5:* Bob Stevens, photo editor at the supermarket tabloid the *Sun* in Boca Raton, Florida, dies from inhaled anthrax, the first anthrax-related death in the United States since 1976. Fear of bioterrorism escalates when anonymous, anthrax-tainted letters are received by the offices of the *New York Post*, NBC-TV news anchor Tom Brokaw, and Senate majority leader Tom Daschle, among others. By the end of November, five deaths have been attributed to exposure to anthrax in the United States. While some authorities believe the letters are the work of foreign terrorists, others suspect that domestic extremists are behind the attacks.

2002

- *January 10:* A federal grand jury in Los Angeles indicts Irv Rubin, national chairman of the Jewish Defense League (JDL), and Earl Krugel, the group's West Coast coordinator, for plotting to bomb the Muslim Public Affairs Council, the King Fahd mosque, and a field office of U.S. Representative Darrel E. Issa, an Arab American.
- *January 16:* Former Symbionese Liberation Army members Sara Jane Olson, Emily Harris, William Harris, and Michael Bortin are arrested and charged with murdering Myrna Lee Opsahl during a bank robbery in Carmichael, California, in 1975. Two days later, Olson, already in custody at the time of her arrest for the murder, is sentenced to 20 years to life in prison for her role in a failed plot to plant bombs in Los Angeles Police Department patrol cars in 1975.

Chronology

- **February 27:** Authorities uncover a major weapon stash and a purported hit list targeting local government officials in Kalispell, Montana. David Burgert and Tracy Brockway are arrested and accused of planning assassinations with the purpose of triggering a revolution during which militia members from throughout the western United States would fight National Guard troops.
- **May 22:** Former Ku Klux Klan member Bobby Frank Cherry, 71 years of age, is convicted in the 1963 bombing of the 16th Street Baptist Church in Birmingham, Alabama. Like fellow conspirators Thomas Blanton, Jr., and Robert "Dynamite Bob" Chambliss, both of whom had been convicted earlier, Cherry faces multiple mandatory life sentences.
- **June 8:** Former Christian Coalition executive director Ralph Reed and orthodox rabbi Yechiel Z. Eckstein announce the formation of Stand for Israel, a nonprofit organization whose goal is to mobilize evangelical Christians in support of Israel.
- **June 11:** A federal jury awards $4.4 million in damages to Earth First! activists Judi Bari and Darryl Cherney after finding that FBI agents and Oakland police officers had violated their First and Fourth Amendment rights during an investigation into a 1990 car bombing. Bari's deposition, recorded on videotape shortly before her 1997 death from breast cancer, was presented to the jury on large-screen monitors in the courtroom.
- **June 25:** A federal judge enters a plea of not guilty on behalf of French-Moroccan defendant Zacarias Moussaoui, the only person charged in the United States in connection with the September 11, 2001, airliner hijackings. Authorities charge that Moussaoui conspired with Osama bin Laden to carry out the attacks and would have been the 20th hijacker had he not been jailed in August 2001 on an immigration violation after acting suspiciously at a flight school in Minnesota.

CHAPTER 4

BIOGRAPHICAL LISTING

This chapter provides brief biographies of important American fundamentalists and extremists. Many of these individuals are or have been affiliated with organizations detailed in Chapter 8. Additional information on these and other activists can be found in the sources listed in the bibliography in Chapter 7.

Jim Bakker, Pentecostal televangelist and founder of the Praise the Lord, or People That Love (PTL), ministry in Charlotte, North Carolina. Jim Bakker, along with wife, Tammy Faye, became widely known outside Christian circles in 1987 when the Charlotte *Observer* revealed that Jim had had an affair with church secretary Jessica Hahn in 1980, after which a co-pastor had paid her $250,000 to keep quiet. The scandal widened when the federal government charged the Bakkers with financially defrauding thousands of people who had bought shares in the couple's Christian theme park, Heritage USA. After revoking the ministry's nonprofit status, the Internal Revenue Service sued for $56 million in back taxes. In 1989, Bakker was convicted on 24 counts of broadcast fraud, mail fraud, and conspiracy, and sentenced to 45 years in federal prison. This was later reduced on appeal to eight years, and he was released in 1994. Divorced from Tammy Faye, Bakker spent a few years out of the public eye writing a memoir. In 1998, he moved to southern California, married for the second time, and began volunteering at a Los Angeles ministry.

Bill Bright, founder of the Campus Crusade for Christ (CCC) at the University of California, Los Angeles, in 1951. Bright used military jargon to promote the CCC as a revolutionary movement with the goal of converting young leftists into anticommunist, pro-American, conservative Christians. Originally emphasizing personal salvation, the CCC became involved in politics in 1964 when it campaigned for conservative presidential candidate Barry Goldwater. In 1967, Bright sent CCC recruits to the Berkeley campus of the University of California to help friend and then-governor Ronald Reagan quell student protests. While CCC flourished, Bright continued to involve himself in conservative politics. He established Christian Embassy in 1975 in Washington, D.C., to evangelize government officials. The following year he helped found Third Century Publishers, which supplied clergy with manuals teaching them how to become involved in politics and influence the electoral process. From 1976 to 1980, with funding from wealthy benefactors, Bright spent millions of dollars renting billboards and distributing bumper stickers with the phrase "I Found It!" above a phone number that connected callers to CCC volunteers. On April 19, 1980, he helped organize Washington for Jesus, a highly successful day-long prayer meeting on the Mall in Washington, D.C., that attracted Pat Robertson, Jim Bakker, and 200,000 other born-again Christians. In 1994, Bright cofounded Alliance Defense Fund to help coordinate legal defense for conservative Christians whose religious rights were in jeopardy.

William Jennings Bryan, fundamentalist politician and lawyer. Bryan was elected to the U.S. House of Representatives in 1890, then faced defeat in three attempts (1896, 1900, and 1908) to run for president of the United States as a Democrat. In 1912, he was named Woodrow Wilson's secretary of state but resigned when he was unable to reconcile the obligations of his political office and his pacifist stance toward World War I. Although Bryan supported such progressive issues as women's suffrage and government control of corporate power, his opposition to the teaching of evolution in public schools led to his appointment as prosecutor in the famous Scopes Monkey Trial. While the jury ultimately decided in the prosecution's favor, defense attorney Clarence Darrow succeeded in undermining Bryan's logic concerning both evolution and Christianity, leading to the decades-long retreat of fundamentalism. The humiliated Bryan died within a week of the trial's conclusion.

Pat Buchanan, fundamentalist politician. After serving as White House director of communications during Ronald Reagan's presidency, Buchanan began a series of unsuccessful attempts at the presidency. In 1992, he ran as a Republican on an ultraconservative platform. Although his strong showing in primaries surprised many, he gained most notice for invoking a "religious war" for the "soul of America" during his speech at the Republican convention in Houston, Texas. Some blamed Buchanan for scaring middle-of-the-road voters away from the Republican Party. As a result, Buchanan, despite another strong showing in the primaries, was prevented from speaking publicly during the 1996 Republican convention in San Diego, California. In 2000, claiming that the Republican

Party had lost its nerve, Buchanan ran for president as a candidate for the Reform Party. In May 2001, he announced that he would not seek election in 2004 out of fear that he would take votes away from President George W. Bush.

Richard Girnt Butler, founder of the white supremacist group Aryan Nations. As a member of Wesley Swift's Church of Jesus Christ Christian in Lancaster, California, during the 1960s, Butler ascended to leadership of the paramilitary Christian Defense League (CDL). He continued leading services at the Lancaster church after Swift died in 1970, then moved to Hayden Lake, Idaho, to establish his own Church of Jesus Christ Christian. In 1974, he built a compound (complete with a church, a school, and a paramilitary training ground) in the area and formed Aryan Nations, a political and paramilitary arm of the church that served as an umbrella organization for a network of Klan, neo-Nazi, and other white supremacist groups. The first Aryan Nations World Congress was held at the compound around 1980. In April 1987, Butler, along with nine others, was charged with "seditious conspiracy to overthrow the government" and to set up an Aryan homeland in the Pacific Northwest. The defendants were acquitted in 1988. In 2000, a state court ordered Butler to pay $6 million to the victims of a 1998 attack by security guards at the compound. Although Butler was forced to sell his compound to raise the money, he vowed to remain in the area and keep Aryan Nations alive.

Frank Collin, founder of the National Socialist Party of America (NSPA) in 1970 after he was dismissed from his position as Midwest coordinator of the National Socialist White People's Party. This ouster was based on a rumor (believed by some to have been part of an FBI smear campaign) that Collin's real last name was Cohn and that he was half Jewish. The NSPA gained notoriety in 1977 when Collin declared his organization's intent to hold a rally in the predominantly Jewish town of Skokie, Illinois. The legal wrangling rose all the way to the U.S. Supreme Court, which refused to prevent the group from marching. Much media attention was dedicated to the fact that the neo-Nazis were defended by ACLU legal director David Goldberger, who was Jewish. In the end, Collin cancelled the Skokie rally in favor of a gathering in Chicago, where the NSPA was shouted down by several thousand counterdemonstrators. In 1980, Collin was arrested and sentenced to seven years in prison for taking indecent liberties with adolescent boys.

Charles E. Coughlin, Catholic priest whose weekly radio sermons from the Shrine of the Little Flower in Royal Oak, Michigan, interwove religious, economic, and political messages. He began his radio program to raise funds for the church and eventually established a network that included 26 independent stations and boasted millions of listeners. Coughlin initially supported leftist social programs, and he was considered influential in getting Franklin Delano Roosevelt elected president in 1932. As the Great Depression wore on, however, the priest became a vehement critic of Roosevelt's New Deal policies and issued warnings about communist conspiracies. In 1934, Coughlin founded the National Union for Social Justice. In 1936, he started the magazine *Social Justice*, which published the anti-Semitic tract "Protocols of the Elders of Zion," endorsed fascism, and called for Roosevelt's impeachment. Two years later, Coughlin formed the Christian Front. Meanwhile, his vast audience began to dwindle in response to his growing extremism. He eventually came under federal grand jury investigation for his opposition to U.S. involvement in World War II. In response, Coughlin's bishop told him to cease all "public pronouncements" or leave the priesthood. Coughlin chose the priesthood and, in 1942, stopped publication of his magazine and signed off the air for good. He retired in 1966 and died in 1979, having maintained his silence in political matters since World War II.

Angela Davis, philosophy teacher at University of California, Los Angeles, and avowed communist and Black Panther sympathizer. After the 1969–70 academic year, California regents opted not to renew her contract based on the content of several speeches she had made. Soon after, a warrant was issued for her arrest for allegedly procuring weapons for Jonathan Jackson. Jackson, a Black Panther sympathizer, had entered a Marin County courtroom, distributed guns to three San Quentin inmates, and taken five hostages in the hopes of securing the release of three inmates from Soledad Prison. The situation ended in a shoot-out and the deaths of Jackson, two of the San Quentin convicts, and a judge who had been taken hostage. Davis went underground, only to be arrested in October 1970 in New York. She was subsequently acquitted and became an iconic figure for communists around the world.

Robert Bolivar DePugh, founder, in 1960, of the Minutemen, a paramilitary group that advocated the stockpiling of food and weapons to guard against communist takeover of the United States. In 1966, DePugh launched the Patriotic Party, the political arm of the Minutemen, but the effort only lasted a few years. In November 1966, DePugh was convicted on firearms charges, which set in motion a convoluted series of additional convictions, dropped charges, short jail terms, and a 17-month stint as a federal fugitive. He was finally captured in July 1969. After his release from prison in 1973, DePugh continued his political career, though his extremism and verbal attacks on others eventually alienated him from the rest of the far Right. In 1982, shortly after the failure of his Committee of

Ten Million organization, he retired from political activity. In 1992, DePugh was convicted of weapons violations when a search of his home, stemming from charges of sexual exploitation of a minor, uncovered a cache of old weapons (including a mortar) dating back to the 1960s.

James C. Dobson, founder of Focus on the Family. After publishing *Dare to Discipline* and other books, Dobson resigned from his professorship at University of Southern California in 1976 and founded Focus on the Family in Colorado Springs, Colorado. Dobson served on several government panels during Ronald Reagan's presidency. In 1994, he co-founded the Alliance Defense Fund to provide legal assistance for conservative Christians. In 2000, Dobson was instrumental in launching the Interfaith Council for Environmental Stewardship, which believed that humans should take precedent over nature and that environmentalism was based on faulty science.

David Duke, white separatist politician. Duke's first foray into racist organization was the formation of the White Youth Alliance (later National Party) in 1969 while attending Louisiana State University. In 1975, he founded the Louisiana Knights of the Ku Klux Klan and advocated a more wholesome image for the racist group. In 1980, he left the KKK and founded the National Association for the Advancement of White People to promote racial separatism. Duke's political career began in 1988 with a short-lived primary campaign for president as a Democrat. The party refused him funding or the chance to take part in party-sponsored debates. Duke eventually ran as the Populist Party's nominee and garnered 150,000 votes. The following year, he was elected to the Louisiana state legislature, after which he continued to sell neo-Nazi literature. Duke failed in his bid for the U.S. Senate in 1990 and for the Louisiana governorship in 1991, although he won a majority of the white vote during the latter campaign. His subsequent political career has been mixed: an unsuccessful run in the Republican presidential primaries in 1992, during which he never won more than 11 percent of the vote in any state; a failed attempt at the Senate in 1996; election as chairman of the Republican Executive Committee in St. Tammany Parish near New Orleans in 1997; and another defeat for a congressional seat in 2000.

Jerry Falwell, founder of the Thomas Road Baptist Church, Moral Majority, Liberty Lobby, and the *Old Time Gospel Hour,* all based in Lynchburg, Virginia. The Thomas Road Baptist Church eventually grew from 35 members at its founding in 1956 to 20,000 by the early 1980s. During the 1960s, as his church grew in influence and power, Falwell strongly criticized integration and the civil rights movement. When he opened the private Lynchburg Christian Academy in 1967, many thought it was part of Falwell's strategy to get around the antisegregation laws that had been imposed on public schools. The 1970s were characterized by increasing political involvement on Falwell's part, particularly in work to overturn the U.S. Supreme Court *Roe v. Wade* decision and to thwart passage of the Equal Rights Amendment. He formed Moral Majority in 1979 to urge conservative Christians to get involved in politics, leading him to become the most prominent spokesman for the Christian Right during 1980s. When Moral Majority began losing its effectiveness, Falwell renamed it the Liberty Federation in 1986 in an attempt to gain wide support beyond the fundamentalist movement, but the new organization never gained the influence of its precursor. In 1987, Falwell took over the People That Love (PTL) Club in the wake of the televangelist scandals, but he soon turned it over to the court overseeing legal proceedings against Jim and Tammy Faye Bakker. Falwell, like most televangelists, lost money in the years following the scandals, leading him to disband the Liberty Federation and assume a lower profile. Falwell was widely criticized in late 2001 when, as a guest on Pat Robertson's *700 Club* TV show, he declared that the ungodliness of gays, pagans, and feminists was partly responsible for the September 11, 2001, terrorist attacks on the World Trade Center in New York City and the Pentagon in Washington, D.C.

Dave Foreman, environmental activist. In 1964, as a student, Foreman campaigned for Barry Goldwater. He later joined the U.S. Marine Corps at the height of the Vietnam War but deserted. He was discharged after spending one month in jail. In 1971, he became involved in environmental activism, eventually working as the chief Washington, D.C., lobbyist for the Wilderness Society. By 1980, however, Foreman was frustrated at making too many compromises during his lobbying efforts and confounded the radical environmental group Earth First! The group's first public protest occurred the following year when members used black plastic to create the illusion of a crack in the Glen Canyon dam, a symbol of the environmental destruction of the American Southwest. In 1987, Foreman published *Ecodefense: A Field Guide to Monkeywrenching*, which provided instructions on how to spike trees, disable heavy equipment, and destroy billboards. Shortly after, Foreman divorced himself from the movement, uncomfortable with the countercultural, leftist bent of many Earth First! members. In 1991, he was arrested and tried on charges of conspiring with four others to sabotage nuclear power plants in California, Colorado, and Arizona. Through a plea bargain, Foreman escaped jail time. The same year, he founded the Wildlands Project, whose purpose was to "re-wild" America by making 50 percent of its land off-limits to human occupation and development. In 1995, he was elected to a three-year term as Sierra Club director. After stepping down, Foreman continued his work with the Wildlands Project.

William Graham (Billy Graham), evangelist who influenced U.S. presidents from the 1950s to the 1970s. Ordained a Southern Baptist minister in 1939, Graham became pastor of the First Baptist Church in Western Springs, Illinois, in 1943. The following year, he became the first official field representative for Youth for Christ. Graham's strong anticommunist rhetoric caught the attention of William Randolph Hearst, who, in 1949, sent a telegram instructing the editors of his magazines and newspapers to "puff Graham." As a result, the evangelist's popularity skyrocketed. Graham was a supporter of U.S. involvement in Vietnam but focused more on personal conversion and social justice. An early supporter of civil rights, he ended segregation at his crusades during the early 1950s and pled for an end to racial injustice in an article for *Life* magazine in 1956. That same year, he established *Christianity Today*, which became the flagship publication of mainstream evangelicalism. Graham is perhaps most well known for his connection to various U.S. presidents. He secured a brief visit with President Harry Truman in 1950, advised Dwight Eisenhower on his inaugural prayer in 1952, recited the opening prayer at Lyndon Johnson's inauguration in 1964, and led Richard Nixon's Sunday services at the White House. Despite this, he never publicly endorsed a candidate for president. The 1973 Watergate scandal caused Graham to end his close associations with politicians. Although he questioned the wisdom of the nuclear arms race during 1980s, Graham refused to involve himself in politics during the rise of the Christian Right.

Billy James Hargis, founder of the Christian Crusade to combine fundamentalism with anticommunism. After several years as a traveling minister, Hargis established Christian Echoes Ministry (later renamed the Christian Crusade) in 1947 in Sapulpa, Oklahoma. From there, he used radio, public appearances, and *Christian Crusade* magazine to spread his anticommunist Christian message. During the early 1950s, he supplied information that Senator Joseph McCarthy used to accuse more liberal ministers of communism. In 1953, along with Carl McIntire, Hargis began the Bible Balloon Project, which involved sending helium-filled balloons carrying biblical passages into Iron Curtain countries. During the 1960s, he instructed his followers to volunteer for conservative political candidates and strongly criticized antiwar and civil rights protesters, at one point referring to Martin Luther King, Jr., as "a stinking racial agitator." He founded American Christian College in Tulsa, Oklahoma, in 1969, but five years later, faced with accusations of sexual misconduct by several students at the college, Hargis admitted guilt while blaming "genes and chromosomes" for his behavior. Shortly thereafter, ill health forced him to step back from his work with the Christian Crusade, resign as president of the college, and move to a farm in Neosho, Missouri. After years of obscurity, he revived the Christian Crusade during the 1990s, running it from his farm.

Bob Jones, Sr., founder of Bob Jones University. Jones became a licensed Methodist minister at the age of 15, but he eventually rejected the established church in favor of fundamentalism. He founded Bob Jones University in 1926, which, after several moves, eventually settled in Greenville, South Carolina, in 1947. Jones is well known for his belief that fundamentalists should not interact with those who do not share their values, a separatist ideal that led him to blast Billy Graham and Jerry Falwell for reaching out to nonfundamentalists.

Theodore Kaczynski, a former mathematics professor identified as the Unabomber, who sent letter bombs to people involved in technology-based industries. Between 1975 and 1995, Kaczynski killed three people and injured 23 using bombs he built in his remote Montana cabin. In 1995, the *Washington Post* and the *New York Times* published the Unabomber's anti-industrial manifesto after being assured that the bombings would stop if they did so. Kaczynski's brother, recognizing Theodore's writing style, tipped off the Federal Bureau of Investigation (FBI). Kaczynski pled guilty, was convicted for the killings, and received four life sentences plus 30 years. A later appeal was unsuccessful.

Robert Jay Matthews, founder of The Order (also known as Bruders Schweigen, or Silent Brotherhood). As a young man, Matthews was a member of the John Birch Society and the survivalist Sons of Liberty. He was also active in the tax protest movement and later joined National Alliance. In September 1983, he founded The Order (based on a white supremacist organization described in William Pierce's *The Turner Diaries*), whose membership largely consisted of people Matthews had met at the Aryan Nations compound in Hayden Lake, Idaho. During 1983 and 1984, the group robbed banks and armored cars to raise funds toward creating an Aryan homeland in the Pacific Northwest. Order members also murdered Jewish talk-radio host Alan Berg in Denver. Based on evidence left behind at an armored car robbery in Ukiah, California, on July 19, 1984, federal authorities eventually caught up with Matthews on Whidbey Island, Washington. He was killed there on December 8, 1984, during a dramatic shoot-out with the FBI.

Timothy McVeigh, Persian Gulf War veteran and mastermind of the Oklahoma City bombing. Upon his return to the United States after the war and failure to pass the rigorous training required for entrance into the

Green Berets, the disillusioned McVeigh traveled the gun show circuit trading weapons and selling copies of *The Turner Diaries* by William Pierce. His anger toward the U.S. government deepened following the FBI's standoff with Randy Weaver at Ruby Ridge, Idaho, and the tragic siege at the Branch Davidian complex in Waco, Texas. McVeigh responded by setting off a bomb at the Alfred P. Murrah Federal Building in Oklahoma City, Oklahoma, on April 19, 1995. The blast killed 168 people, the worst incident of terrorism on U.S. soil up to that time. Sentenced to death, McVeigh was executed on June 11, 2001.

Tom Metzger, founder of White Aryan Resistance. He joined David Duke's Knights of the Ku Klux Klan in 1975 and quickly rose to the rank of grand dragon. In 1978, he ran unsuccessfully for San Diego County supervisor. The following year, Metzger broke from Duke's Klan to form his own California Knights of the Ku Klux Klan. He continued his political career, however, winning the Democratic primary for Congress in 1980 but losing the general election. Two years later, he ran for the Democratic nomination for U.S. Senate, gaining 75,000 votes but once again losing the election. In 1983, Metzger changed the name of his group to White Aryan Resistance. He actively sought and received support from young skinheads and began broadcasting the weekly television show *Race and Reason.* In October 1990, a court ruled that Metzger, along with his son John, had motivated skinheads in Portland, Oregon, to murder an Ethiopian man in 1988. The $12.5-million ruling forced Metzger to sell his home and pay an undisclosed percentage of his organization's income to the son of the deceased in Africa. Despite this setback, Metzger continued to run White Aryan Resistance from Fallbrook, California.

Huey Newton, confounder, along with Bobby Seale and David Hilliard, of the Black Panther Party in 1966 to patrol and protect the black community in Oakland, California. In 1967, Newton was involved in a shoot-out with police during which he and a police officer were wounded, and another police officer was killed. Although Newton was found guilty of murder, the California Supreme Court later reversed the decision based on irregularities involving the jury. He was freed on $50,000 bail in 1970, and two subsequent trials ended in hung juries. After facing nearly continuous legal trouble through the 1970s, Newton was shot and killed in 1989 in Oakland. Although he had remained politically active, the murder was thought to be drug related.

William Pierce, founder of the National Alliance. A former University of Oregon physics professor, Pierce was an officer of the National Socialist White People's Party, as well as editor of *National Socialist World,* at the time of George Lincoln Rockwell's assassination in 1967. In 1968, he joined the anti-Semitic National Youth Alliance (NYA), an outgrowth of Willis Carto's Youth for Wallace organization in support of Governor George Wallace. When the NYA split in 1971, Carto's faction was re-named Youth Action, while Pierce's faction became the National Alliance. Originally located in Arlington, Virginia, the National Alliance relocated to Hillsboro, West Virginia, in 1985. Pierce was well known as the author of *The Turner Diaries* (1978), a novel thought by many to have influenced the violent tactics of The Order, as well as Timothy McVeigh's bombing of the Oklahoma City federal building. Pierce also wrote the novel *Hunter* (1989), which advocated individual acts of violence against the government. He died in July 2002 of renal failure.

Ralph Reed, cofounder of the Christian Coalition. Reed became a born-again Christian shortly after graduating from the University of Georgia in 1982. He moved to North Carolina in 1984 and formed Students for America, which supported Jesse Helms in his senatorial race against Jim Hunt. After earning a Ph.D. in history from Emory University, Reed be-came executive director of Christian Coalition in 1989. During his time there, Reed promoted grassroots electoral campaigns and often down-played such volatile issues as abortion and school prayer in order to broaden the organization's appeal. In 1993, in the wake of Bill Clinton's election to the presidency, the organization's membership more than dou-bled. Despite ongoing success, Reed announced in April 1997 that he was stepping down as executive director of the Christian Coalition to begin Century Strategies, a consulting firm dedicated to helping "pro-family, pro-life, and pro–free enterprise candidates at every level of government." Despite his poor record during the 1998 election, he remained the Repub-lican Party's most sought-after adviser for the 2000 election. Among those who retained his services was George W. Bush. That same year, Reed won election to the chairmanship of the Georgia Republican Party.

Oral Roberts, televangelist and founder of Oral Roberts University in Tulsa, Oklahoma. Roberts pioneered the use of television for preaching and faith healing during the 1940s and 1950s. He gained notoriety in March 1987 when he claimed that God would kill him if he failed to raise $8 million in donations within a specified time. A few days before time was up, a dog-track owner sent the money and recommended that Roberts see a psychiatrist. Roberts had no qualms about the fact that the money had been earned by gambling, stating upon receipt that "all money is green."

Marion Gordon Robertson (Pat Robertson), televangelist who founded the Christian Broadcasting Network and confounded the Christian Coali-tion. Robertson became a charismatic evangelical while attending the

Biblical Seminary in New York City from 1956 to 1959. The year after graduating, he founded the Christian Broadcasting Network (CBN) in Portsmouth, Virginia. In 1963, as part of a fund-raising strategy, Robertson founded the *700 Club* television program. After years of avoiding politics, he supported Jimmy Carter for president in 1976. Disappointed that Carter did not live up to his expectations, Robertson again stepped back from politics. He concentrated instead on building CBN University in Virginia Beach, which opened in 1979. In 1981, despite previous pronouncements that politics and religion did not mix, Robertson founded the Freedom Council to teach evangelical Christians "how they could be effective in the political process." He gained some notoriety in 1985 when, on his *700 Club* program, he commanded Hurricane Gloria to veer away from the Virginia coastline; the storm obediently swerved, causing damage to Long Island instead. The Freedom Council closed its doors in 1986 after the Internal Revenue Service warned that, as a tax-exempt organization, it could no longer be used to support Robertson's political aspirations, which culminated in his failed attempt at the U.S. presidency in 1988. The following year, he helped create the Christian Coalition to defeat politicians who opposed his Christian Right agenda. In 2000, 13 years after dropping the title "reverend" during his bid for presidency of the United States, Robertson started using it again.

George Lincoln Rockwell, founder of the American Nazi Party. Rockwell's racist philosophies were heavily influenced by Gerald L. K. Smith, whose virulent anti-Semitism prompted Rockwell to read Adolf Hitler's *Mein Kampf.* Rockwell started several racist organizations and supported Senator Joseph McCarthy before forming the American Nazi Party (ANP) in Arlington, Virginia, in 1959. Rockwell spent most of the 1960s gaining attention through his public-speaking tours and activism. In 1965, he ran unsuccessfully for governor of Virginia, after which he changed the name of the ANP to the National Socialist White People's Party. Rockwell was assassinated in Arlington on August 25, 1967, by party dissident John Patler.

Phyllis Schlafly, pro–family values activist. She first gained national attention with her self-published book *A Choice Not an Echo* (1964), which purported to show how nominations at the Republican presidential conventions have historically been controlled by East Coast big money. The book eventually sold 3 million copies. In 1967, Schlafly started publishing her monthly newsletter, the *Phyllis Schlafly Report.* In 1972, she founded the pro-family organization Eagle Forum, which she used as a vehicle to wage a successful 10-year battle against the Equal Rights Amendment. Since then, the Eagle Forum has broadened its focus to

119

include such issues as patent reform, computer encryption, and trade legislation.

Gerald L. K. Smith, founder of the racist and anti-Semitic Christian Nationalist Crusade in 1942. Smith worked for Senator Huey Long until the latter was assassinated in 1935. An early member of William Dudley Pelley's Silver Shirt Legion during the 1930s, Smith provided a vital link between prewar fascist groups and the white supremacist organizations that began springing up during the 1960s and 1970s. In 1948, he formed the Christian Nationalist Party (CNP) in St. Louis, Missouri, and ran on a Christian Identity platform that promised to destroy Jewish organizations and deport all Zionists and African Americans. In 1952, as part of its anti-Eisenhower campaign, the CNP named General Douglas MacArthur as its presidential candidate. The general ignored the nomination. Smith eventually moved his base of operations to Los Angeles, from which he mailed his magazine *The Cross and the Flag* and other racist literature. During the mid-1960s, he moved to Eureka Springs, Arkansas, where he spent the last decade of his life staging passion plays and constructing a seven-story statue of Jesus, among other projects. He died in 1976 and was buried at the foot of the statue.

Jimmy Swaggart, charismatic televangelist. In 1987, he pressured Jim Bakker to admit having had an affair with a church secretary years before, precipitating the downfall of the PTL (People That Love) Club. The following year, while the Bakker scandal was still unfolding, Swaggart was blackmailed by a fellow Assemblies of God preacher (who had photographic evidence) to admit that he had solicited a prostitute in New Orleans, Louisiana. Soon, other prostitutes came forward and claimed they had also been visited by the preacher. A few months after Swaggart's tearful confession on national television, he was caught with another prostitute in New Orleans.

Robert H. W. Welch, Jr., founder of the John Birch Society in 1958 along with 11 other businessmen. The organization, whose purpose was to combat a supposed communist conspiracy to subvert American government and society, was named after a Baptist missionary killed by Chinese communists at the end of World War II. Welch considered Birch to be the first casualty of World War III. Welch published the principles of the society in the *Blue Book*, in which he declared that the United States was a republic, not a democracy, and that democracy was "merely a deceptive phrase, a weapon of demagoguery, and a perennial fraud." Through the years, Welch accused Dwight Eisenhower, Franklin Roosevelt, Harry Truman, and Ronald Reagan, among others, of being part of the communist plot to subvert America. Although his fame declined during the

1960s, Welch maintained his uncompromising anticommunist stance until his death in 1985.

Paul Weyrich, founder of the Heritage Foundation and the Committee for the Survival of a Free Congress. In 1971, Weyrich established a policy analysis organization with the financial backing of Joseph Coors with the goal of supplying Richard Nixon's administration with more conservative alternatives to its policies. The group was named the Heritage Foundation in 1973. The following year, Weyrich established a political action organization called the Committee for the Survival of a Free Congress. Throughout the early 1970s, he urged, without much initial success, conservative Christians to involve themselves in politics. Though not himself a member of the religious Right, Weyrich recognized fundamentalists as an untapped pool of conservative voters who could unite on such issues as abortion, prayer in public schools, and anticommunism. During the late 1970s, he assisted in the successful fight to force the Internal Revenue Service to abandon its attempts to regulate Christian schools. He later advised Jerry Falwell on how to get involved in politics and has been credited with coining the phrase *moral majority*, which Falwell used as the name of his organization. Weyrich was also involved, in an advisory capacity, with the founding of the Christian Coalition. By the late 1990s, however, Weyrich had renounced political involvement for Christians, declaring that fundamentalists "probably have lost the culture war" and urging them to "drop out of this culture" to live "godly, religious, and sober lives."

CHAPTER 5

GLOSSARY

This chapter provides definitions for relevant terms that often arise in discussions and literature concerning fundamentalism and extremism.

anarchism   From the Greek term meaning "without a chief or head," this political philosophy asserts that government is inherently corrupt and that justice can only be brought about through the abolition of the state and all other authoritarian institutions. These formal power arrangements should be replaced by organization based on cooperative agreement among autonomous individuals. Most early anarchists advocated peaceful means to bring about change; during the 19th century, however, anarchists such as Mikhail Bakunin began advocating the use of violence against political leaders as the essential first step in building a better society.

apocalypse   From the Greek for "to reveal the future," for Christians this term refers to the catastrophic events prophesied to occur just before the Second Coming of Christ: the deliverance of true believers from a brief tribulation period during which the Antichrist will rule the earth and the end of human time. Examples of apocalyptic passages in the Bible include Mark 13:3–31, 2 Thessalonians 2:3–12, and the books of Revelation and Daniel.

Baptist Church   Calvinist sect originating in England during the 1630s that rejected the authority of the mainstream church. Among the core beliefs is that salvation is a highly personal, subjective experience and that church structure should tend toward the democratic rather than the hierarchical. Faced with persecution in their home country, many Baptists immigrated to the American colonies during the early 17th century.

born-again Christian   Someone who has had a personal, emotional, and life-changing encounter with God through Jesus. The term comes from John 3:3, in which Jesus tells a Pharisee named Nicodemus, "Except a man be born again, he cannot see the kingdom of God."

charismatic movement   Christian sect originating during the 20th century characterized by emotional and ecstatic outbursts. Worship services often include such practices as speaking in tongues, healing, and prophesying. The movement has influenced both Protestants and Catholics.

Christian Identity   A religious sect whose followers believe that white Aryans are the true descendants of the biblical tribes of Israel and therefore constitute God's chosen people, that Jews are the literal offspring of Satan, and that the biblical apocalypse, during which God's "good" Aryans will fight a bloody war against Satan's "evil" Jews in North America, is imminent. These beliefs motivate much of the violent behavior and survivalist tendencies exhibited by many of the white supremacist groups in the United States.

communism   Political and economic system based on the 19th-century writings of Karl Marx and Friedrich Engels that calls for the overthrow of capitalist systems in favor of a collective society based on equal distribution of goods and property. Russian revolutionary Vladimir Lenin imposed an authoritarian character on the ideology, and later proponents of communism (also known as Marxism-Leninism), such as Joseph Stalin and Mao Zedong, added further modifications to the original doctrine.

Congregationalist Church   Calvinist sect that broke away from the established church to declare and maintain the sovereignty of the local congregation. The denomination became one of the primary bases of the Puritan's religious structure in New England during the early 17th century.

Counterintelligence program (COINTELPRO)   Federal Bureau of Investigation (FBI) effort, primarily during the 1960s and early 1970s, to harass, disrupt, and impede the activities (both legal and illegal) of domestic radicals. Largely focused on left-wing groups, the program was disbanded in 1974 when a government committee found that COINTELPRO had conducted illegal surveillance and disinformation campaigns against a number of dissidents, including Martin Luther King, Jr. Documents uncovered under the Freedom of Information Act have further discredited the FBI's tactics.

dispensational premillennialism   Theory, popularized during the 19th century by John Nelson Darby, that human history is divided into seven dispensations, or eras, each ending with God's judgment. Proponents believe humanity is approaching the end of the sixth dispensation, which will be marked by the Second Coming of Jesus and the commencement of his thousand-year reign on earth.

ecotage (ecosabotage, ecoterror, monkeywrenching)   Sabotage for the purpose of protecting the environment from development or overuse. Such tactics include the destruction of heavy equipment, arson, tree spiking, removing survey stakes, defacing or destroying billboards, and slashing the tires of off-road vehicles.

evangelicalism   From the Greek for "good news," a movement within North American Protestantism whose followers emphasize a personal, born-again relationship with Jesus, believe the Bible is the inerrant word of God, and actively indulge in the practice of witnessing or sharing the gospel with others.

Greensboro Five   The five members of the U.S. Communist Workers Party who were shot and killed by members of the Ku Klux Klan at an anti-Klan march in Greensboro, North Carolina, on November 3, 1979.

Higher Criticism   A scholarly approach to studying the Bible that originated in Germany during the 19th century. Many conservative Christians believe such attempts to determine the historical and scientific bases of biblical passages undermine inerrant readings of scripture.

inerrancy   Belief that the Bible contains the literal word of God and stands as the sole source of truth regarding matters of religion, morality, human history, and science.

jihad   Arabic term meaning "struggle"; although most Muslims adhere to the concept of *jihad al nafs* (the internal struggle to reform negative behavior in the individual or local community), many Islamic fundamentalists favor *jihad bi al saif*, or war waged in the service of religion.

millennium   A 1,000-year period of peace during which Jesus will preside over earth, followed by the Last Judgment.

neo-Nazis   Post–World War II groups that subscribe to Adolf Hitler's National Socialist (Nazi) ideology.

Pentecostalism   A movement within Protestantism based on Acts 1:1–5 and 2:4–21, in which the apostles are baptized "with the Holy Spirit" on the day of Pentecost and begin to "speak with other tongues." Contemporary followers believe that the Holy Spirit can imbue true believers with the powers of glossolalia (speaking in tongues), prophecy, healing, and exorcism.

postmillennialism   Optimistic belief that Jesus will return only after virtuous Christians have succeeded in establishing and maintaining a 1,000-year era of peace on earth.

predestination   The Calvinist belief that God decided the ultimate fate of all people at the beginning of time.

premillennialism   Fundamentalist belief that God, recognizing that humans are too corrupt and imperfect to establish the millennium themselves, will intervene by sending Jesus back to earth. Only after the apocalyptic battle foretold in the book of Revelation will Jesus establish his 1,000-year kingdom of peace, which will be followed by the Last Judgment and the end of human history.

pro-life movement   Organized protest against abortion that originated among Catholics as a reaction against the Supreme Court's 1973 *Roe v. Wade* decision. The movement eventually grew to include Protestants and other groups.

providence   The belief, common among Puritans and revived by fundamentalists, that the will of God can be determined by signs and omens in the material world.

Puritans   Members of late-16th-century Church of England who, unhappy with the Anglican Church's similarities to Catholicism, broke away to return to a purer form of Protestantism. Facing persecution from the mainstream church, many immigrated to North America during the early 17th century.

Rapture   For Christian fundamentalists, the moment when all righteous people will ascend into heaven, leaving the earth under control of Satan for seven years (the Tribulation), after which the Second Coming of Christ will occur. Proponents of Christian Identity, many of whom stockpile food and weapons in anticipation of the Tribulation, reject belief in the Rapture.

reconstructionism   Theological doctrine based on the premise that Christians have a mandate to rebuild all of human society according to the blueprint offered by the Bible in general and Mosaic law (a theocratic system of strict moral, ceremonial, and civil regulations that governed the nation of Israel during biblical times) in particular.

Sagebrush Rebellion   Conservative, antienvironmentalist movement that began during the 1970s with the purpose of claiming state sovereignty over federally owned public lands. Proponents sought to replace the conservationist ethic with a system that would allow private mining, logging, and ranching interests to utilize the land for personal profit.

secular humanism   Belief in the importance of human values (such as reason, science, art, and philosophy) rather than reliance on God. As utilized by Christian fundamentalists, it is a vague, catchall term encompassing every value and belief perceived to replace God-centered absolutes with moral relativism. Just as communism once replaced modernism as the primary enemy of fundamentalists, so too has secular humanism replaced communism.

skinheads   Mainly white males with shaved heads who make up a subculture that originated among disaffected working-class youths in England during the 1970s. Since then, the movement has spread to the United States and other European countries, and many skinheads have come to espouse white supremacist ideals and use violence as a mean to achieve their ends. However, there are many skinhead groups, such as Skinheads Against Racial Prejudice (SHARP), that subscribe to left-wing, nonracist philosophies.

Glossary

white supremacists   People who believe that the white race is superior to all other races. Many white supremacists are also white separatists, advocating a separate white nation, usually situated in the Pacific Northwest of the United States.

Zionist Occupation Government (ZOG)   White supremacist term for the U.S. federal government, based on the conspiracy theory that the nation is controlled by a secret committee of Jews who intend to create a new world order by turning control of the government over to the United Nations.

PART II

GUIDE TO FURTHER RESEARCH

CHAPTER 6

How to Research Fundamentalism and Extremism

Before beginning any research project, it is important to have a topic or theme, a list of key terms and searchable words, and a general idea of how to use the variety of research tools that are now available. This chapter suggests a number of web sites, indexes, and catalogs that will help organize and define the research process and will provide a wide range of information, from a variety of points of view, pertaining to religious fundamentalism and political extremism.

THE INTERNET

The Internet and the World Wide Web offer virtually unlimited amounts of information on fundamentalist and extremist groups. Keep in mind, however, that web sites reflect the agenda and biases of their creators. This is particularly important to keep in mind when visiting sites created by extremists and fundamentalists. Much of the information presented on these sites falls into the realm of conspiracy theory and character assassination and should therefore should be weighed against opposing points of view supplied by other web sites and non-Internet resources. By the same token, some watchdog groups have been known to inflate statistics and exaggerate the danger posed by extremist groups. For this reason, it is also important, when using statistical information in a report, to cite the source in case questions of validity arise.

Like any research tool, the Internet is most useful if time is taken to learn the various tricks that will allow the researcher to efficiently tap into all the resources and information it has to offer. It is important to remem-

131

ber, however, that although the World Wide Web is an incredible resource, it is best used as a supplement to, rather than a replacement for, research materials that are available only by visiting a public or school library.

Unlike books, newspapers, periodicals, and video documentaries, the Internet is a nonlinear research medium, meaning that the information is not offered in a straight line. The user, therefore, rather than the author or producer, decides where to search for information and in what order the information will be received and reviewed. A single web site can provide links to a number of other sites, each of which may, in turn, lead to additional sites. One site that does not appear relevant to the topic at hand may provide access to one or more sites that deal precisely with the subject matter being researched. Therefore, diligence is important. Navigating in this manner can provide large amounts of information, but following a seemingly endless array of links can also cause the researcher to lose track of useful pages. Most web-hosting services aid in research organization by offering the ability to store "favorite" or "bookmarked" sites that are likely to be revisited in the future. The exact method of bookmarking a web site may vary between Internet providers, but generally there is an icon in the upper right-hand corner that will save the web page being viewed to a "favorites" folder. Another useful feature is the "history" menu, which is a linear list of all sites visited during a research session or in the recent past. This acts as a sort of "bread-crumb trail" that allows surfers to retrace their steps or revisit any site or link that has been hit along the way.

"Surfing the web" by following links can, as has already been mentioned, lead to large amounts of information, but this inherently haphazard method can also cause researchers to miss important web sites altogether. Using web indexes and search engines can fill in these information gaps.

INDEXES

A web index, or guide, is a site that offers a structured, hierarchical listing or grouping of key terms or subject areas relating to the topic requested. This allows researchers to focus on a particular aspect of a subject and find relevant links and web sites to explore.

Web indexes possess several advantages over random or blind Internet surfing. First, they offer a structured hierarchy of topics and terms that simplify the process of honing in on a specific topic, related subtopic, or link. Second, sites are screened and evaluated for their usefulness and quality by those who compile the index, giving the researcher a better chance of finding more substantial and accurate information. This feature also has its downside, however, which is that the user is at the mercy of the indexer's judgment about which sites are worth exploring. As with all other research tools, web indexes should therefore be used in conjunction with other tools and methods.

The most popular and user-friendly web index is Yahoo! (http://www.yahoo.com). Researchers can use the home page's top-level list of topics and follow them to more specific areas, or they can type one or more key words into the search box and receive a list of matching categories and sites. To explore fundamentalism via Yahoo!, for example, the researcher would click on the "Society and Culture" link, then the "Religion and Spirituality" link. From there, the user could choose such subtopics as "Church-State Issues," "Creation vs. Evolution," and "Organizations," depending on the focus of the research. Extremism could also be explored through the "Society and Culture" link, followed by "Crime," then "Types of Crime," and finally "Hate Crimes" or "Terrorism." These topics are just suggestions to get started, of course. Since fundamentalism and extremism are such broad topics, it is useful to keep an open mind about where information can be found. Don't limit research to the obvious, and supplement browsing with a direct search to ensure the most comprehensive results.

About.com (http://www.about.com) is similar to Yahoo! but gives greater emphasis to guides prepared by experts in various topics. Information on both fundamentalism and extremism can be found by browsing "News and Issues," then "Crime/Punishment," and following such links as "Abortion," "First Amendment," "Guns," and "Race/Hate Crimes." Issues relevant to fundamentalism can also be found by clicking "Religion and Spirituality," then "Christianity—General." From there, many of the topics may prove useful, including "Beliefs," "Creationism," and "God in Our Schools."

Another example of a useful web index is AskJeeves (http://askjeeves.com). This site attempts to answer questions posed in plain, everyday English, such as "What year was the Ku Klux Klan formed?" Sometimes it directly answers the question, and other times it provides a number of possibly useful links it obtains by scanning a series of search engines.

SEARCH ENGINES

When beginning an online research project, several organization's web sites may come to mind, but many more out there may not be so well known but are highly valuable. This is where search engines come into the picture. A search engine scans web documents for key words or terms provided by the researcher and comes up with a list of relevant web sites to explore. Instead of organizing topically in a top-down fashion, search engines work their way from the bottom up, meaning that they search the web for key terms and compile their findings into an index. Next, the search engine takes that index and matches the search words to those links that have been flagged as key term matches. Finally, the engine compiles a list based on the sites within the index that match the entered searchable words.

There are hundreds of search engines. Among the most user-friendly and popular are

Alta Vista (http://www.altavista.com)
Excite (http://www.excite.com)
Go (http://www.go.com)
Google (http://www.google.com)
Hotbot (http://hotbot.lycos.com)
Lycos (http://www.lycos.com)
Northern Light (http://www.northernlight.com)
WebCrawler (http://www.webcrawler.com)

Search engines are easy to use by employing the same kinds of key words that work with web indexes and library catalogs. A variety of web search tutorials are available online, including a downloadable one published by Complete Planet (http://www.brightplanet.com/deepcontent/index.asp).

There are some basic rules for using search engines. When looking for something, use the most specific term or phrase. For example, when looking for information about white supremacists, using the phrase *"white supremacists"* will result in more useful information than simply typing in *"racists."* Note that phrases should be placed in quotation marks in the search field if you want them to be matched as phrases rather than as individual words.

When searching for a more general topic, use several descriptive words (nouns are more reliable than verbs), such as *"hate crime statistics."* Most search engines will automatically list first pages that match all three terms.

Use "wildcards" when a search term may have more than one ending. For example, typing in *"supremac*"* will match both *supremacist* and *supremacy*.

Almost all search engines support Boolean (and, or, not) operators that can be used to broaden or limit a search topics. Use *and* to narrow a search: *"abortion AND bomb"* will match only pages that have both terms. Use *or* to broaden a search: *"skinhead OR neo-nazi"* will match any page that has either term. Use *not* to exclude unwanted results: *"neo-Nazi NOT Germany"* finds articles about neo-Nazis except those in or relating to Germany.

Each search engine has its own method of finding and indexing results and will come up with a unique list. It is therefore a good idea to use several different search engines, particularly for a general query. Several "metasearch" programs automate the process of submitting search terms to multiple search engines. These include Metacrawler (http://www.metacrawler.com) and Search.com (http://www.search.com).

FINDING ORGANIZATIONS AND PEOPLE

Web sites of organizations can often be found by entering the name into a search engine. Generally, the best approach is to put the name of the organization into quotation marks, such as "Earth Liberation Front." If this does not yield satisfactory results, another approach is to take a guess at the organization's likely web address. Earth Liberation Front's site, for example, is www.earthliberationfront.com. The American Civil Liberties Union is commonly known by the acronym ACLU, so it is no surprise that the organization's web site is www.aclu.org. (Keep in mind that noncommercial organization sites normally use the *.org* suffix, government agencies use *.gov*, educational institutions use *.edu*, and businesses use *.com*.)

There are several ways to find people on the Internet. One can enter the person's name (in quotes) in a search engine and may find that person's home page on the Internet. Another way is to contact the person's employer, such as a university for an academic or a corporation for a technical professional. Most such organizations have web pages that include a searchable faculty or employee directory. Finally, one could try one of the people-finder services such as Yahoo! People Search (http://people.yahoo.com) or BigFoot (http://www.bigfoot.com). This may yield an e-mail address, regular address, and/or phone number.

SPECIFIC RESOURCES

A variety of government, educational, and private web sites offer background material, news, analysis, and other material on topics, groups, and people associated with fundamentalism and extremism. The following are some of the more useful major sites, broken down by category.

Government Sites

The Federal Bureau of Investigation (http://www.fbi.gov) has information on domestic terrorism. Particularly useful is the annual report *Terrorism in the United States* (http://www.fbi.gov/publications/terror/terroris.htm).

The Bureau of Alcohol, Tobacco and Firearms (http://www.atf.treas.gov) is in charge of suppressing traffic in illegal use of explosives and controlling the sale and registration of firearms. The web site contains information relevant to extremist criminal activity.

Academic Sites

Academic sites are primarily concerned with research and building databases of archival information. The Terrorism Research Center (http://www.terrorism.com) includes links to many other organizations and agencies. The

Fundamentalists and Extremists

Air University Library at Maxwell Air Force Base in Alabama (http://www.au. af.mil/au/aul/bibs/tergps/tgdom.htm) has a list of domestic extremist groups, each accompanied by a book and periodical bibliography.

Civil Liberties Groups

Extremists often target minority groups for whom civil liberties are an important consideration. In addition, many of these organizations (both fundamentalist and extremist) feel that laws intended to curb their activities violate their own civil liberties. The American Civil Liberties Union (http://www.aclu.org) is a good source for news and advocacy materials. The web site has a number of issue pages that are relevant to fundamentalism and extremism:

> Criminal Justice: http://www.aclu.org/issues/criminal/hmcj.html
> Cyber-Liberties: http://www.aclu.org/issues/cyber/hmcl.html
> Free Speech: http://www.aclu.org/issues/freespeech/hmfs.html
> Lesbian and Gay Rights: http://www.aclu.org/issues/gay/hmgl.html
> National Security: http://www.aclu.org/issues/security/hmns.html
> Racial Equality: http://www.aclu.org/issues/racial/hmre.html
> Religious Liberty: http://www.aclu.org/issues/religion/hmrf.html
> Reproductive Rights: http://www.aclu.org/issues/reproduct/hmrr.html
> Women's Rights: http://www.aclu.org/issues/women/hmwo.html

Civil liberties groups that focus on computer-related issues are also relevant, since much of the legislation concerning extremism and counterterrorism is aimed at increasing law enforcement capabilities in eavesdropping on and monitoring communication. The Electronic Privacy Information Center (http://www.epic.org), the Electronic Frontier Foundation (http://www.eff.org), and the Center for Democracy and Technology (http://cdt.org) are all useful for keeping up with these issues.

Watchdog and Antihate Groups

Among the groups that focus on hate crimes based on ethnicity, gender, and other biases are the Anti-Defamation League (http://www.adl.org), which tracks anti-Semitic activity, and the Southern Poverty Law Center (http://www.splcenter.org), which monitors the activities of extremist groups. The former's site lists hate groups and militias and includes a chronology of hate incidents. The Center for Democratic Studies (http://cdsresearch.org) has a religion and democracy program that researches emergent religious organizations and their impact on American democracy.

Fundamentalist and Extremist Sites

Many fundamentalist and extremist groups have their own web sites. Addresses for many of these sites can be found in Chapter 8. Discretion is advised when deciding whether to visit or use sites that may be involved in the promotion of extremist ideologies.

BIBLIOGRAPHIC RESOURCES

Although the Internet and World Wide Web provide virtually unlimited resources for the researcher, libraries and bibliographic resources are still vital assets to any research project. A bibliographic resource is any type of index, catalog, or guide that lists books, texts, periodicals, or printed materials containing articles or chapters related to a subject.

LIBRARY CATALOGS

Most public and academic libraries have placed their card catalogs online. This allows the user to access a library's catalog from any Internet connection, even from home. Viewing a library catalog in advance enables the researcher to develop a comprehensive bibliographic resource list and reserve these resources before signing offline, saving time and frustration.

The Library of Congress (http://lcweb.loc.gov/catalog) is the largest library catalog available. This site provides advice on search techniques, lists of resources, and catalogs of books, periodicals, maps, photographs, and more.

Online catalogs can be searched by author, title, and subject headings, as well as by matching keywords in the title. Thus a title search for "militia" will retrieve all books that have that word somewhere in their title. However, since all books about militias may not have that word in the title, it is still necessary to use subject headings to get the best results.

General Library of Congress subject headings for fundamentalism and extremism include, but certainly are not limited to, the following:

Christianity and Politics—United States
Communism—United States
Conservatism—Religious Aspects—United States
Evangelicalism—United States
Fundamentalism—United States
Hate Crimes—United States
Hate Groups—United States
Militia Movements—United States
Neo-Nazis—United States

New Left—United States
Racism
Radicalism—United States
Right and Left (Political Science)
Right-Wing Extremists—United States
Skinheads—United States
Social Movements—United States
Terrorism
United States Church History—20th Century
White Supremacy Movements—United States

Once the record or a book or other item has been found, it is a good idea to check for additional subject headings and name headings that may have been previously overlooked. These can be used for additional research.

BOOKSTORE CATALOGS

Another valuable resource is online bookstore catalogs such as Amazon.com (http://www.amazon.com) and Barnes&Noble.com (http://www.barnes andnoble.com). These sites not only offer a new way to purchase books related to fundamentalism and extremism but also provide publisher information, lists of related topics and books, and customer reviews. These features allow online bookstore catalogs to be used as another source for annotated bibliographies.

PERIODICAL DATABASES

Most public libraries subscribe to various database services, such as Info-Trac, which offer detailed indexes of hundreds of current and back-issue periodicals. These databases can perform searches based on titles, authors, subjects, or keywords from within the text. Depending on the service, the database can provide a listing of bibliographical information (author, title, pages, periodical name, issue, and date), a synopsis and abstract (a brief description of the article), or the article in its entirety.

Many public and academic libraries now have dial-up or Internet access, allowing these periodical databases to be searched from home, school, or the local cybercafé. The periodical database search can often be found in the library's catalog menu or on its home page. Sometimes a library membership card may be necessary to access the information available on a library's web site, so always check with the desired library for its specific policies.

Another extensive but somewhat time-consuming option for searching for periodicals is to visit the web site of a specific periodical related to fundamentalist or extremist topics. Often the web address is the periodical's name plus *.com* (if commercial), *.gov* (if it is a governmental publication), *.edu* (if it is a university published journal), or *.org* (if it is a publication produced by a public organization). Some of these publications may have several years of back issues online.

LEGAL RESEARCH

Since the Bill of Rights and the First Amendment in particular are so crucial to the continued viability of many fundamentalist and extremist groups, it is often useful for researchers to obtain the text and summary of laws and court decisions that pertain to them. Gathering and understanding legal research can be more difficult than simply reading through bookstore catalogs and bibliographical indexes. Once again, the Internet proves to be extremely useful by offering a variety of user-friendly ways to research laws and court cases without paging through volumes of court cases in legal libraries (to which the public may not have access to begin with).

FINDING LAWS

When federal legislation passes, it becomes part of the United States Code, a massive compendium of federal law. The U.S. Code can be searched online at several locations. Perhaps the easiest and most comprehensive is the U.S. Code database compiled by the Office of the Law Revision Counsel (http://uscode.house.gov). Another option is the web site of Cornell University Law School (http://www4.law.cornell.edu/uscode/). The fastest way to retrieve a law is by its title and section citation, but phrases and keywords can also be used.

The codes of many states' laws are also available online. Links to the codes for specifics states can be found at the 'Letric Law Library (http://www. lectlaw.com/inll/l.htm).

KEEPING UP WITH LEGISLATIVE DEVELOPMENTS

When performing legal research, some pertinent legislation may be pending. Pending legislation can frequently be found by looking at advocacy group sites for both national and state issues.

The Library of Congress's Thomas web site (http://thomas.loc.gov) is a web-based user-friendly interface that has many valuable features for keeping up with legislative developments and legal research. The Thomas site allows the user to access proposed legislation to each congress by entering key terms or a bill number. For example, if the researcher is looking for abortion legislation, either the bill number can be entered or, if that is not known, key words (*"abortion rights,"* for example) can be searched, and a listing of relevant legislation will be compiled.

Clicking on the bill number of one of the items found will display a summary of the legislation, the complete text, its current status, any floor actions, and any other information available. If the bill number is known from the beginning, the legislation can be accessed directly by entering it into the search field.

FINDING COURT DECISIONS

Similar to laws, legal decisions are recorded and organized using a uniform system of citations. The basic elements are *Party 1 v. Party 2*, followed by the volume number, the court, the report number, and the year in parentheses. Here are two examples to illustrate the naming method.

Roe v. Wade, 410 U.S. 113 (1973)   In this example, the parties are Roe (plaintiff) and Wade (defendant). The case can be found in volume 410 of the *United States Supreme Court Reports*, report number 113, and the case was decided in 1973. (The name of the court is not indicated in Supreme Court decisions.)

Good News Club v. Milford Central School, 202 F. 3d 502 (1999)   In this U.S. Court of Appeals citation, the parties are the Good News Club (plaintiff) and Milford Central School (defendant), and the case can be found in volume 202 of the *Federal Reporter* (covering U.S. Circuit Court and U.S. Court of Appeals decisions) on page 502. The U.S. Court of Appeals decided the case in 1999.

To locate a decision made by the federal court, the level of the court involved must first be determined: district (lowest level, first stage for most trials), circuit (the main court of appeals), or the Supreme Court. Once this is known, the case and the court's ruling can be located on a number of web sites by searching for either the citation or the names of the parties. There are two sites in particular that are useful in calling up cases.

The first, the Legal Information Institute web site (http://supct.law. cornell.edu/supct/), contains every Supreme Court decision made since 1990, plus 610 of the most well-known and referenced Supreme Court cases. The site also provides several links to other web sites that contain earlier Supreme Court decisions.

The other site, Washlaw Web (http://www.washlaw.edu/), maintains a comprehensive database of decisions made at all court levels. In addition, the site has a large list of legal topics and links, making it an excellent resource for any type of legal research.

For more information and tips on researching legal issue, read the "Legal Research FAQ" at http://www.eff.org/legal/law_research.faq. The EFF site also explains advanced research techniques such as Shepardizing, so called for *Shepard's Case Citations*, which explains how a decision is cited in subsequent cases and whether or not the case was later overturned.

CHAPTER 7

ANNOTATED BIBLIOGRAPHY

Numerous books and articles have been published on fundamentalism and extremism in recent years, particularly since the rise in political power of the Christian Right during the 1980s and the increased interest in right-wing extremist groups following the bombing of the Murrah Federal Building in Oklahoma City in 1995. This bibliography lists a representative sample of sources on both subjects, ranging from scholarly sociological studies to opinion pieces aimed at the general public. Sources have been selected for usefulness to the general reader, currency (most material dates from 1995 and later), and variety of points of view.

Listings are divided between fundamentalism and extremism and, within each of these subjects, by type (books, articles, and videos). Internet documents have not been included, as they tend to change frequently or disappear altogether. Such resources can be found by searching web sites listed in Chapter 6 and Chapter 8.

FUNDAMENTALISM

BOOKS

Albert, James A. *Jim Bakker: Miscarriage of Justice?* Chicago: Open Court, 1998. Albert argues that Bakker did not receive a fair trial. He bases this on the contention that rather than intentionally committing fraud, Bakker was merely the victim of his own enterprises, which grew too big, too fast and eventually got out of control.

Armstrong, Karen. *The Battle for God.* New York: Ballantine, 2000. This national best-seller provides a detailed yet readable history of the development of fundamentalist thought among Jews, Muslims, and Christians, from the late 15th century to the early 21st century. It includes footnotes, a bibliography, and a glossary of terms.

Baird-Windle, Patricia, and Eleanor J. Bader. *Targets of Hatred: Anti-Abortion Terrorism.* New York: Palgrave, 2001. Baird-Windle, a retired abortion provider, and Bader, a social worker, provide a history of the antiabortion movement dating back to the years before the Supreme Court's landmark *Roe v. Wade* decision. Based largely on interviews with nearly 200 abortion providers across the United States, the book chronicles 40 years of harassment, arson, bombing, and murder, and demonstrates the consistent failure of law enforcement officials to provide adequate protection for clinics. It includes reviews of important laws and court cases, plus excerpts from literature commonly distributed by antiabortionists.

Balmer, Randall. *Blessed Assurance: A History of Evangelicalism in America.* Boston: Beacon Press, 1999. This short book traces the development of the American evangelical tradition, illustrating how the movement, despite its image as backward and old fashioned, has always been in tune with the times. The author also poses the interesting idea that the high level of tolerance for religious experimentation in the United States has helped maintained the nation's stability by steering malcontents away from politics and into the religious sphere.

———. *Mine Eyes Have Seen the Glory: A Journey into the Evangelical Subculture in America.* New York: Oxford University Press, 1989. Born and raised within an evangelical household, Balmer eventually walked away from religion out of curiosity about the rest of the world. In this book, he journeys back into the subculture to gain a better understanding of the role that evangelicalism plays in American culture. First-person accounts of visits to churches, organizations, and gatherings are interspersed with background information on the historical development of evangelicalism in the United States. In researching the book, Balmer avoided big names such as Falwell, Swaggart, and Graham and instead traveled around the country to provide views into the beliefs and behaviors of smaller congregations in different geographic regions. Each chapter has endnotes.

Bawer, Bruce. *Stealing Jesus: How Fundamentalism Betrays Jesus.* New York: Crown, 1997. The author claims that fundamentalist beliefs, rather than being traditional as adherents claim, are recent legalistic inventions that have replaced the values that Jesus actually preached.

Beale, David O. *In Pursuit of Purity: American Fundamentalism Since 1850.* Greenville, S.C.: Unusual Publications, 1986. Beale, who teaches church history at Bob Jones University, provides a history of fundamentalism from a conservative Christian perspective. The book includes a bibliography and appendixes.

Boston, Robert. *The Most Dangerous Man in America? Pat Robertson and the Rise of the Christian Coalition.* Amherst, N.Y.: Prometheus, 1996. An exploration of Robertson's political and theological beliefs from the perspective that implementation of the Christian Coalition's agenda would mean the end of religious and political freedom in the United States. This extremely critical view leads the author to conclude that Robertson should be labeled an enemy of the state.

———. *Right Is Wrong: About Separation of Church and State*. Amherst, N.Y.: Prometheus, 1993. Boston examines U.S. history and constitutional law and concludes that the religious Right is erroneous in its attempts to break down the wall of separation between church and state. The book includes a section on common myths about the separation of church and state, a short history of the religious Right, a list of major religious Right organizations, and suggestions for further reading.

Bumsted, J. M., and John E. Van de Wetering. *What Must I Do to Be Saved? The Great Awakening in Colonial America*. Hinsdale, Ill.: Dryden, 1976. This study focuses on the evolution of the Great Awakening from an urban phenomenon to a rural movement that helped shape Protestant religion on the American frontier.

Capps, Walter H. *The New Religious Right: Piety, Patriotism, and Politics*. Columbia: University of South Carolina Press, 1990. This book assesses the meaning of the conservative Christian movement in the context of the larger sociopolitical and religious framework of the United States. It includes notes and a bibliography.

Caudill, Edward; Edward J. Larson; and Jesse Fox Mayshark. *The Scopes Trial: A Photographic History*. Knoxville: University of Tennessee Press, 2000. The 38 photographs in this book provide a local context for a trial that has grown to mythic proportions over the years. Historical details are provided in an introduction, an afterword, and extensive captions for each photograph.

Church, F. Forrester. *God and Other Famous Liberals: Reclaiming the Politics of America*. New York: Simon and Schuster, 1991. As a counterargument to the traditional fundamentalist position, this book contends that the Bible, rather than advocating conservative politics, is the ultimate liberal document and that fundamentalism should be based on charity and tolerance. It also explores the idea that the Bible lies at the root of liberal democracy, having inspired such documents as the Declaration of Independence, the Constitution, and the Bill of Rights.

Cromartie, Michael. *Disciples and Democracy: Religious Conservatives and the Future of American Politics*. Washington, D.C.: Ethics and Public Policy Center, 1994. These essays explore the beliefs, goals, and social agendas of religious conservatives. Each one is accompanied by responses and comments. Among the contributors are Ralph Reed and Michael Farris.

———, ed. *No Longer Exiles: The Religious New Right in American Politics*. Washington, D.C.: Ethics and Public Policy Center, 1993. Nine essays analyze the achievements and potential of the Christian Right in the wake of the 1992 elections.

D'Antonio, Michael. *Fall from Grace: The Failed Crusade of the Christian Right.* New Brunswick, N.J.: Rutgers University Press, 1992. The author presents a collection of essays detailing his encounters with people involved in the Christian Right, including students at Oral Roberts University and visitors to the Bakkers' Heritage USA theme park. Combining first-person narrative with journalistic asides, the book offers a compelling view of the Christian Right during and shortly after the period of televangelist scandals in the late 1980s. Although well-written and informative, D'Antonio's book is somewhat premature in sounding the death knell of the conservative Christian movement.

Detweiler, Fritz. *Standing on the Premises of God: The Christian Right's Fight to Redefine America's Public Schools.* New York: New York University Press, 2000. Detweiler provides an overview of the Christian Right's view of education, the theological basis of these views, the leaders who have mobilized conservative Christians to implement these ideas, and the tactics they use to do so.

Diamond, Sara. *Facing the Wrath: Confronting the Right in Dangerous Times.* Monroe, Me.: Common Courage Press, 1996. Approaching her subjects from a decidedly leftist position (the short essays in this book were originally published in such liberal periodicals as the *Nation, Z Magazine* and the *Humanist*), Diamond covers a wide range of topics relevant to the Christian Right—including abortion, the Promise Keepers, dominion theology, and Focus on the Family—in Part 1. Essays in Part 2 cover the influence of right-wing think tanks, while Part 3 deals with the Patriot movement.

———. *Not By Politics Alone: The Enduring Influence of the Christian Right.* New York: Guilford Press, 1998. In this book, Diamond studies the ebb and flow of the relationship between conservative Christians and the Republican Party from the 1970s to the late 1990s. Much attention is given to the influence of national organizations and the evangelical media, from talk-radio programs to publishing companies and music studios. Here Diamond presents a much more balanced, objective view than in her book *Facing the Wrath.*

———. *Roads to Dominion: Right-Wing Movements and Political Power in the United States.* New York: Guilford Press, 1995. This book focuses on the rise of right-wing politics in the post–World War II era. The author divides her subject into four categories—the anticommunist conservative movement, the racist Right, the Christian Right, and the neoconservatives—but does a good job of tying these strands together to present a coherent view of the political climate in the United States during the 50-year period covered. It includes an extensive bibliography.

Annotated Bibliography

Gorney, Cynthia. *Articles of Faith: A Frontline History of the Abortion Wars.* New York: Simon and Schuster, 1998. This well-balanced view of the abortion controversy focuses on two Missouri activists: pro-choice leader Judith Widdicombe and antiabortion activist Samuel Lee. It provides an overview of the history of the struggle while giving the reader insight into what drives the activism of people on both sides of the issue.

Green, John C.; Mark J. Rozell; and Clyde Wilcox, eds. *Prayers in the Precincts: The Christian Right in the 1998 Elections.* Washington, D.C.: Georgetown University Press, 2000. Each essay focuses on a particular state, examining the strategies used by the Christian Right, opposition to the conservative agenda, and the outcome of the election.

Harding, Susan Friend. *The Book of Jerry Falwell: Fundamentalist Language and Politics.* Princeton, N.J.: Princeton University Press, 2000. This book, using Jerry Falwell as its primary example, studies how evangelists use the language of the Bible—in sermons, speeches, books, and radio and television broadcasts—to negotiate their engagement with the world in general and with politics specifically. It includes long passages quoted from speeches and sermons, followed by in-depth analysis of the specific language and rhetoric involved. It also includes source notes for Falwell's speeches, a copy of his church's statement of doctrine, and a bibliography.

Heineman, Kenneth J. *God Is a Conservative: Religion, Politics, and Morality in Contemporary America.* New York: New York University Press, 1998. The author traces the concurrent revivals of fundamentalist Christianity and political conservatism from the 1960s to the late 1990s.

Herman, Didi. *The Antigay Agenda: Orthodox Vision and the Christian Right.* Chicago: University of Chicago Press, 1997. Combining sociology, legal studies, political science, history, and literary criticism, Herman analyzes the fundamentalist mobilization against gay rights. The book includes endnotes and a list of references.

Hunter, James Davison. *American Evangelism: Conservative Religion and the Quandary of Modernity.* New Brunswick, N.J.: Rutgers University Press, 1983. Hunter draws from both scholarly and evangelical sources to present a study of the ongoing tension between conservative Christians and modernity. In addition to its informative text, the author utilizes numerous tables to illustrate demographic profiles, beliefs and practices, and more. Chosen as a main selection of the Religious Book Club, this volume provides a good counterbalance to the many books that approach the study of the Christian Right from a hostile perspective.

Jelen, Ted G. *The Political Mobilization of Religious Beliefs.* New York: Praeger, 1991. This technical sociological study of how religious beliefs manifest themselves in electoral politics includes numerous tables, a survey of beliefs of specific congregations, and a list of references.

Kaplan, Jeffrey. *Radical Religion in America: Millennarian Movements from the Far Right to the Children of Noah.* Syracuse, N.Y.: Syracuse University Press, 1997. Kaplan analyzes the beliefs of three apocalyptic religious movements: Christian Identity, Odinism, and the anti-Christian B'nai Noah. The book includes a chapter on how anticult and antihate groups, such as the Anti-Defamation League, Klanwatch, and the Cult Awareness Network, monitor the activities of these organizations.

Kintz, Linda. *Between Jesus and the Market: The Emotions That Matter in Right-Wing America.* Durham, N.C.: Duke University Press, 1997. Kintz analyzes the psychological makeup of born-again Christians, focusing on the role of women in conservative Christian churches and organizations. She also discusses the connection between fundamentalism and the proliferation of militia groups. The book includes notes and a bibliography.

Kuzenski, John C.; Charles S. Bullock III; and Ronald Keith Gaddie. *David Duke and the Politics of Race in the South.* Nashville, Tenn.: Vanderbilt University Press, 1995. This collection of essays is informative but assumes that the reader has some prior knowledge of David Duke. It includes a number of tables, figures, and maps.

Lambert, Frank. *Inventing the Great Awakening.* Princeton, N.J.: Princeton University Press, 1999. Lambert shows how the Great Awakening was carefully orchestrated by enthusiastic religious promoters through the use of commercial strategies and the latest technologies, particularly print media. The book includes notes, a bibliography, tables, and illustrations.

Larson, Edward J. *Summer for the Gods: The Scopes Trial and America's Continuing Debate over Science and Religion.* Cambridge, Mass.: Harvard University Press, 1998. This detailed, Pulitzer Prize–winning book focuses less on the courtroom drama and more on the events leading up to it and the ways it has impacted U.S. society since, including its influence on the development of the American Civil Liberties Union and the Christian Right. Well researched, the book also attempts to provide an even-handed account while debunking myths perpetuated by the film *Inherit the Wind* and other sources.

Martin, William. *With God on Our Side: The Rise of the Religious Right in America.* New York: Broadway Books, 1996. A companion volume to the public television series of the same name, this book provides an objective and comprehensive overview of the important people, organizations, and events that have shaped the Christian Right and led it to where it is today. It draws on an impressive list of more than 100 interviews with many of the major figures of the movement, including Jerry Falwell, Ralph Reed, Pat Robertson, and Phyllis Schlafly. It includes photographs, endnotes, and an index.

Nardo, Don. *The Scopes Trial.* San Diego, Calif.: Lucent, 1997. This brief overview of the Scopes trial begins with the publication of Charles Darwin's

On the Origin of Species, follows the rise of Christian fundamentalism, and details the legal events leading up to the trial before dealing with the trial itself. It includes sidebars, black-and-white photographs, a bibliography, and a works-cited list.

Oberman, Heiko A. *The Reformation: Roots and Ramifications*. Trans. Andrew Colin Gow. Grand Rapids, Mich.: William B. Eerdmans, 1994. This collection of essays includes profiles of Martin Luther, an examination of the Reformation's philosophical roots, and a study of the ways in which Luther's ideas continue to influence religion, politics, and culture.

Reiter, Jerry. *Live from the Gates of Hell: An Insider's Look at the Anti-Abortion Movement*. Amherst, N.Y.: Prometheus, 2000. Ostensibly the work of a conservative insider, this book harshly criticizes antiabortionists as gun-toting hatemongers whose beliefs have little, if anything, to do with Christianity. The author is particularly critical of mainstream antiabortionists who go to great lengths to distance themselves from the radicals but readily spread confrontational rhetoric used by zealots to defend their actions.

Rozell, Mark J., and Clyde Wilcox, eds. *God at the Grassroots: The Christian Right in the 1994 Elections*. Lanham, Md.: Rowman and Littlefield, 1995. Each of the essays explores the tactics and success of the Christian Right in a particular state. Among those covered are California, Florida, Georgia, Iowa, Michigan, Minnesota, Oklahoma, Oregon, South Carolina, Texas, and Virginia.

Solinger, Rickie, ed. *Abortion Wars: A Half Century of Struggle, 1950–2000*. Berkeley: University of California Press, 1998. The 18 essays in this volume approach the history of abortion from the pro-choice perspective. Contributors range in occupation from journalists and scholars to lawyers, activists, and doctors, and the wide range of topics—including strategy, activism, and abortion before *Roe v. Wade*—reflects this diversity.

Spring, Joel H. *Political Agendas for Education: From the Christian Coalition to the Green Party*. Mahwah, N.J.: Lawrence Erlbaum, 1997. Spring provides a balanced view of the various religious and social groups that struggle to shape public education in America.

Sutton, Jerry. *The Baptist Reformation: The Conservative Resurgence in the Southern Baptist Convention*. Nashville, Tenn.: Broadman and Holman, 2000. The author discusses the manner in which fundamentalists usurped power in the Southern Baptist Convention and their response to what they perceived as a liberal leadership that dealt too closely with such divisive issues as feminism, homosexuality, and abortion. He approaches the subject from a conservative point of view.

Terry, John Mark. *Evangelism: A Concise History*. Nashville, Tenn.: Broadman and Holman, 1994. Terry, an associate professor of missions and evangelism at the Southern Baptist Theological Seminary, approaches the subject from a Christian perspective. Using the Bible as his primary source, he traces the movement from the birth of Jesus through to the use of television and radio as means to spread the Gospel. Each chapter is followed by a set of study questions intended to guide readers in their understanding of the text.

Watson, Justin. *The Christian Coalition: Dreams of Restoration, Demands for Recognition*. New York: St. Martin's Griffin, 1999. An in-depth look at the Christian Coalition and its primary motive, which the author concludes is a desire to transform the United States into a Christian nation. The book includes biographical information on founders Ralph Reed and Pat Robertson, coverage of major political elections in which the coalition has been involved, and studies of the group's tactics, from lobbying campaigns to the manner in which they promote themselves as a minority group persecuted by a society that has fallen prey to secular humanism. Among the book's major strengths are its extensive notes and bibliographic sections, which provide plenty of direction for additional study.

White, Mel. *Stranger at the Gate: To Be Gay and Christian in America*. New York: Simon and Schuster, 1994. White was born into a conservative Christian home and ghostwrote books and speeches for such Christian Right figure as Jerry Falwell, Pat Robertson, and Billy Graham. From an insider's perspective, he delves into the tactics used by fundamentalists to campaign against gay rights. Among the appendices are "Six Letters to the Religious Right," a list of gay and lesbian religious organizations, and ideas to help communities protect themselves from influence by the Christian Right.

Wilcox, Clyde. *Onward Christian Soldiers? The Religious Right in American Politics*. Boulder, Colo.: Westview, 1996. Wilcox examines the role conservative Christians have played in electoral politics and speculates about the future of the Christian Right. A glossary, notes, and a bibliography are included.

Winship, Michael P. *Seers of God: Puritan Providentialism in the Restoration and Early Enlightenment*. Baltimore, Md.: Johns Hopkins University Press, 1996. This scholarly review of early European settlers in the Americas focuses on the Puritans' reliance on signs from God in their daily lives. Although it may be too detailed for the casual reader, it does provide insight into many of the theological issues that were revived by fundamentalists during the 20th century. It includes extensive endnotes and an index.

ARTICLES

Albert, Tanya. "Ruling Favors Anti-Abortion Web Site." *American Medical News*, vol. 44, April 23–30, 2001, pp. 16ff. Physician groups argue that a federal appeals court ruling in California allowing antiabortion activists

to post "wanted" posters of abortion providers on the Internet poses a
threat to the lives of those listed. Others claim that since the postings do
not directly tell people to kill doctors, their web site is protected by the
First Amendment.

Bendyna, Mary E., et al. "Uneasy Alliance: Conservative Catholics and the
Christian Right." *Sociology of Religion,* vol. 62, Spring 2001, pp. 51–64.
Using data from a survey of Republican activists in Virginia, Bendyna examines the level of support for Christian Right groups and leaders among
Catholics, evangelicals, and mainstream Protestants; the political views of
Catholics and Protestants affiliated with the Christian Right; and sources
of support for the Christian Right among Catholics and Protestants. The
results of the survey, presented in five tables that accompany the text, indicate that Catholics hold conservative views on several issues important
to the Christian Right (such as abortion) but differ on such issues as the
death penalty and social welfare programs. Although there is strong support for Christian Right politicians among Republican Catholics, differences in opinion make it unlikely that the Christian Right will be able to
mobilize large numbers of mainstream Catholics in their favor in the near
future. The article includes sample questions from the survey.

Boston, Rob. "Preachers, Politics, and Campaign 2000." *Church and
State,* vol. 53, September 2000, pp. 8–13. The author accuses members
of the religious Right, particularly Jerry Falwell and Pat Robertson, of
stepping into legally precarious territory by using their tax-exempt
ministries to campaign on behalf of George W. Bush during the 2000
presidential campaign.

Bridges, Tyler. "Southern Comfort." *New Republic,* vol. 220, February 22,
1999, pp. 13–14. This article discusses the varied reactions of politicians
in the Republican Party to David Duke's announcement that he would
seek a congressional seat in Louisiana during the 2000 election.

Carnes, Tony. "Republicans, Christian Right Stunned by Voter Rebuke."
Christianity Today, vol. 42, December 7, 1998, p. 20. Carnes reports on the
results of the 1998 midterm election, in which fallout from President
Clinton's sex scandal with Monica Lewinsky was expected to lead to big
gains for Republicans. Instead, the Republicans fared worse than any
party not holding the presidency in 64 years. The article also discusses
why the turnout of voters identifying themselves with the Christian Right
dropped 10 to 20 percent from the previous election.

Cherry, Matt. "Raving Robertson." *Free Inquiry,* vol. 18, Fall 1998, p. 18.
This is a scathing report of Pat Robertson's denouncement of Orlando,
Florida, for its Gay Day celebrations. The preacher had warned that the
city could face hurricanes, terrorist bombs, earthquakes, tornadoes, "and
possibly a meteor" if it didn't repent.

Cohen, Mark Francis. "Born Yet Again." *National Journal*, vol. 31, May 1, 1999, pp. 1,164–67. Ralph Reed, head of an Atlanta-based political consulting firm, was the Republican Party's most sought-after campaign adviser during the 2000 election despite his poor record during the 1998 election. The article studies this, as well as giving an overview of Reed's years as top man of the Christian Coalition.

Confessore, Nicholas. "Born Again." *American Prospect*, vol. 12, August 13, 2001, pp. 10–11. The author examines Ralph Reed's post–Christian Coalition record as a political consultant, as well as his prospects as chairman of the Republican Party in Georgia.

Conn, Joseph L. "Exploiting Tragedy." *Church and State*, vol. 52, June 1999, pp. 7–8. The author accuses Pat Robertson, Jerry Falwell, and James Dobson of exploiting the school shootings in Littleton, Colorado, by using the tragedy to promote such conservative issues as vouchers, school prayer, and homeschooling.

———. "Rift on the Right." *Church and State*, vol. 52, April 1999, pp. 4–6. The article explores the debate between Paul Weyrich, who has claimed the Christian Right has lost the culture war and has disavowed mixing politics and religion, and leaders of the religious Right who claim that the battle is just beginning.

Conniff, Ruth. "Left-Right Romance." *Progressive*, vol. 64, May 2000, pp. 12–15. Conniff reports on the odd alliance between Green Party presidential candidate Ralph Nader and antifeminist, family-values crusader Phyllis Schlafly in order to get the Channel One television network out of public schools.

Davis, Derek H. "Thoughts on the Possible Realignment of the Christian Right in Twenty-First Century America." *Journal of Church and State*, vol. 41, Summer 1999, pp. 433–43. Davis reports on the retreat of two major leaders of the Christian Right from political activism: Paul Weyrich (cofounder of both the Moral Majority and the Christian Coalition) and syndicated conservative columnist Cal Thomas. Citing the corrupting effect of politics, both Weyrich and Thomas counsel a return to a simpler, more personal version of Christianity. Gary Bauer, Pat Robertson, Jerry Falwell, and others not yet ready to "lay down the sword" have responded bitterly to this decision. The author argues that careful reading of the New Testament reveals no mandate for political action on the part of Christians.

DeYoe, Jeffrey. "Homegrown Extremism." *Christian Century*, vol. 118, October 2001, pp. 7ff. DeYoe examines the range of subject matter and emotion in church sermons following the September 11, 2001, terrorist attacks. He is particularly disturbed by the preacher at the First Baptist Church in Daytona Beach, Florida, who told 2,000 parishioners that those behind the terrorist attacks, when caught, should be "executed on the spot," while nations harboring terrorists should face "massive and disproportionate retaliation."

Dobson, James. "The New Cost of Discipleship." *Christianity Today*, vol. 43, September 6, 1999, pp. 56–58. In response to several leaders of the Christian Right who had recently disavowed mixing religion and politics, Dobson reaffirms his stance that it is the duty of all Christians to voice their views in public.

"Dobson, Religious Right Join Forces with Pope to Push 'Family' Agenda." *Church and State*, vol. 54, February 2001, pp. 14–15. The article details a November 2000 trip to Vatican City by Focus on the Family president James Dobson to meet Pope John Paul II and attend a conference on families and the world economy. It stresses the common ground that fundamentalists and Catholics have found in recent years.

"Dobson's FOF Attacks JFK for Stand in Favor of Church State Separation." *Church and State*, vol. 54, January 2001, pp. 16–17. This article reports on comments published by Focus on the Family blaming former president John F. Kennedy for ushering in an era of secularism with his strong stance on church-state separation. It points out that Kennedy's comments in support of separation of church and state were made to calm the fears of Protestant leaders, who thought Kennedy, if elected, would transform the White House into an extension of the Vatican.

Donovan, Gill. "Falwell Apologizes for Remarks on Terrorist Attacks." *National Catholic Reporter*, vol. 37, September 28, 2001, p. 10. Two days after the September 11, 2001, terrorist attacks on the United States, Jerry Falwell went on Pat Robertson's *700 Club* television program and blamed the destruction on homosexuals, abortionists, and secular humanists, among others, while Robertson concurred. After public outcry against the remarks, including a rebuke from the White House, Falwell issued a public apology, while a spokeswoman for Robertson claimed he "didn't really realize" what Falwell was saying while they were on the air.

Dreyfuss, Robert. "The Holy War on Gays." *Rolling Stone*, March 18, 1999, pp. 38–41. Dreyfuss focuses on the Christian Right's attempts to stem the tide of increasing tolerance of homosexuality in the United States through the work of such organizations as the National Pro-family Forum, Focus on the Family's Family Research Council, and Americans for the Truth About Homosexuality.

"Evangelicals Attack Environmentalists." *Christian Century*, vol. 117, May 3, 2000, pp. 497–98. This article reports on the launch of the Interfaith Council for Environmental Stewardship, which declares that "humans should take priority over nature" and that environmentalists are misguided by "faulty science."

"The Falwell Follies." *Church and State*, vol. 53, May 2000, pp. 7–9. The article traces Jerry Falwell's enterprises and media gaffes, from the formation of the Moral Majority in 1979 to his 1999 warning to parents that Tinky Winky, a character on the children's television show *Teletubbies*, might be gay.

Fineman, Howard, "Return of the 'Reverend.'" *Newsweek*, vol. 135, April 24, 2000, pp. 41–43. Thirteen years after dropping the title "reverend" to run for president in 1988, Pat Robertson reattached the honorific to his name. In light of this, the author explores the pivotal role Robertson played in George W. Bush's 2000 presidential campaign and questions the importance of fundamentalists to the Republican Party.

"Focus on Family Executive Admits Affair, Resigns." *Christian Century*, vol. 117, November 1, 2000, pp. 1105ff. This article reports on the resignation from Focus on the Family of Mike Trout after "admitting to an inappropriate relationship with a woman other than his wife." This came only weeks after Focus on the Family official John Paulk, who has described himself as a former homosexual and claims that gay people can change, was criticized for visiting a Washington, D.C., bar and then lying about it.

Frey, Hillary, and Miranda Kennedy. "Abortion on Trial: The Prosecution of Dr. Pendergraft." *Nation*, vol. 272, June 18, 2001, pp. 12–16. The authors cover the story of renowned abortion doctor James Scott Pendergraft, who was sentenced to jail but who claims that local officials and federal prosecutors falsely convicted him of extortion, conspiracy, and mail fraud for the sole purpose of shutting down his abortion clinic in the conservative community of Ocala, Florida.

Friedman, Dorian. "New Position, Same Mission." *U.S. News and World Report*, vol. 122, May 5, 1997, p. 16. The article reports on Ralph Reed's announcement that he will step down as director of the Christian Coalition and launch a consulting firm to help "pro-family" candidates get elected.

Green, Joshua. "Apocalypse Now." *American Prospect*, vol. 11, January 17, 2000, pp. 23ff. The author discusses the similarities in the plots of four apocalyptic novels written by Larry Burkett, Pat Robertson, Paul Colson, and Paul Meier. All of them include incompetent liberal presidents whose terms are cut short by the Second Coming.

Harwood, John. "Focus on Family Leader Dobson Emerges as Christian Right's Most Powerful Voice." *Wall Street Journal*, May 26, 2000, pp. A24ff. The article provides a brief biographical overview of James Dobson and reports on his warnings to presidential candidate George W. Bush not to compromise on such conservative issues as abortion and family values.

Isikoff, Michael. "Taxing Times for Robertson." *Newsweek*, vol. 133, June 21, 1999, p. 39. The decline of Pat Robertson's Christian Coalition is reflected in dropping membership numbers, growing debts, an exodus of top officials, and loss of tax-exempt status.

Ivins, Molly, and Lou Dubose. "Dubya's Dance with the Right." *Time*, vol. 155, March 13, 2000, pp. 37–38. This article consists of an excerpt from Molly Ivins and Lou Dubose's book *Shrub: The Short but Happy Political Life of George W. Bush* in which the authors discuss the then Texas governor's relationship with the Christian Right. They claim that although Bush often votes in support of fundamentalists, he just as often ignores their advice and is usually reluctant to advertise any ties with them.

Jacobsen, Louis. "The Eagle Has Landed." *National Journal*, vol. 29, October 25, 1997, pp. 2,154–55. Jacobsen discusses the political agenda of Phyllis Schlafly's Eagle Forum.

———. "There's Something About David." *National Journal*, vol. 31, January 30, 1999, pp. 290–91. The author discusses David Duke's bid for a congressional seat during the 2000 election and the discomfort of many politicians concerning the possibility of his election.

Junod, Tom. "365 Days to the Apocalypse and We Still Don't Know Where to Hide the Jews . . . and Other Notes from Pat Robertson's Y2K conference." *Esquire*, vol. 131, January 1999, pp. 94–99. The author provides tongue-in-cheek coverage of his visit to Pat Robertson's Preparing for Y2K conference. Among the discussions are tips on how to store food and develop survival skills for the apocalypse and the theory that President Clinton has done nothing to prevent Y2K disasters so that the ensuing civil unrest will give him an excuse to declare martial law and federalize food distribution.

Kaminer, Wendy. "American Gothic." *American Prospect*, vol. 11, December 18, 2000, pp. 38–39. This editorial argues that the Christian Right's crusade against the occult and New Age spirituality is strongly tied with the far Right's history of condemning feminism.

Lerner, Sharon. "A New Kind of Abortion War." *Village Voice*, vol. 46, January 1, 2002, pp. 47–48. Lerner discusses several lobbying campaigns that have been mounted by antiabortion activists, including efforts to promote bills that would discourage education about contraception and force welfare recipients with children to marry. Right-to-life partisans have also convinced lawmakers in Louisiana, Alabama, Florida, and South Carolina to approve "choose life" license plates, which carry antiabortion messages and raise money for pregnancy crisis centers that counsel women not to have abortions.

Lugg, Katherine A. "Reading, Writing, and Reconstructionism: The Christian Right and the Politics of Public Education." *Educational Policy*, vol. 14, November 2000, pp. 622–37. This article begins by supplying a brief overview of the history of fundamentalism and detailing the radical beliefs of Christian reconstructionists before discussing the implications of these groups' distrust of public education. It covers attempts to re-Christianize schools, as well as deinstitutionalization (strategies to disestablish public education) and the use of stealth tactics to secure the election of Christians to school boards.

Malcolm, Teresa. "Robertson's Comments Draw Fire." *National Catholic Reporter*, vol. 34, November 14, 1997, p. 6. The Council on American-Islamic Relations asks Pat Robertson to apologize after he accuses Muslims of being a "religion of slavers" and of persecuting Christians around the world.

Mardesich, Jodi. "Safety Net." *Advocate*, September 25, 2001, pp. 28–29. The magazine article profiles Marc Adams, a gay man who attended Liberty University because he heard Jerry Falwell preach that homosexuality could be "cured." Instead, he fell in love with another male student and eventually dropped out of the college. Together, he and his boyfriend moved to Seattle and started HeartStrong, an organization that provides counseling to gay students at antigay religious schools.

Marks, Alexandra. "In Abortion Fight, Lines Have Shifted Ten Years After a Historic Rally." *Christian Science Monitor*, July 16, 2001, pp. 1ff. Marks details the changes that have occurred in the abortion fight since antiabortion activists gathered in Wichita, Kansas, in 1992 to picket women's health clinics. Her article focuses on Wichita citizens who were involved in demonstrations and counterdemonstrations at the time, and their reactions to an approaching rally intended to commemorate the 10th anniversary of the protests.

Marsh, Katherine. "Scandal in the Family." *Good Housekeeping*, vol. 228, January 1999, p. 85. This article profiles Jim and Tammy Faye Bakker's son, Jay, who reminisces about his reactions to his parents' scandals during the late 1980s and his father's subsequent jail term. He is now the pastor of Revolution, an Atlanta-based organization that ministers to street kids.

Maudlin, Michael G. "The Bible Stud at the End of the World." *Christianity Today*, vol. 41, September 1, 1997, pp. 22–26. The author reviews evangelical novels by Paul Meier, Tim LaHaye, and Pat Robertson and discusses how the authors use fiction to expound views and opinions that would be too controversial to air in any other manner.

McGee, Brian R. "Witnessing and Ethos: The Evangelical Conversion of David Duke." *Western Journal of Communication*, vol. 62, Summer 1998, pp. 217–43. This article explores how white supremacist David Duke, during his 1989 through 1991 political campaigns, used evangelical language to mask his past Klan affiliations and reinvent himself as a born-again Christian to widen his appeal to voters. It includes extensive footnotes and a list of works cited.

Annotated Bibliography

Micah, Joshua. "The Firewall Next Time." *American Prospect*, vol. 11, January 31, 2000, pp. 9–10. Micah reports on Ralph Reed's status as a paid consultant for George W. Bush's presidential campaign. His article focuses on the South Carolina primary and Reed's prospects for rallying conservative Christians in the state to vote for his candidate.

Miller, Kevin D. "The Re-Education of Jim Bakker." *Christianity Today*, vol. 42, December 7, 1998, pp. 62–64. The article recounts Bakker's activities since his release from jail, which include volunteering at a ministry in Los Angeles and writing a book warning that the apocalypse may take the form of an asteroid hitting the earth.

Miller, Samantha, and Ron Arias. "New Testament." *People Weekly*, vol. 51, May 17, 1999, pp. 167–68. The authors trace Bakker's downfall and his postprison resurgence as a teacher of Bible classes in Los Angeles.

"Pat Robertson Condones China's Forced Abortion Policy, Angers Right." *Church and State*, vol. 54, June 2001, pp. 12–16. The Christian Right's angry reaction to Robertson's comments that although he doesn't agree with China's one-child policy, it is necessary to avoid overpopulation. Several conservative leaders point out that the evangelist's statements in support of China's policies have paralleled his attempts to launch business ventures within the communist nation. The article also notes the cancellation of the Christian Coalition's 2001 conference, as well as its declining budget.

Podhoretz, Norman. "The Christian Right and Its Demonizers." *National Review*, vol. 52, April 3, 2000, pp. 30–32. Podhoretz argues that the Christian Right has many positive virtues, including serving as a reminder of the religious beliefs upon which the United States was founded. He claims that the formation of such groups as the Moral Majority and Christian Coalition has been based not on an aggressive attempt to impose Christian views on Americans but rather a defensive strategy intended to protect Christians from a dominant liberal society.

"Ralph Reed Firm Draws Criticism for Dirty Tricks in Virginia Race." *Church and State*, vol. 53, October 2000, p. 16. Faith and Family Alliance, created by the vice president of Ralph Reed's Century Strategies, sent out a mailing that critics say distorted the financial record of congressional candidate Eric I. Cantor.

"Ralph Reed Seeks to Lead Georgia State Republicans." *Church and State*, vol. 54, April 2001, p. 20. The article reports on Reed's plan to run for chairmanship of the Republican Party in Georgia.

"Reed Apologizes for Lobbying Bush on Behalf of Microsoft." *Church and State*, vol. 53, May 2000, pp. 18–19. Reed apologizes after it becomes public that Microsoft paid him to lobby presidential hopeful George W. Bush, even while he served as a paid consultant to the Republican candidate.

157

"The Religious Right Silent at GOP Convention." *Christian Century*, vol. 117, August 16–August 23, 2000, pp. 824–25. Written before the 2000 election, this article observes that although evangelical voters supported George W. Bush three to one over Al Gore and the religious conservative vote was vital to Bush's election chances, leaders of the Christian Right were largely invisible at the Republican National Convention in Philadelphia. This was part of the Republican Party's attempt to appeal to more moderate voters.

"Robertson, IRS Settle Tax Case." *Christian Century*, vol. 115, April 22–April 29, 1998, p. 425. The Internal Revenue Service will allow the Christian Broadcasting Network to retain its tax-exempt status if it pays back taxes for 1986 and 1987, during which time it violated tax laws with its political activities.

Schaffer, Michael. "Say a Prayer for the Christian Coalition." *U.S. News and World Report*, vol. 130, May 28, 2001, pp. 25ff. The author traces the declining revenue and membership of the Christian Coalition after the departure of Ralph Reed. Meanwhile, the ascendance of George W. Bush to power has changed the fortunes of Christian conservatives for the better.

Schlafly, Phyllis. "Why Education Is Americans' Number-One Worry." *Contemporary Education*, vol. 68, Summer 1997, pp. 213ff. Eagle Forum founder Schlafly discusses the failure of the public school system, which she primarily blames on "refusal to teach basic skills and knowledge in the elementary grades and the dumbing down of the textbooks and courses of study." In particular, she targets Outcome-Based Education, Goals 2000 funding, and School-to-Work programs for criticism.

Schmidt, Peter. "A Clash of Values in the Heartland." *Chronicle of Higher Education*, vol. 47, April 16, 2001, pp. A25–A28. After antiabortion activists discovered that the University of Nebraska's medical center used tissue from aborted fetuses in research, they began lobbying for a bill to ban the practice. The university's president maintains that such research is vital to help AIDS and Alzheimer's patients.

Selle, Robert. "Activist Grandmother." *The World and I*, vol. 14, May 1999, pp. 56–59. Selle profiles family values activist and Eagle Forum founder Phyllis Schlafly.

———. "Family Advocate." *The World and I*, vol. 14, April 1999, pp. 76–79. An in-depth profile of Focus on the Family founder James Dobson.

Shenk, Joshua Wolf, and Gary Cohen. "Right-Wing-Conspiracy Facts and Fiction." *U.S. News and World Report*, vol. 124, February 9, 1998, pp. 28ff. Investigating Hillary Rodham Clinton's claim that President Clinton has been victimized by a "vast right-wing conspiracy," the authors conclude that well-synchronized efforts to take down the president are linked more by common aims than by "active conspiratorial intent."

Annotated Bibliography

Slone, Chris. "Robertson Shakes up the Empire." *Christianity Today*, vol. 41, July 14, 1997, p. 60. On the same day, Pat Robertson sells International Family Entertainment to Rupert Murdoch for $1.9 billion and announces his resignation as president of the Christian Coalition.

"Tate Replaces Reed at Christian Coalition." *Christian Century*, vol. 114, June 18–June 25, 1997, p. 585. The article reports on the transfer of power in the Christian Coalition in the wake of Ralph Reed's departure.

Van Biema, David. "Faith After the Fall." *Time*, vol. 158, October 8, 2001, pp. 76ff. The author reports on church attendance, spirituality, and booming sales of apocalyptic Christian novels during the days immediately following the September 11, 2001, terrorist attacks.

Weyrich, Paul. "Should Conservatives Refocus Their Energies Away from Politics?" *Insight on the News*, vol. 15, March 29, 1999, pp. 24–25ff. Weyrich argues that conservative Christians have lost the culture war and should therefore explore ways of "bypassing altogether the institutions controlled by the enemies of Western culture." He urges readers to turn off television, video games, and other "avenues for consuming cultural decadence," and to drop out of mainstream culture and "find places, even if in the sanctity of your own home, to educate your children and live godly, righteous, and sober lives."

Williams, Rhys H. "Introduction: Promise Keepers: A Comment on Religion and Social Movements." *Sociology of Religion*, vol. 61, Spring 2000, pp. 1–10. Approaching the study of the Promise Keepers from a sociological perspective, the author claims that the movement is much more complex and personal than would appear from reports by the mainstream press. He takes a scholarly approach that cites a number of articles and books and includes a reference list.

Zoba, Wendy Murray. "Daring to Discipline America." *Christianity Today*, vol. 43, March 1, 1999, pp. 30–38. The author profiles Focus on the Family founder James Dobson and explores his growing influence both inside and outside the Christian Right community.

VIDEOS

"Adoption Vigilantes." A&E Television Networks, n.d. Video (VHS). 50 minutes. Part of A&E's *Investigative Reports* series, this video goes underground, providing a look into the kidnapping of adopted babies to return them to their birth parents on moral and religious grounds.

"Billy Graham: A Personal Crusade." A&E Television Networks, n.d. Video (VHS). 50 minutes. This profile, part of A&E's *Biography*, depicts the spiritual development of Graham, from the revival that changed his life at age 16 to his becoming the most well-known preacher in the United States. It includes interviews with former presidents Gerald Ford and George Bush, who discuss Graham's influential role as "pastor to the presidents." Graham's son Franklin reveals the private side of the famous preacher.

"Jimmy Swaggart: Fire and Brimstone." A&E Television Networks, n.d. Video (VHS). 50 minutes. Another profile in A&E's *Biography* series, this follows Swaggart from his honest beginnings as a singing preacher to his years as the head of a multimillion-dollar televangelical ministry and finally his downfall after twice being caught with prostitutes. It includes interviews with Tammy Faye Bakker and Jerry Falwell.

"Ourselves, Our Bodies: The Feminist Movement and the Battle over Abortion." A&E Television Networks, 1999. Video (VHS). 50 minutes. Part of the History Channel's *20th Century with Mike Wallace* television series, this video tells the dramatic, contentious, and often violent story of the battle between feminists and antiabortion activists. Using *Roe v. Wade* as a focal point, Wallace shows how the struggle changed after the Supreme Court's famous decision.

"Pat Robertson: Preaching Politics." A&E Television Networks, n.d. Video (VHS). 50 minutes. In this A&E *Biography* profile, interviews with associates, journalists, and political commentators are used to show how failed businessman Pat Robertson transformed himself into an influential minister and helped launch the revolution that ensured the Christian Right would become a political force.

"The Televangelists." A&E Television Networks, 1999. Video (VHS). 50 minutes. Part of the *20th Century with Mike Wallace* History Channel series, this video shows how the invention of television allowed evangelists to reach wide audiences and gain power. It includes interviews with Jerry Falwell, Oral Roberts, Pat Robertson, Robert Schuller, and Jimmy Swaggart.

"With God on Our Side: The Rise of the Religious Right." Alexandria, Va.: PBS Video, 1996. Video (VHS). 360 minutes. This six-tape series uses numerous interviews and archival footage to follow the development of the religious right movement from its early days as an anticommunist force during the 1950s to its highly organized political maneuverings of the Christian Coalition during the 1990s.

EXTREMISM

BOOKS

Abanes, Richard. *American Militias: Rebellion, Racism and Religion.* Downers Grove, Ill.: Intervarsity Press, 1996. Abanes, founder of the Religious Information Center of Southern California, analyzes the militia movement, providing background and insight into members' beliefs and conspiracy theories. The book includes photographs, notes, and bibliography.

Able, Deborah. *Hate Groups.* Rev. ed. Berkeley Heights, N.J.: Enslow, 2000. Written for the teenage reader, this book explores the roots of modern hatred, details several of the hate groups active today, and delves into the motives of racists. It includes chapter notes, contact information for organizations that study hate groups, a glossary, an index, and photographs.

Abt, John J. *Advocate and Activist: Memoirs of an American Communist Lawyer.* Urbana: University of Illinois Press, 1993. Abt was a longtime lawyer for the Communist Party USA, and his memoir is a virtual who's who of the American left during the 20th century, from repeat presidential candidate Gus Hall to Angela Davis, whom Abt helped defend during the 1970s. Abt's reputation as a left-wing lawyer was such that Lee Harvey Oswald requested him for his defense following the assassination of President John F. Kennedy. The book includes an index and photographs.

Anderson, Terry H. *The Movement and the Sixties: Protest in America from Greensboro to Wounded Knee.* New York: Oxford University Press, 1995. This book covers the broad leftist protest movement of the 1960s that encompassed civil rights sit-ins, anti-Vietnam protests, and the black power struggle, among other crusades. The first chapter provides an overview of 1950s America and the cold war era for context. Extensive notes, a select bibliography, and an index are provided.

Andrews, Geoff, et al., eds. *New Left, New Right and Beyond: Taking the Sixties Seriously.* New York: St. Martin's, 1999. The essays in this book investigate the ongoing influence of both right-wing and left-wing activities of the 1960s.

Andryszewski, Tricia. *The Militia Movement in America: Before and After Oklahoma.* Brookfield, Conn.: Millbrook Press, 1997. Intended for seventh-through 12th-grade students, Andryszewski's book uses the 1995 bombing of the Alfred P. Murrah Federal Building in Oklahoma City as its point of departure for an informative discussion of the antigovernment militia movement in the United States. Similarities among the Ku Klux Klan, neo-Nazi groups, and militias are explored, and several leaders of these right-wing extremist groups are profiled. It includes detailed chapter notes, a bibliography, and black-and white photographs.

Arnold, Ron. *Ecoterror: The Violent Agenda to Save Nature/The World of the Unabomber.* Bellevue, Wash.: Free Enterprise Press, 1995. A critical look at the radical environmental movement written by a supporter of the wise-use movement, which believes that public lands should be open to exploitation by private companies. Although Arnold goes to great lengths to catalog abuses of the law by environmentalists, conspicuously absent are accounts of similar tactics, including arson and death threats, that have been perpetrated by wise-use proponents.

Avrich, Paul. *The Haymarket Tragedy.* Princeton, N.J.: Princeton University Press, 1984. Avrich details the political and labor climate that led to the famous bomb-throwing incident in Chicago, as well as the trial that sent four anarchists to their deaths and several more to jail. His critical view of the trial is backed by the fact that the convicted were later pardoned by the governor of Illinois. Illustrations, photographs, and notes are included.

————, ed. *Anarchist Voices: An Oral History of Anarchism in America.* Princeton, N.J.: Princeton University Press, 1995. Avrich, who interviewed a number of anarchists, allows them to speak for themselves about their often-misunderstood beliefs. Included are a list of periodicals, suggestions for further reading, and illustrations.

Ayers, Bill. *Fugitive Days: A Memoir.* Boston: Beacon Press, 2001. Ayers takes his readers from his normal childhood to his days as a member of Students for a Democratic Society and beyond to his years as an active part of the Weathermen's Revolutionary Youth Movement.

Barkun, Michael. *Religion and the Racist Right: The Origins of the Christian Identity Movement.* Rev. ed. Chapel Hill: University of North Carolina Press, 1997. The first section of this book traces the development of Christian Identity theology from it roots in 19th-century British Israelism to its birth as a distinct belief system in Los Angeles. The second part details Christian Identity doctrine, while Part Three examines ways in which the movement's major proponents have challenged the political system of the United States. The revised edition includes a 35-page epilogue that explores connections between the Oklahoma City bombing, the militia movement, and Christian Identity. It includes an extensive notes section and index.

Bell, Daniel. *Marxian Socialism in the United States.* Ithaca, N.Y.: Cornell University Press, 1996. Originally published in 1952, this book traces the early years of the American socialist movement, providing portraits of important people and accounts of the numerous factions and splinter groups. A new introduction and afterword for this edition put the original text in historical perspective.

Berlet, Chip, ed. *Eyes Right! Challenging the Right Wing Backlash.* Boston: South End Press, 1995. A number of essays provide a critical analysis of the political Right, from mainstream conservatives to neo-Nazis. Included are lists of organizations and books to read.

Berlet, Chip, and Matthew N. Lyons. *Right-Wing Populism in America: Too Close for Comfort.* New York: Guilford, 2000. This book examines the antielitist rhetoric, conspiracy theories, and ethnic scapegoating utilized by right-wing groups. It also shows how the populism of extremist organizations such as Posse Comitatus and the Ku Klux Klan have infiltrated the electoral campaigns of George Wallace, Pat Buchanan, and others. There is an extensive bibliography.

Blee, Kathleen M. *Women of the Klan: Racism and Gender in the 1920s.* Berkeley: University of California Press, 1991. The author explores how female members of the Klan often juggled far-right views of race with progressive ideas about gender equality, working to preserve both white women's suffrage and white Protestant cultural supremacy. The book includes extensive notes.

Braun, Aurel, and Stephen Scheinberg, eds. *The Extreme Right: Freedom and Security at Risk.* Boulder, Colo.: Westview, 1997. These far-ranging essays from a variety of contributors analyze and assess right-wing extremism in Canada, France, Germany, Hungary, Poland, Russia, and the United States. Other essays attempt to define extremism and discuss the internationalization of the Far Right. Included are a list of research interviews and a bibliography.

Buhle, Paul. *Marxism in the USA from 1870 to the Present Day: Remapping the History of the American Left.* London: Verso, 1987. Buhle follows the development of communism in the United States from the immigrant socialism of the 19th century to the New Left revival of the 1960s and 1970s.

Buhle, Paul, and Dan Georgakas, eds. *The Immigrant Left in the United States.* Albany: State University of New York Press, 1996. A series of essays explores the roles that immigrants from Poland, Greece, Germany, Italy, the Middle East, Asia, Haiti, and Central America have played in radical American politics.

Bushart, Howard L.; John R. Craig; and Myra Barnes. *Soldiers of God: White Supremacists and Their Holy War for America.* New York: Kensington, 1998. This book focuses on the beliefs of various white supremacist groups, such as the Ku Klux Klan, Aryan Nations, and White Aryan Resistance. It includes extensive chapters on Christian Identity and conspiracy theories, a bibliography, selected readings, and photographs.

Cawley, R. McGreggor. *Federal Land, Western Anger: The Sagebrush Rebellion and Environmental Politics.* Lawrence: University Press of Kansas, 1993. In-depth analysis of the causes and connotations of the rebellion against tighter federal regulation of land in the western states. The author contends that "the Sagebrush Rebellion deserves to be listed with the conservation movement and the environmental movement as pivotal events in shaping the history of U.S. federal land policy," although the fact that it is only one chapter in the long history of land grabs by states and private interests in the West makes this a dubious claim at best.

Chalmers, David M. *Hooded Americanism: The History of the Ku Klux Klan.* 3d ed. Durham, N.C.: Duke University Press, 1987. Originally published in

1965, this lengthy historical overview focuses heavily on the Ku Klux Klan's heyday during the 1920s, including a number of brief chapters that each detail Klan activity in a single state. Subsequent editions have added chapters on Klan revivals during the 1960s and 1980s, plus a chapter dedicated to the 1979 shoot-out in Greensboro, North Carolina, between members of the Klan and the Communist Workers Party that left five people dead. It includes photographs and a bibliography.

Churchill, Ward, and Jim Vander Wall. *Agents of Repression: The FBI's Secret Wars Against the Black Panther Party and the American Indian Movement.* Boston: South End Press, 1990. This traces the history of the FBI's controversial Counterintelligence Program (COINTELPRO) and contends that the federal government continued using similar repressive tactics against minority rights groups for years following the official disbanding of the program in 1971. The book includes numerous photographs and illustrations, as well as a glossary, endnotes, and a bibliography.

Cockburn, Alexander; Jeffrey St. Clair; and Allan Sekula. *Five Days That Shook the World: Seattle and Beyond.* New York: Verso, 2000. The authors provide eyewitness accounts of leftist protests in Seattle; Washington, D.C.; Philadelphia; Los Angeles; Prague; and other cities, claiming that this new activism heralds the birth of a new radical movement in the United States and beyond.

Collier, Peter, and David Horowitz. *Deconstructing the Left: From Vietnam to the Persian Gulf.* Lanham, Md.: Second Thoughts, 1991. The authors, both of whom are ex-leftist radicals turned political conservatives, declare that Marxism is no longer relevant as a global political force and critique its continued importance in U.S. universities.

Coppola, Vincent. *Dragons of God: A Journey Through Far Right America.* Atlanta, Ga.: Longstreet Press, 1996. A journalist's firsthand account of his encounters with individuals affiliated with right-wing extremist organizations, such as the Ku Klux Klan, Aryan Nations, and Posse Comitatus. Includes several samples of white supremacist literature.

Cozic, Charles P., ed. *The Militia Movement.* San Diego, Calif.: Greenhaven, 1997. These essays defend a wide range of viewpoints relevant to the issue of militias, from the views that militias have a constitutional right to own guns and that citizen militias defend liberty, to the beliefs that citizen militias threaten democracy and that the militia movement is misguided. Included are a list of organizations and a bibliography.

Davis, Daryl. *Klan-Destine Relationships: A Black Man's Odyssey in the Ku Klux Klan.* Fort Hills, N.J.: New Horizon Press, 1998. Grammy Award–winning pianist Davis's account of his attempts to understand the racist mind by meeting and talking to members of the Ku Klux Klan. Most interesting are the dialogues between Davis, an African American, and such racists as Roger Kelly, imperial wizard of the Invincible Empire Knights of the Ku Klux Klan. The sheer audacity of the project is accentuated by the black-and-white photographs showing Davis posing with various white supremacists.

Dees, Morris, and Steve Fiffer. *Hate on Trial: The Case Against America's Most Dangerous Neo-Nazi*. New York: Villard Books, 1993. Dees describes how he brought Tom Metzger to trial for his role in the Portland skinhead murder case.

Delgado, Richard, and Jean Stefancic. *Must We Defend Nazis? Hate Speech, Pornography, and the New First Amendment*. New York: New York University Press, 1997. The authors argue that First Amendment rights to free speech should not be absolute but rather should take into account the psychological harm that words can cause to minorities and women. This book is oriented toward the legal aspects of free speech. Notes and an index are included.

Diggins, John Patrick. *The Rise and Fall of the American Left*. New York: W. W. Norton, 1992. Diggins divides his study of the American Left into four eras: the Lyrical Left of the World War I era, the Old Left of the Depression and early cold war era, the New Left of the 1960s, and the Academic Left of the Republican-dominated 1980s. Of particular interest is the section on the New Left, which encompasses the civil rights and student antiwar struggles.

Donner, Frank. *Protectors of Privilege: Red Squads and Police Repression in Urban America*. Berkeley: University of California Press, 1990. This book exposes the repressive tactics that police have used to undermine leftist organizations since the Haymarket bombing in Chicago during the 1880s. It focuses largely on undercover law enforcement in Chicago, Los Angeles, New York, and Philadelphia.

Dyer, Joel. *Harvest of Rage: Why Oklahoma City Is Only the Beginning*. Boulder, Colo.: Westview, 1997. Dyer approaches the subject of the antigovernment Patriot movement from an alarmist perspective, warning that rural America is a hotbed of right-wing violence just waiting to happen.

Emerson, Steve. *American Jihad: The Terrorists Living Among US*. New York: Simon and Schuster, 2002. Emerson spent most of the 1990s studying U.S.-based groups that fund and manage terrorist organizations. In this disturbing book, he examines the extent of Islamic fundamentalist networks in the United States, showing how the Palestinian terrorist group Hamas maintains operations in five U.S. states, revealing the connection between Islamic Jihad and the University of South Florida, and citing convincing, if circumstantial, evidence suggesting that Osama bin Laden once applied for a U.S. visa. According to Emerson, the United States continues to harbor hundreds, if not thousands, of such terrorists.

Ezekial, Raphael S. *The Racist Mind: Portraits of American Neo-Nazis and Klansmen.* New York: Viking Penguin, 1995. Part 1 of this book details the author's visits to a Klan rally in Georgia, the 1988 Arkansas sedition trial, and the Aryan Nations Congress. Part 2 consists of in-depth interviews with Tom Metzger of White Aryan Resistance, Dave Holland of Southern White Knights, and Richard Butler of Aryan Nations. Part 3 is a series of interviews with young members of a Detroit neo-Nazi group. The author, a Jewish psychologist, analyzes not only the mindset of the American racist but also his own feelings while confronting the American white supremacist movement. He includes a list of suggested readings.

Faryna, Stan; Brad Stetson; and Joseph G. Conti, eds. *Black and Right: The Bold New Voice of Black Conservatives in America.* Westport, Conn.: Praeger, 1997. Contributors, including Supreme Court Justice Clarence Thomas and former representative Gary Franks, discuss the growing number of African Americans who, discontent with the current state of the civil rights establishment, favor smaller government, lower taxes, tougher crime laws, welfare reform, and personal initiative. The book includes a list of media and organizational resources for the study of African-American conservatism, a bibliography, and contributor biographies.

Feldman, Glenn. *Politics, Society, and the Klan in Alabama, 1915–1949.* Tuscaloosa: University of Alabama Press, 1999. This detailed state study documents the Ku Klux Klan's violent history in Alabama. Feldman discusses how industrial boosters initially welcomed the Klan as an instrument for law and order, only to turn against them when the organization's violence began to tarnish the state's image. Also explored are Hugo Black's membership in the Klan before he became a liberal Supreme Court justice and the racist organization's transformation from an anti-Catholic and anti-immigrant group to an anticommunist crusader, all the while maintaining its central focus on white power.

Feuerlicht, Roberta Strauss. *Joe McCarthy and McCarthyism: The Hate That Haunts America.* New York: McGraw-Hill, 1972. This critical account of the McCarthy era blames both Republicans and Democrats for allowing the hunt for communists to get out of hand. Strauss also contends that McCarthyism never completely died and that Americans must remain vigilant to prevent similar events in the future. It includes photographs; the bibliography is outdated.

Foreman, Dave. *Confessions of an Eco-Warrior.* New York: Crown, 1991. Although the title suggests an autobiographical work, Earth First! cofounder Foreman instead presents a series of essays that set forth his agenda and beliefs concerning the defense of the environment. He includes several chapters on the virtues of monkeywrenching and tree spiking.

Foreman, Dave, and Bill Haywood, eds. *Ecodefense: A Field Guide to Mon-keywrenching.* Tucson, Ariz.: Nedd Ludd, 1985. Prefaced with the dis-claimer that no person involved in the book's production "encourages anyone to do any of the stupid, illegal things contained herein," *Ecodefense* proceeds to supply the reader with detailed instructions on how to spike trees, disable heavy equipment, topple billboards, free wild animals from snares, and flatten the tires of off-road vehicles, among other things. It in-cludes a foreword by Edward Abbey, whose novel *The Monkey Wrench Gang* helped inspire the Earth First! movement.

Fried, Albert, ed. *Communism in America: A History in Documents.* New York: Columbia University Press, 1997. This expansive collection of essays traces the development of communist activity in the United States from the 1920s through the end of the cold war. Among the writers and activists who pro-vide historical perspectives are Clarence Darrow, Langston Hughes, Ernest Hemingway, John Dos Passos, James Agee, and W. E. B. DuBois.

———. *McCarthyism, The Great American Red Scare: A Documentary History.* Oxford: Oxford University Press, 1997. Fried has compiled a collection of speeches, congressional hearings, court decisions, official reports, ex-ecutive orders, letters, memoirs, and essays, that, taken together, provide a comprehensive overview of McCarthyism and the Red Scare of the late 1940s to mid-1960s. It includes a bibliographic essay.

George, John, and Laird Wilcox. *American Extremists: Militias, Supremacists, Klansmen, Communists, and Others.* Amherst, N.Y.: Prometheus Books, 1996. One of the most complete overviews of American extremism avail-able, this book focuses on the period between the 1960s and the late 1990s. The section on the Far Left includes chapters on such groups as the Communist Party USA, Socialist Workers Party, Black Panther Party, Workers World Party, and Revolutionary Communist Party, while the Far Right portion studies the activities and motives of the John Birch So-ciety, Christian Right, Minutemen, Jewish Defense League, Nation of Islam, neo-Nazis, Ku Klux Klan, militia groups, and more. Each chapter is followed by a notes section. Among the useful appendices are a run-down of fake quotes that extremists use to defend their beliefs and tactics, a list of principal characteristics associated with extremists (such as "ha-tred of opponents" and "consistent indulgence in irresponsible accusa-tions and character assassination"), and a chart comparing differing characteristics of leftists, rightists, and nonextremists.

Gibbs, Nancy, et al. *Mad Genius: The Odyssey, Pursuit, and Capture of the Un-abomber Suspect.* New York: Warner, 1996. Written by a team of *Time* magazine journalists, this book traces the path that led Theodore Kaczyn-ski to isolate himself in a Montana cabin and begin his 18-year letter-bomb campaign. It includes 16 pages of photographs, a list of items seized

____

in Kaczynski's cabin and used as evidence against him during the trial, and the complete manuscript of the Unabomber's antitechnology manifesto.

Glassgold, Peter, ed. *Anarchy! An Anthology of Emma Goldman's* Mother Earth. Washington, D.C.: Counterpoint, 2001. A collection of essays and stories that originally appeared in Emma Goldman's *Mother Earth*, an anarchist magazine dedicated to "social science and literature" published from 1906 to 1917. Contributors include Margaret Sanger and Peter Kropotkin.

Graysmith, Robert. *Unabomber: A Desire to Kill.* Washington, D.C.: Regnery, 1997. Graysmith not only traces the bombing career of Theodore Kaczynski but also critiques the FBI's handling of the 18-year investigation and attempts to answer such conspiracy-oriented questions as whether the Unabomber had an accomplice who is still at large. It includes eight pages of color photographs.

Guerin, Daniel, ed. *No Gods, No Masters.* Trans. Paul Sharkey. 2 vols. Oakland, Calif.: AK Press, 1998. This set traces the history of anarchism up to the Spanish Civil War through documents, essays, letters, and other writings. Among those included are Emma Goldman, Max Stirner, Pierre-Joseph Proudhon, Mikhail Bakunin, and Peter Kropotkin.

Hamm, Mark S. *Apocalypse in Oklahoma: Waco and Ruby Ridge Revenged.* Boston: Northeastern University Press, 1997. This book recounts the events leading up to the bombing of the Murrah federal building in Oklahoma City, then explores how the far Right's anger was fueled during the 1990s by federal mishandling of the standoff with Branch Davidians in Waco, Texas, and the siege of Randy Weaver's cabin in Ruby Ridge, Idaho.

Haynes, John Earl. *Red Scare or Red Menace? American Communism and Anticommunism in the Cold War Era.* Chicago: Ivan R. Dee, 1990. This book traces changing attitudes toward communism in the United States beginning in the 1920s.

Heineman, Kenneth J. *Put Your Bodies Upon the Wheels: Student Revolt in the 1960s.* Chicago: Ivan R. Dee, 2001. Heineman provides an even-handed examination of the social, philosophical, and moral roots of the 1960s civil rights and student protest movements, exploring questions of violence and the drug culture along the way. The final chapter discusses the ongoing impact the tumultuous decade has had on U.S. culture.

Hilliard, David, and Lewis Cole. *This Side of Glory: The Autobiography of David Hilliard and the Story of the Black Panther Party.* Boston: Little, Brown, 1993. The reader follows Hilliard from his childhood in the rural South to his role as cofounder of the Black Panther Party in Oakland, California, during the 1960s and beyond. Included are photographs and a useful "Cast of Characters" that lists important members of the Black Panthers and the roles they played in the party.

Hinshaw, John H., and Paul Leblanc. *U.S. Labor in the 20th Century: Studies in Working-Class Struggles and Insurgency.* Amherst, N.Y.: Prometheus, 2000. The 25 essays in this book explore the connection between radicalism and the revitalization of the labor movement, particularly in relation to class, gender, and ethnic issues.

Hixson, William B., Jr. *Search for the American Right Wing: An Analysis of the Social Record, 1955–1987.* Princeton, N.J.: Princeton University Press, 1992. Overview of the primary analytical models that American social scientists have used to study the right wing in the United States.

Hodgson, Godfrey. *The World Turned Right Side Up: A History of the Conservative Ascendancy in America.* Boston: Houghton Mifflin, 1996. Hodgson explores the post–World War II history of conservative politics in the United States and supplies notes and bibliography.

Hoffman, Bruce. *Inside Terrorism.* New York: Columbia University Press, 1998. The author traces the history of terrorism from the Reign of Terror that followed the French Revolution to the late 1990s. Among the contemporary subjects are Timothy McVeigh, American militia groups, white supremacists, and the Weathermen. The book includes an extensive bibliography.

Hoffman, David. *The Oklahoma City Bombing and the Politics of Terror.* Venice, Calif.: Feral House, 1998. Another book that purports to expose the conspiracy behind the bombing of the Murrah building in Oklahoma City. It includes information on supposed connections between Timothy McVeigh and Middle Eastern terrorists, as well as evidence that something more powerful than a truck bomb made of fertilizer was involved in the explosion. It includes photographs, diagrams, and documents that are presented as evidence of the author's theories.

Hoffman, Jack, and Daniel Simon. *Run Run Run: The Lives of Abbie Hoffman.* New York: G. P. Putnam's Sons, 1996. This biography of Abbie Hoffman was written by his brother, who interweaves a generally sympathetic account of the Yippie radical's life with insight into important events of the 1960s and early 1970s, including the 1968 Democratic National Convention and ensuing trial. It includes notes and photographs.

Horowitz, David. *Radical Son: A Generational Odyssey.* New York: Free Press, 1997. Horowitz documents his transformation from 1960s radical and important player in the rise of the New Left to an intellectual leader of 1990s conservatism. The book includes firsthand accounts of the author's meetings with Bertrand Russell, Tom Hayden, and Black Panther cofounder Huey Newton. It includes photographs.

Horowitz, David A., ed. *Inside the Klavern: The Secret History of the Ku Klux Klan of the 1920s.* Carbondale: Southern Illinois University Press, 1999. Horowitz has collected and annotated the minutes of the 300-member

Ku Klux Klan of La Grande, Oregon, from 1922 to 1924. The documents provide a detailed view of the inner workings of the Klan at the height of its power, including admission requirements, officer selection criteria, and enforcement of moral standards. The editor provides notes and context for the documents.

Isserman, Maurice. *If I Had a Hammer: The Death of the Old Left and the Birth of the New Left*. New York: Basic Books, 1987. The author explores the links between the leftist movement that flourished during the 1930s and the one that arose from student protests during the 1960s. In particular, Isserman sheds light on how the movement quietly survived through the Red Scare of the late 1940s and 1950s.

Jeansonne, Glen. *Women of the Far Right: The Mothers' Movement and World War II*. Chicago: University of Chicago Press, 1996. This book explores the role of women in American groups that sympathized with the Nazi regime before, during, and after World War II. Photographs, notes, and a bibliographic essay are included.

Johanningsmeier, Edward P. *Forging American Communism: The Life of William Z. Foster*. Princeton, N.J.: Princeton University Press, 1994. This book recounts the life of an important American professional revolutionary and labor agitator. It includes extensive endnotes and some photographs.

Kaczynski, Ted. *The Unabomber Manifesto: Industrial Society and Its Future*. Berkeley, Calif.: Jolly Roger Press, 1995. Originally published in the *Washington Post* and *New York Times* under the pseudonym FC, which was thought at the time to be a terrorist group rather than an individual, this unedited version of Kaczynski's manuscript allows readers to judge for themselves the philosophy that led to violence and murder.

Kaplan, Jeffrey, and Leonard Weinburg. *The Emergence of a Euro-American Radical Right*. New Brunswick, N.J.: Rutgers University Press, 1998. The authors argue that recent demographic, social, economic, and technological trends have facilitated the development of a new radical Right that spans the Atlantic Ocean and transcends national boundaries. This has resulted in the establishment of several American groups, such as the Ku Klux Klan and Aryan Nations, in Europe. The book includes extensive notes.

Keith, Jim. *Okbomb! Conspiracy and Cover-Up*. Lilburn, Ga.: IllumiNet, 1996. Purporting to be the definitive exposé of a government coverup, this analysis of the Oklahoma City bombing places great emphasis on the fact that many eyewitnesses to the events surrounding the attack have contradicted one another. To support his conspiracy theory, the author offers a number of quotes and pieces of information that are intended to be thought-provoking but seem little more than coincidence.

Klehr, Harvey, and John Earl Haynes. *The Secret World of American Communism*. Trans. Timothy D. Sergay. New Haven, Conn.: Yale University Press,

1996. Utilizing a combination of narrative and documents from the archives of the former Soviet Union, the authors contend that the Communist Party of the United States of America was involved in espionage and subversion on behalf of the Soviets. The book includes illustrations.

Kovel, Joel. *Red Hunting in the Promised Land: Anticommunism and the Making of America.* New York: Basic Books, 1994. Written shortly after the fall of the Soviet Union, this book takes a critical view of the anticommunist struggle that dominated American politics from the Red Scare of 1919 to the early 1990s. During his examination, the author connects the anticommunist movement to deeper beliefs inherent in Western Christianity and philosophy.

Lee, Martin A. *The Beast Reawakens.* Boston: Little, Brown, 1997. Lee examines the worldwide, post–cold war resurgence of fascism, focusing on the role that American neo-Nazis played in keeping the National Socialist agenda alive after World War II. Photographs, bibliography, and extensive notes are included.

Lerner, Michael. *The Socialism of Fools: Anti-Semitism on the Left.* Oakland, Calif.: Tikkun, 1992. While acknowledging that anti-Semitism largely originates on the radical Right, Lerner studies the anti-Semitism inherent in liberal critiques of Israeli policies toward Palestinians, as well as the growth of dangerous anti-Semitic trends in some Third World communities. Illustrations and photographs are included.

Levy, Peter B. *The Civil Rights Movement.* Westport, Conn.: Greenwood Press, 1998. An excellent place to start any study of the civil rights movement, this detailed introduction includes six essays that each explain an important aspect of the movement, a chronology of events, biographies of major personalities, excerpts from important documents, a glossary of terms, and an annotated bibliography.

Lewis, Martin W. *Green Delusions: An Environmentalist Critique of Radical Environmentalism.* Durham, N.C.: Duke University Press, 1992. Lewis, a moderate environmentalist, argues that radical environmentalism is based on ill-conceived notions that, if enacted, would exacerbate ecological problems rather than correct them. The book includes an appendix that compares extreme "Arcadian" environmentalism with its more moderate "Promethean" counterpart and an extensive bibliography.

Linenthal, Edward T. *The Unfinished Bombing: Oklahoma City in the American Memory.* New York: Oxford University Press, 2001. Based on more than 150 interviews with survivors, family members of victims, and rescuers, this book analyzes the aftermath of the Oklahoma City bombing. Linenthal focuses on the ways Americans have tried to come to terms with the atrocity and on the different ways the bombing has been interpreted. Coping mechanisms have ranged from cultivating a sense of civic renewal and religious redemption to dispensing apocalyptic warnings of greater evils to come. One section of the book is dedicated to the design and construction of the Oklahoma City National Memorial. There are numerous photographs.

List, Peter C., ed. *Radical Environmentalism: Philosophy and Tactics.* Belmont, Calif.: Wadsworth, 1993. Essays in this collection explore radical environmentalism largely through the eyes of its proponents, including Arne Naess, Carolyn Merchant, Murray Bookchin, Dave Foreman, Edward Abbey, and Paul Watson. Among the topics explored are the philosophies of deep ecology, ecofeminism, social ecology, and bioregionalism, as well as the tactics of Greenpeace, Earth First!, Sea Shepherd Society, and others.

Lloyd, Brian. *Left Out: Pragmatism, Exceptionalism, and the Poverty of American Marxism, 1890–1922.* Baltimore, Md.: Johns Hopkins University Press, 1997. Lloyd explores the problems that radicals in the United States faced when they tried to apply Marxist doctrines to American culture, particularly during the early 20th century. Endnotes are included.

Lutholtz, M. William. *Grand Dragon: D. C. Stephenson and the Ku Klux Klan in Indiana.* Reprint. West Lafayette, Ind.: Purdue University Press, 1994. An account of the career of the grand dragon of the powerful Indiana Klan, who, at the height of his power, was convicted of murder in 1925.

Macdonald, Andrew. *The Turner Diaries.* 2d ed. New York: Barricade Books, 1996. Written by National Alliance founder William Pierce under the pseudonym Andrew Macdonald and originally published in 1978, *The Turner Diaries* was one of Timothy McVeigh's favorite books. The fictional account of the bombing of the FBI building in Section VI contains a number of eerie parallels with McVeigh's 1995 assault on the Alfred P. Murrah Federal Building in Oklahoma City, from the approximate time of the explosion to the use of ammonium nitrate fertilizer. For this edition, the publisher has added a disclaimer on the cover indicating that the book contains racist propaganda, a warning that sensitive readers would do well to take seriously. An introduction by the publisher explains that although the house disagrees with Pierce's message, it is a testament to the strength of American democracy that the publisher is able to disseminate unpopular sentiments without threat of censorship by the government.

Marks, Kathy. *Faces of Right Wing Extremism.* Boston: Branden, 1996. This book provides a useful rundown of various right-wing groups, including comprehensive lists of Ku Klux Klan, neo-Nazi, skinhead, militia, and Christian Identity groups. It also includes a chapter on relevant U.S. Supreme Court rulings; however, the book does contain several blatant factual errors, such as the claim that the Greensboro, North Carolina, shoot-out occurred in 1969 rather than 1979.

Annotated Bibliography

Martinez, Thomas, and John Guinther. *Brotherhood of Murder.* New York: McGraw-Hill, 1988. A former member of the white supremacist group The Order tells his story.

Mayer, Henry. *All on Fire: William Lloyd Garrison and the Abolition of Slavery.* New York: St. Martin's Press, 1998. Although previous biographers have painted Garrison as an extremist who had little impact on the course of history, in Mayer's view he was one of the most important figures of 19th-century America. The author includes detailed accounts of the internal politics of the abolitionist groups Garrison organized, as well as an analysis of the contents of the *Liberator* newspaper.

McCuen, Gary E. *The Militia Movement and Hate Groups in America.* Hudson, Wisc.: Gary McCuen Publications, 1996. Twenty-one essays present a variety of points of view on the subject of militias and hate groups. Formatted to promote classroom discussion, each chapter begins with a list of points to consider while reading. Interspersed throughout the book are exercises to develop reasoning skills, such as interpreting editorial cartoons, and recognizing editorial bias and authors' points of view. It includes a bibliography.

Mckivigan, John R., ed. *Abolitionism and American Religion.* New York: Garland, 1999. A collection of important essays on the American abolitionist movement's attempts to garner support from religious institutions.

Michael, Lew, and Dan Herbeck. *American Terrorist: Timothy McVeigh and the Oklahoma City Bombing.* New York: Regan Books, 2001. This book is primarily an account of Timothy McVeigh's life, from childhood to the Oklahoma City bombing and beyond. Based on the authors' interviews with more than 150 people, as well as 75 hours of conversation with McVeigh, the text allows McVeigh to tell his own story with little to no analysis on the part of the writers. Some readers may be offended by the attempt to put a human face on the perpetrator of one of the worst crimes in U.S. history, but the authors do so without glorifying McVeigh's ideology or suggesting that the bombing can be justified in any way. Published shortly before McVeigh's execution, the book does not cover the investigation into the FBI's mishandling of court documents or the change of execution dates. It includes black-and-white photographs, source notes, a list of the victims of the bombing, and a copy of a letter that convicted Unabomber Ted Kaczynski sent to the authors concerning his impressions of McVeigh during the time they were incarcerated together.

Nash, Jay Robert. *Terrorism in the 20th Century: A Narrative Encyclopedia from the Anarchists, Through the Weatherman, to the Unabomber.* New York: M. Evans, 1998. Consisting of 10 chapters, each dedicated to a single decade of the 20th century, this book offers a narrative overview of terrorism in the United States. It begins with the assassination of President

William McKinley in 1901 and ends with Timothy McVeigh and the Oklahoma City bombing, covering both famous and lesser-known personalities and events in between. It includes a chronology, glossary, and bibliography.

Nelson, Jack. *Terror in the Night: The Klan's Campaign Against the Jews.* New York: Simon and Schuster, 1993. Pulitzer Prize–winning author Nelson provides a gripping, journalistic account of the FBI's attempt to catch a Klansman suspected of bombing synagogues in Mississippi. There are an index and a list of sources.

The New Lexicon of Hate: The Changing Tactics, Language and Symbols of America's Extremists. Los Angeles: Simon Wiesenthal Center, 1997. This slim volume is packed with up-to-date information on the Ku Klux Klan, neo-Nazis, skinheads, militia groups, and Christian Identity groups. It includes diagrams of tattoos commonly worn by racists, a list of racist popular-music bands, important dates on the racist calendar, and a sampling of hate-oriented web sites.

Newton, Huey. *Revolutionary Suicide.* New York: Harcourt Brace Jovanovich, 1973. Newton's autobiography begins with his grandparents and ends with his release from jail and subsequent visit to China in 1971. In between lies a fascinating account of a troubled youth and the discontent with the U.S. power structure that led to the formation of the Black Panthers. Underlying the narrative is the idea that members of a revolutionary group must sacrifice their individuality for the greater good of the cause in question.

9:02 A.M. April 19, 1995: The Official Record of the Oklahoma City Bombing. Rev. ed. Oklahoma City, Okla.: *Oklahoma Today* Magazine, 2000. This touching tribute contains color photographs, essays, diagrams, and transcripts of speeches relevant to the bombing. Forming the centerpiece of the book are photographs and brief biographies of each of the victims of the blast.

Noble, Kerry. *Tabernacle of Hate: Why They Bombed Oklahoma City.* Prescott, Ont.: Voyageur, 1998. Author Noble details the years he spent as a member of the Covenant, the Sword and the Arm of the Lord (CSA), as well as his negotiations with the FBI that helped prevent a bloody gun battle between the CSA and federal agents. After discussing the history and philosophy of the organization, Noble explores ideas held in common by CSA members and other extremists that may have motivated Timothy McVeigh and Terry Nichols to bomb the Murrah federal building in Oklahoma City. The book includes photographs, recommended readings, and a list of people killed in Oklahoma City.

Peace, Roger C. *A Just and Lasting Peace: The U.S. Peace Movement from the Cold War to Desert Storm.* Chicago: Noble Press, 1991. The author, an activist and writer for peace and justice causes, focuses on the development of the movement during the 1980s and early 1990s, particularly protests against U.S. foreign policy in Central America, the Middle East, and South Africa. He includes a directory of organizations working for peace and justice, a chart illustrating the interconnection among various peace issues, and endnotes.

Perea, Juan F., ed. *Immigrants Out! The New Nativism and the Anti-Immigrant Impulse in the United States.* New York: New York University Press, 1997. Nearly 20 essays explore the recent resurgence of anti-immigrant sentiment in the United States in light of the prominent role that that nativism has played in the nation's history.

Powers, Richard Gid. *Not Without Honor: The History of American Anticommunism.* New York: Free Press, 1995. Powers traces the American anticommunist movement from the post–World War I years to the fall of the Berlin Wall and collapse of the Soviet Union. Extensive notes, bibliography, and photographs are included.

Quarles, Chester L. *The Ku Klux Klan and Related American Racialist and Antisemitic Organizations: A History and Analysis.* Jefferson, N.C.: McFarland and Company, 1999. This book traces the history and developing philosophies of the Klan, as well as the proliferation of related white supremacist groups from the 1970s onward. It also includes chapters on Christian Identity religion and right-wing terrorism, appendices that consist of various Ku Klux Klan documents, endnotes, a bibliography, and an index.

Radosh, Ronald. *Commies: A Journey Through the Old Left, the New Left and the Leftover Left.* San Francisco: Encounter, 2001. Raised in a communist household in New York, Radosh was an important spokesman for the American Left until research for his book *The Rosenberg File* (written with Joyce Milton) forced him to conclude that the couple was indeed guilty of espionage. After the book's publication Radosh was labeled a traitor by his former left-wing colleagues, forcing him to reevaluate the beliefs he had held for his entire life. *Commies* recounts a childhood spent attending May Day rallies and progressive youth camps, as well as the later anguish that accompanied his disenchantment with the Left.

Ridgeway, James. *Blood in the Face: The Ku Klux Klan, Nazi Skinheads, and the Rise of a New White Culture.* 2d ed. New York: Thunder's Mouth Press, 1995. This basic overview of the racist Right contains a large number of photographs, as well as reproductions of volatile tracts and flyers distributed by the Ku Klux Klan, Aryan Nations, White Aryan Resistance, and others. It also includes bibliographic notes and a useful chart that illustrates the web of connections between the people and groups mentioned in the book.

175

Fundamentalists and Extremists

Roleff, Tamara L.; Brenda Stalcup; and Mary E. Williams, eds. *Hate Groups: Opposing Viewpoints.* San Diego, Calif.: Greenhaven Press, 1999. These essays provide differing points of view on such questions as Are hate crimes a serious problem? Do certain groups promote hate and violence? Does the militia movement pose a serious threat? How can hate crimes and terrorism be reduced? Among the contributors are Bill Clinton, William Pierce, and Klanwatch. A bibliography, ideas for further discussion, a list of organizations, and an index are included.

Ronson, Jon. *Them: Adventures with Extremists.* London: Picador, 2002. Simultaneously funny and alarming, this book chronicles British humorist Jon Ronson's encounters with various Islamic fundamentalists, Christian separatists, and white supremacists around the world. Among the U.S.-based extremists covered are a Ku Klux Klan leader and participants in the Ruby Ridge and Waco standoffs. The common thread among all the extremists is their belief that a secret organization known as the Bilderberg Group rules the world. In the final chapter, Ronson attempts to infiltrate a Bilderberg meeting in Portugal to find out if the extremists' fears of conspiracy have any basis in fact.

Sargent, Lyman Tower, ed. *Extremism in America.* New York: New York University Press, 1995. A collection of ideological writings from a wide variety of extremist groups, beginning with the late-19th-century Populist Party. Subsequent sections include writings about communism, anticommunism, race, social concerns, economic questions, intentional communities, radical decentralization, and tactics. Although each section begins with a brief introduction by Sargent, the readings are largely allowed to stand on their own with a minimum of editorial commentary. Since many of these writings are difficult to come by, this book is an excellent resource for researchers interested in studying the undiluted message of such groups as the Ku Klux Klan, Aryan Nations, and the Communist Party USA. It includes a bibliography.

Scarce, Rik. *Eco-Warriors: Understanding the Radical Environmental Movement.* Chicago: Noble Press, 1990. Approaching the subject from a sympathetic point of view, Scarce covers the beliefs, tactics, and personalities that form the foundation of such groups as Earth First!, the Sea Shepherd Conservation Society, Greenpeace, and the Animal Liberation Front.

Schrank, Robert. *Wasn't That a Time? Growing Up Radical and Red in America.* Cambridge, Mass.: MIT Press, 1998. This is an autobiographical account of a man whose radical political career began in the Youth Communist League during the 1930s and led him through some of the major social and political upheavals in 20th century America. It includes photographs.

Shipman, Charles. *It Had to Be Revolution: Memoirs of an American Radical.* Ithaca, N.Y.: Cornell University Press, 1993. The author gives an autobiographical account of a radical leftist career that spanned many of the social struggles of the United States during the 20th century. He includes photographs.

Singer, Peter. *Animal Liberation.* 2d ed. New York: Random House, 1990. Originally published in 1975, this book is considered by many to have inspired the worldwide animal rights movement. Singer argues that inflicting suffering on animals for scientific study and meat production is morally indefensible and wasteful. The second edition includes Singer's thoughts on the development of the radical animal rights movement between 1975 and 1990, as well as an updated list of books and organizations and suggestions for where to buy "cruelty-free" products.

Smith, Jennifer B. *An International History of the Black Panther Party.* New York: Garland, 1999. This offers a brief introduction to the birth and growth of the Black Panthers in the United States and other countries. It includes an extensive bibliography.

Stern, Jessica. *The Ultimate Terrorists.* Cambridge, Mass.: Harvard University Press, 1999. This overview of post–cold war global terrorism includes information on the Ku Klux Klan, Aryan Nations, Timothy McVeigh, and other North American extremists, putting them into the context of larger trends. It includes notes and tables.

Stern, Kenneth S. *A Force Upon the Plain: The American Militia Movement and the Politics of Hate.* New York: Simon and Schuster, 1996. Chapters discuss the standoff between federal agents and Randy Weaver at Ruby Ridge, Christian Identity, paramilitary training, gun rights, conspiracy theories, Timothy McVeigh and the Oklahoma City bombing, tax protest, and other aspects of the extreme Right in the United States. It includes a list of sources.

Stewart, Gail B. *Militias.* San Diego, Calif.: Lucent Books, 1998. This basic overview includes chapters on the roots of the militia movement and conspiracies, a list of organizations to contact, suggestions for further reading, and plenty of black-and-white photographs.

Stewart, James Brewer, and Eric Foner. *Holy Warriors: The Abolitionists and American Slavery.* Rev. ed. New York: Hill and Wang, 1997. Focusing on the pre–Civil War years, this book shows the important roles that the American Revolution and Great Awakening played in the formation of the abolitionist movement. Also of interest is the space devoted to the vital role that women played in the struggle to outlaw slavery in North America.

Strand, Rod, and Patti Strand. *The Hijacking of the Humane Movement.* Wilsonville, Ore.: Doral, 1993. This scathing critique of animal rights activism contends that the movement has been taken over by hateful radicals whose violent tactics cause more harm than good to animals. Case studies involving such organizations as People for the Ethical Treatment of Animals and Animal Liberation Front are included. The authors' biased views are revealed by the fact that complete addresses are supplied for organizations that advocate animal testing and experimentation, while animal rights groups are identified only by name and city. A list of 20th-century medical advances through animal research and testing is provided.

Thomas, Janet. *The Battle in Seattle: The Story Behind the WTO Demonstrations.* Golden, Colo.: Fulcrum, 2000. Thomas provides an eyewitness account of events in Seattle from the perspective of a protester and passionate antiglobalization activist.

Tourish, Dennis, and Tim Wohlforth. *On the Edge: Political Cults Right and Left.* Armonk, N.Y.: M. E. Sharpe, 2000. This book examines organizations that use charismatic, guru-style leadership normally associated with religious sects to achieve political ends. Among the belief systems and groups studied are Christian Identity, followers of Lyndon LaRouche, and Marlene Dixon's leftist Democratic Workers Party.

Tucker, Richard K. *The Dragon and the Cross: The Rise and Fall of the Ku Klux Klan in Middle America.* Hamden, Conn.: Archon, 1991. This book details the growing power of the 300,000-strong Indiana Ku Klux Klan during the 1920s, followed by its rapid decline after Grand Dragon David C. Stephenson was convicted for the murder of a woman in 1925.

Wade, Wyn Craig. *The Fiery Cross: The Ku Klux Klan in America.* Reprint. New York: Oxford University Press, 1998. This in-depth analysis follows the Klan from its founding after the Civil War to its late-20th-century association with neofascist groups. It includes black-and-white photos, as well as appendices consisting of samples of Klan documents.

Walters, Jerome. *One Aryan Nation Under God: How Religious Extremists Use the Bible to Justify Their Actions.* Naperville, Ill.: Sourcebooks, 2001. This book provides an in-depth description and examination of the beliefs of the Christian Identity movement, with numerous references to the Bible passages on which extremists base their religion. Endnotes and an index are also included.

Weller, Worth H., and Brad Thompson. *Under the Hood: Unmasking the Modern Ku Klux Klan.* North Manchester, Ind.: DeWitt, 1998. Weller, a journalist, and Thompson, former Indiana grand dragon of the American Knights of the Ku Klux Klan, seek to provide a tool to defeat the Klan by demystifying the organization. Rather than being a historical account, the book focuses on the Ku Klux Klan in Indiana during the 1990s, illustrating the means by which they organized rallies and the tactics they used to carry them out. Appendices include Klan documents, Klan presence on the Internet, regalia and officers, and an account of Thompson's appearance on the *Jerry Springer* television show while Thompson was still associated with the Klan.

Wood, Gordon S. *Radicalism of the American Revolution.* New York: Random House, 1993. Contending that the Revolution was "the most radical and far-reaching event in American history," Wood sets out to illustrate how the cultural and political concepts behind the rebellion led to fundamental and important changes in the American way of life.

Zerzan, John. *Elements of Refusal.* Seattle, Wash.: Left Bank Books, 1988. Anarchist Zerzan, thought by many to have been one of the driving forces behind the 1999 protests against the World Trade Organization in Seattle, ruminates on the origins of human alienation. Among the topics covered in his essays are time, agriculture, technology, unionism, Marxism, and war.

ARTICLES

Back, Les. "White Fortress in Cyberspace." *The UNESCO Courier*, vol. 54, January 2001, pp. 44–46. The author traces the rise of the Internet as a recruiting tool for white supremacists and wonders whether these new, educated, white-collar devotees will prove to be even more dangerous than classic skinhead racists.

"Back on Form." *Economist*, vol. 361, October 20, 2001, p. 34. This reports on a sermon in which Louis Farrakhan, leader of the Nation of Islam, blamed the September 11, 2001, terrorist attacks on the "liars, whoremongers, lesbians, pimps and hustlers" who have led America astray and, just as Jerry Falwell claimed, courted divine retribution.

Bai, Matt, and Vern E. Smith. "Evil to the End." *Newsweek*, vol. 133, March 8, 1999, pp. 22–24. The authors cover the trial during which John William King was sentenced to death for the murder of James Byrd in Jasper, Texas. They speculate on the reasons behind the rise of young, middle-class racists.

Barclay, David, and Ron Wakabayashi. "Hate Crimes and the Business Community." *Diversity Factor*, vol. 8, Spring 2000, pp. 32–37. This study operates on the premise that as diversity in the workplace increases, so too will incidences of hate crimes. For the purposes of the article, the authors use a broad definition of the term *hate crime* that includes ethnic slurs, distribution of racist propaganda, graffiti, and vandalism.

Barone, Michael. "A Brief History of Zealotry in America." *U.S. News & World Report*, vol. 118, May 8, 1995, pp. 44ff. The article traces the history of violent assaults on federal authority, from the Whiskey Rebellion of the 1790s, through John Brown's raid on the Harper's Ferry arsenal and the birth of the Ku Klux Klan during the 1800s, through 20th-century anarchist and leftist rebellion, and finally to the present-day militia movement.

"The Battle in Congress: Security v. Liberty." *Economist,* vol. 361, October 20, 2001, pp. 31–34. This explores several of the civil liberties issues raised by antiterrorism legislation drafted in response to the September 11, 2001, attacks on New York City and Washington, D.C.

Bello, Walden. "Lilliputians Rising—2000: The Year of the Global Protest Against Corporate Globalization." *Multinational Monitor,* vol. 22, January/February 2001, pp. 33–36. The author looks at the history of the World Trade Organization and the issues that led thousands of people to protest its policies and practices in Seattle and Washington, D.C., as well as several cities overseas.

Beltrame, Julian. "Fortress North America: How Our World Will Change." *Maclean's,* vol. 114, October 15, 2001, pp. 23–27. This article examines, from the Canadian perspective, the repercussions of heightened security along the Canada-U.S. border to protect both nations from terrorist infiltration. The author worries that in the process of harmonizing laws and procedures to maximize the efficiency of such a project, Canada may lose some of its national sovereignty and may eventually be viewed, in the eyes of the world, as having merged with the United States.

Bergman, B. J. "Wild at Heart." *Sierra,* vol. 83, January/February 1998, pp. 24–29ff. The author profiles Dave Foreman, cofounder of Earth First! and, at the time of the article's writing, a director of the Sierra Club. The article intersperses biographical information about Foreman with an account of a rafting trip on the Colorado River with the subject of the article.

Betsworth, Kirsten. "Legacy of Hate." *Good Housekeeping,* vol. 233, July 2001, pp. 117–20. A woman who married a member of William Pierce's National Alliance gives a firsthand account. Now divorced, she is trying to prevent her children from becoming bigots like their father, with whom the author shares joint custody. Although the author's achievements in escaping the National Alliance and starting her life anew are admirable, her account lacks insight into the bigger issues of white supremacy and the problem of racism.

Block, Alan W. "Weekend Warriors." *National Review,* vol. 47, May 29, 1995, pp. 39ff. The author warns against giving the Federal Bureau of Investigation and the Bureau of Alcohol, Tobacco and Firearms more funding and authority as a response to the growing threat of militia groups after the Oklahoma City bombing.

Blume, Howard, and Christine Pelisek. "Three Guys and a Megaphone: The JDL's Shrinking Role in Jewish Extremism." *L.A. Weekly,* vol. 24, January 11–17, 2002, pp. 10–12. Nearly nonexistent for several years, the Jewish Defense League returned to the headlines in January 2002 when members Earl Krugel and Irv Rubin were accused of plotting to bomb the King Fahd mosque in Los Angeles and the Orange County office of Darrell

Issa, a Republican congressman of Lebanese descent. The authors detail the events surrounding the arrests and provide brief biographies of Krugel and Rubin. They also worry that the events of September 11, 2001, and renewed violence in the Middle East might energize the Jewish extremist movement in both the United States and Israel.

Blythe, Will. "The Guru of White Hate." *Rolling Stone*, June 8, 2000, pp. 98–106. A firsthand account of a visit to William Pierce at the West Virginia headquarters of his white supremacist organization, the National Alliance. It includes biographical information, as well as a rundown of the influence of Pierce's novel *The Turner Diaries*. Although Pierce is painted as a hardcore, unrepentant racist, he also comes across as an unremarkable man filled with self-doubt. The article is accompanied by a sidebar covering white supremacist music.

Boynton, Robert S. "Powder Burn." *Outside*, vol. 24, January 1999, pp. 44–49. This is an examination of Earth Liberation Front's 1998 arson attack on a ski resort in Vail, Colorado.

Campbell, R. K. "Investigating Hate Groups on the Internet." *Law & Order*, vol. 47, November 1999, p. 40. This is a guide for police officers interested in researching hate groups on the Internet. It provides a brief list of web sites and addresses, including those of David Duke and the Black Panthers.

Cannon, Angie. "Justice at Long Last? Ex-Klansmen Are Held in '63 Church Bombing." *U.S. News & World Report*, vol. 128, May 29, 2000, p. 23. This brief article discusses the revival of legal proceedings against Bobby Frank Cherry and Thomas Blanton, Jr., two former Ku Klux Klansmen accused of murdering four young African-American girls in the 1963 bombing of the 16th Street Baptist Church in Birmingham, Alabama.

Cannon, Angie, and Warren Cohen. "The Church of the Almighty White Man." *U.S. News & World Report*, vol. 127, July 19, 1999, pp. 22–23. This article, which profiles Matthew Hale, head of the white supremacist World Church of the Creator, was written shortly after Benjamin N. Smith, a member of Hale's church, went on a shooting rampage that targeted minorities, killing two people and wounding nine before he committed suicide.

"Civil Liberties Watch: The Criminalization of Hatred." *Humanist*, vol. 54, May 1994, pp. 38ff. This article chronicles the enactment of hate-crime laws in many states during the early 1990s, describes the characteristics of these laws, and discusses accompanying law enforcement issues and civil liberties implications.

Cloud, John. "Is Hate on the Rise?" *Time*, vol. 154, July 19, 1999, p. 33. The author discusses the growing violence of white supremacists, focusing on World Church of the Creator leader Matthew Hale and his devotee Benjamin N. Smith.

Cockburn, Alexander. " 'New' and 'Left' Are Not Oxymoronic." *Los Angeles Times*, April 20, 2000, p. B11. The author of this editorial commentary lauds the rise of the new leftist radicalism evidenced in well-attended antiglobalism protests in Seattle and Washington, D.C.

Cohen, Adam. "All You Need Is Hate." *Time*, vol. 158, Fall 2001 Special Issue, pp. 46ff. This article discusses National Alliance leader William Pierce's acquisition of Resistance Records, "the world's leading purveyor" of racist, or "hate-core," music. Although Pierce sells music CDs as a tool to recruit young people into the white supremacist movement, he does claim to have qualms about using rock and roll, which he regards as "black music," to attract teenagers to the Aryan cause. However, he takes great pride in not contributing to the trend of selling rap music to white kids.

Cooper, Marc, and Lisa Westberg. "Montana's Mother of All Militias." *Nation*, vol. 260, May 22, 1995, pp. 714ff. In the wake of Timothy McVeigh's bombing of the Oklahoma City federal building, the authors take a comprehensive look at the beliefs of members of the Militia of Montana, considered to be one of the more radical militia groups and the organization after which many others have been modeled. The article also discusses the history and development of the militia movement in the United States. It includes a list of organizations that track the activities of militia groups.

Cose, Ellis. "An Uneasy Sense of Outrage." *Newsweek*, vol. 133, March 8, 1999, p. 24. This editorial suggests that merely condemning John William King to death for the dragging murder of James Byrd does not solve America's deeper racial problems.

"Counter Movement Backs Wise Use." *Christian Science Monitor*, January 12, 1993, p. 11. This traces the antienvironmental wise-use movement from its roots in the Sagebrush Rebellion of the 1970s to its rise in power during the early 1990s. It cites leaders of several organizations within the movement, as well as spokespersons for a few of the environmental groups that oppose them.

Dana, Will. "Civil Liberties Under Attack." *Rolling Stone*, November 8, 2001, pp. 54ff. Dana interviews Vermont senator Patrick Leahy, head of the Judiciary Committee and one of the few politicians to speak out against Attorney General John Ashcroft's proposed antiterrorism laws in the wake of the September 11, 2001, terrorist attacks on New York City and Washington, D.C. In the interview, Leahy speaks of potential civil liberties abuses if the U.S. Constitution is undermined in the name of national security.

De Borchgrave, Arnaud. "Grim Graduates of Terrorist U." *Insight on the News*, vol. 17, October 22, 2001, pp. 29ff. The article links radical Muslims in Pakistan with Afghanistan's ruling Taliban militia through the fundamentalist University for the Education of Truth in Khattak, Pakistan.

Nine of the Taliban's top 10 leaders studied there, where Osama bin Laden is hailed as a hero to Islam second only to Muhammad himself.

Decker, Twila. "Unbroken." *Los Angeles Times Magazine*, August 5, 2001, pp. 16–18. This documents the events leading up to the impending court case of Sara Jane Olson, a former member of the Symbionese Liberation Army, which is widely known for its 1974 kidnapping of Patricia Hearst. Olson, who eluded capture by the police for 24 years, faced charges of conspiring to kill two police officers. The article provides background information on the SLA, delves into Olson's life as a well-respected member of her St. Paul, Minnesota, community, and also focuses on her vehement denials of any responsibility for the murders.

Dillow, Gordon. "Supremacist Money Goes to Africa." *Orange County Register,* March 19, 1995, pp. A1ff. The author reports on White Aryan Resistance leader Tom Metzger's obligation to pay $12.5 million to the estate of an Ethiopian man killed by Oregon skinheads in 1988. He comments on the irony that an undisclosed percentage of donations to White Aryan Resistance are sent to Africa to support the son of the deceased.

Dogar, Rana. "Women of the Militias." *New Woman*, vol. 27, February 1997, pp. 120–23ff. The author explores the beliefs and motives of the women who make up 30 percent of the membership of militia groups in the Midwest.

Elliott, Michael. "A Clear and Present Danger." *Time*, vol. 158, October 8, 2001, pp. 26–39. The article follows the U.S. government's attempt, in the wake of the September 11, 2001, terrorist attacks on New York City and Washington, D.C., to strike a balance between building a sense of homeland security and maintaining civil rights promised by the Constitution. It also discusses the history of noncooperation among various federal agencies, as well as between federal and state offices.

Elvin, John. "Wild-Eyed in the Wilderness." *Insight on the News*, vol. 17, April 23, 2001, pp. 21–23. This article profiles Earth First! cofounder Dave Foreman, who discusses his long-term efforts to "re-wild" America through The Wildlands Project (TWP).

Gordon, Diana R. "The Politics of Anti-Terrorism." *Nation*, vol. 260, May 22, 1995, pp. 20ff. The author examines proposals for antiterrorism legislation that arose in the wake of the Oklahoma City bombing and warns that the tragedy should not be exploited in order to enact laws that would seriously undermine the Bill of Rights.

Gwynne, S. C. "The Second Coming of a Nightmare." *Time*, vol. 153, March 1, 1999, p. 8. Gwynne describes the small logging town of Jasper, Texas, during the trial of white supremacist John William King, illustrating how it was overrun by the media, entrepreneurs hawking souvenirs, and radicals on all sides of the race issue who wished to air their views.

Fundamentalists and Extremists

Haider-Markel, Donald P., and Sean P. O'Brien. "Creating a Well-Regulated Militia: Policy Responses to Paramilitary Groups in the U.S." *Political Research Quarterly*, vol. 50, September 1997, pp. 551–65. This is a somewhat-tedious academic discussion of the ways in which politicians must respond to the threat of antigovernment militia while addressing the more mainstream conservative issues that these groups raise. It includes footnotes and a list of references.

Hawken, Paul. "On the Streets of Seattle." *Amicus Journal*, vol. 22, Spring 2000, pp. 29–33ff. This eyewitness account of a protester at the 1999 anti–World Trade Organization (WTO) rally in Seattle is interspersed with background information on the WTO that will help readers understand exactly what thousands of people were demonstrating against.

Irvine, Reed. "FBI Missed Red Flags About Terrorists' Plans." *Insight on the News*, vol. 17, October 29, 2001, pp. 44ff. In 1995, police in the Philippines uncovered a plot by Islamic fundamentalists to plant bombs in a dozen U.S. airliners and crash an airplane into Central Intelligence Agency (CIA) headquarters. Irvine claims that had this warning, among others, been heeded by the Federal Bureau of Investigation and the CIA, the events of September 11, 2001, might have been avoided.

Jackson, David S. "When ELF Comes Calling." *Time*, vol. 157, January 15, 2001, p. 35. This provides a brief overview of the Earth Liberation Front's history and tactics, in addition to reporting the group's first actions in the eastern United States.

Jenkins, Philip. "Home-Grown Terror." *American Heritage*, vol. 46, September 1995, pp. 35ff. The article explores the connections between 1990s antigovernment militias and groups that, during the 1930s, claimed to be patriotic even while they espoused Nazi ideology and advocated violent revolution.

Jensen, Derrick, and Chris Dodge. "You May Be an Anarchist—and Not Even Know It." *Utne Reader*, May/June 2001, pp. 48ff. This is a lengthy interview with John Zerzan, an Oregon-based anarchist and author who is thought to be one of the masterminds behind the 1999 anti–World Trade Organization protests in Seattle, Washington. Sidebars to the interview provide biographical information on Zerzan and attempt to define anarchism. The article ends with a list of anarchist resources, such as books, magazines, and web sites.

Johnson, Chalmers. "Blowback." *Nation*, vol. 273, October 15, 2001, pp. 13–15. Johnson insists that U.S. foreign policy is partly to blame for the September 11, 2001, terrorist attacks. Toward supporting his point, he describes the CIA concept of "blowback" and illustrates how covert overseas operations have repeatedly come back to haunt the United States.

Annotated Bibliography

Johnson, Denis. "The Militia in Me." *Esquire*, vol. 124, July 1995, pp. 38–45. Johnson discusses the affinity between his loss of faith in the U.S. government and the beliefs of militia members.

Jordan, June. "The Hunters and the Hunted." *Progressive*, vol. 63, October 1999, pp. 17–19. Written in the wake of Aryan Nations member Buford O. Furrow's Los Angeles shooting spree, the author briefly profiles the Phineas Priesthood before launching into a personal account of her visit to a rabbi in Berkeley three days after Furrow's rampage.

Kaplan, David E., et al. "Nazism's New Global Threat: The Internet Helps Build a Sophisticated Web of Violent, Well-Funded Racists." *U.S. News & World Report*, vol. 129, September 25, 2000, pp. 34–35. One of many articles exploring the use of the Internet by white supremacists, this essay focuses on the potential to create new global information and travel networks. It discusses the recent "Nazification" of American white supremacists, as well as the ability of German skinheads to access foreign web sites containing information that is illegal in their own country.

Kelly, Michael. "The Road to Paranoia." *New Yorker*, vol. 71, June 19, 1995, pp. 60ff. The author chronicles the rise of the U.S. militia movement and its philosophical basis in paranoia, and focuses on Militia of Montana members John Trochmann and Bob Fletcher.

Kimmel, Michael. "Gender, Class, and Terrorism." *Chronicle of Higher Education*, vol. 48, February 8, 2002, pp. B11–12ff. Kimmel claims that events such as the 1995 Oklahoma City bombing and the September 11, 2001, terrorist attacks result from a combination of "the massive male displacement that accompanies globalization, the spread of American consumerism, and the perceived corruption of local political elites." His argument rests on the idea that Oklahoma City bomber Timothy McVeigh and September 11 terrorist Mohammed Atta had both aired similar complaints about the growing global influence of Western values.

Lemonick, Michael D., et al. "Deadly Delivery." *Time*, vol. 158, October 22, 2001, pp. 32–38. This early report on the dimensions of and danger posed by the anthrax outbreaks in New York City delves into the recent history of anthrax misuse and speculates about Iraq's biological warfare capability and its possible connections to bioterrorist attacks in the United States. The article also details the different symptoms and treatments for anthrax contracted through skin contact, eating tainted meat, and inhalation. A sidebar answers such questions as How do you catch anthrax? Is anthrax contagious? Is anthrax treatable?

Levi, Margaret, and David Olson. "The Battle in Seattle." *Politics and Society*, vol. 28. September 2000, pp. 309–29. This is the introductory essay of a special issue of *Politics and Society* dedicated to the history of labor strife in Seattle, Washington. As such, it undermines perceptions of Seattle as a predominantly white, middle-class city and puts the 1999 anti–World Trade Organization protests in the context of a long tradition of militant Industrial Workers of the World (IWW) activity and radical labor practices, particularly among waterfront workers.

Loeb, Harlan A. "Words Have Consequences: Re-Framing the Hate Speech Debate." *Human Rights*, vol. 26. Fall 1999, pp. 11–12. Using the case of Matthew Hale and Benjamin N. Smith as a point of departure, Loeb discusses the limits of the right to free speech in the United States and whether those who spread racist literature should be held responsible for the violent actions of those who read it.

McCain, Robert Stacy. "Hate Debate." *Insight on the News*, vol. 16, June 19, 2000, p. 33. This article reports on Laird Wilcox, researcher and author of books about fringe groups, and his belief that watchdog groups use faulty research methods that lead them to exaggerate the dangers posed by racist groups.

McDonald, Marci; Joe Chidley; and E. Kaye Fulton. "The Enemy Within." *Maclean's*, vol. 108, May 8, 1995, pp. 34ff. The article examines the growth in the number of hate groups in Canada during the 1990s.

Miller, Mark. "From Villain to Victim." *Newsweek*, vol. 139, February 4, 2002, p. 29. This article outlines the importance of Patty Hearst's role in the upcoming trial of Emily Harris, William Harris, Michael Bortin, and Sara Jane Olson, former members of the Symbionese Liberation Army accused of murdering Myrna Opsahl during a 1975 bank robbery.

Mollins, Carl. "At Home with a Racist Guru." *Maclean's*, vol. 108, May 8, 1995, pp. 42ff. This profile of National Alliance leader and *The Turner Diaries* author William Pierce explores his connection to the militia movement in the United States and his influence on white racists in Canada.

Morse, David. "Beyond the Myths of Seattle." *Dissent*, vol. 48, Summer 2001, pp. 39–43. Morse discusses how the media created a version of the 1999 anti–World Trade Organization protests in Seattle that made the protesters seem more violent than they actually were. In turn, police forces in cities where later protests were planned (such as Washington, D.C.; Philadelphia; and Los Angeles) used this myth of violence to justify undermining civil liberties in the name of "keeping the peace."

Morse, Jodie. "Middle-Aged Radicals, plucked from Suburbia." *Time*, vol. 159, January 28, 2002, p. 4. Morse reports on the arrests of four former members of the Symbionese Liberation Army (SLA) accused of murdering a woman during a 1975 bank robbery. The article provides a brief history of SLA activity and of the lengthy police investigation into the murder.

Murphy, Kim. "Disruption Is Activists' Business." *Los Angeles Times*, April 25, 2000, pp. A1ff. This profiles the activities of the Earth Liberation Front and its spokesperson Chris Rosebraugh, as well as unsuccessful efforts by law enforcement officials to arrest the perpetrators of the acts of ecosabotage for which the group claims responsibility.

O'Brien, Sean P., and Donald P. Haider-Markel. "Fueling the Fire: Social and Political Correlates of Citizen Militia Activity." *Social Science Quarterly*, vol. 79, June 1998, pp. 456–65. This is an academic study of the political motivations and social status of members of militia groups.

O'Sullivan, John. "Their Amerika." *National Review*, vol. 53, October 15, 2001, pp. 28–30. The author, while acknowledging the usefulness of reasonable criticism of U.S. foreign policy, emphatically reputes the idea that America is partially responsible for the terrorist attacks on New York City and Washington, D.C.

Sandberg, Jared. "Spinning a Web of Hate." *Newsweek*, vol. 134, July 19, 1999, pp. 28–29. This article on the use of the Internet by white supremacists focuses on how such groups use language that exploits the anger of rebellious teens and entice children with online games, comic strips, music, and friendly pitches from other children.

Sharpe, Tanya Telfair. "The Identity Christian Movement: Ideology of Domestic Terrorism." *Journal of Black Studies*, vol. 30, March 2000, pp. 604–23. The first half of this lengthy, endnoted essay is devoted to extrapolating the white supremacist doctrines of the Christian Identity; the second half covers organizations that subscribe to the belief system, focusing on their communication strategies and violent activities.

Smith, Vern E. "The Ghosts of Mississippi." *Newsweek*, vol. 135, June 12, 2000, p. 39. The reopening of several Mississippi cases involving the murders of civil rights activists by members of the Ku Klux Klan during the 1960s is seen by many as a chance to exorcise historical ghosts.

Smolowe, Jill. "Enemies of the State." *Time*, vol. 145, May 8, 1995, pp. 58ff. This chronicles the history of the growing antigovernment militia and white supremacist movements in the United States. It was written within weeks of the Oklahoma City bombing.

Spake, Amanda, et al. "Confusion in Spades: The Anthrax Scares Reveal a Public-Health System in Disarray." *U.S. News & World Report*, vol. 131, October 29, 2001, pp. 42–48. This article discusses the U.S. public-health system's inadequate framework for dealing with bioterrorist attacks. It includes a sidebar listing organisms likely to be used in a bioterrorist attack (anthrax, smallpox, botulism, and plague), with prevention prospects, signs of infection, and treatments listed for each.

Stream, Carol. "Guns and Bibles." *Christianity Today*, vol. 39, June 19, 1995, pp. 34ff. This explores how many right-wing extremist groups combine Christian faith and the right to bear arms, resulting in a blurring of the line between fundamentalist end-times rhetoric and the apocalyptic conspiracy and racist theories expounded by many militia and white supremacist groups.

Thomas, Evan. "Cracking the Terror Code." *Newsweek*, vol. 138, October 15, 2001, pp. 42–46. The author reports on the Federal Bureau of Investigation and Central Intelligence Agency's process of uncovering information about the terrorists who crashed jetliners into the World Trade Center and Pentagon on September 11, 2001.

"Today Los Angeles, Tomorrow . . ." *Time*, vol. 142, (July 26, 1993), p. 49. This details a plot foiled by the Federal Bureau of Investigation in which white supremacists planned to start a race war by killing the pastor and congregation of an African-American church in Los Angeles and murdering such prominent African Americans as Rodney King, Al Sharpton, and the rap group Public Enemy.

"United States: Hatred Unexplained." *Economist*, vol. 352, July 10, 1999, pp. 25–26. This article profiles Benjamin Smith, the World Church of the Creator member who went on a three-day, two-state shooting spree against minorities during which he killed two people and wounded nine others.

Valdez, Al. "Nazi Low Riders." *Police*, vol. 23, March 1999, pp. 46–48. Intended for law enforcement personnel, this article discusses the rise in power of the Nazi Low Riders skinhead gang and their connection with the methamphetamine trade. It includes suggestions on how to identify members, warnings about their violent reputation, and information about recruitment drives.

Veenker, Jody. "Church Leader Worships Whites." *Christianity Today*, vol. 43, October 25, 1999, p. 91. Veenker focuses on the theological basis for Matthew Hale's World Church of the Creator.

"A Violent Priesthood." *Christian Century*, vol. 116, September 8–September 15, 1999, pp. 842–43. Members of the Phineas Priesthood, often closely affiliated with Christian Identity doctrine, use an obscure passage in the Bible to justify violent action, including murder.

Vlahos, Michael. "Understanding the Enemy." *Rolling Stone*, November 8, 2001, pp. 50ff. The author offers his opinion about the U.S. response to the September 11, 2001, terrorist attacks based on his interpretation of Osama bin Laden's motivations. Vlahos makes a distinction between terrorism and insurgency, claiming that the terrorist attacks belong in the latter category and can be placed in a centuries-old pattern of trying to unite Islam and return it to a pure, incorrupt form.

Witkin, Gordon, and Joseph P. Shapiro. "An Epidemic of Fear and Loathing." *U.S. News & World Report*, vol. 118, May 8, 1995, pp. 37ff. This article discusses the philosophy, structure, and tactics of the U.S. militia movement in the wake of the Oklahoma City bombing. It includes sidebars listing conspiracy beliefs that many militia members hold in common and comparing the conspiracy and government versions of what happened at the Branch Davidian compound in Waco, Texas.

VIDEOS

"Assault on Gay America." Alexandria, Va.: PBS Video, 2000. Video (VHS). 60 minutes. Using the murder of gay computer programmer Bill Jack Gaither by a white supremacist in Alabama as the point of departure, this documentary explores the roots of homophobia in the United States.

"Attack at Waco." A&E Television Networks, n.d. Video (VHS). 50 minutes. Part of A&E's *American Justice* series, this analyzes the U.S. government's attack on the Branch Davidian compound in Waco, Texas, and includes interviews with federal officials and survivors of the fire.

"Blood in the Face." Directed by Kevin Rafferty, Anne Bohlen, and James Ridgeway. New York: First Run Features, 1991. Based on James Ridgeway's book of the same name, this film documents a gathering of neo-Nazis in the woods of Michigan for workshops and lectures. Interspersed is footage of such prominent white supremacists as George Lincoln Rockwell and David Duke.

"The Bombing of America." South Burlington, Vt.: Nova Videos, 1996. This focuses on the science of bomb explosions and the forensic evidence that helped solve bombings by the Unabomber and of the Oklahoma City federal building in 1995, the World Trade Center in 1993, and several abortion clinics in the Washington, D.C., area. It also looks into the technique of criminal profiling to pinpoint the identity of bombers.

"Crossing the Bridge." A&E Television Networks, n.d. Video (VHS). 50 minutes. The History Channel focuses on the March 7, 1965, incident during which Alabama police used violence to prevent civil rights activists from approaching the state capitol building. The police assault horrified the nation, adding momentum to the already powerful civil rights movement.

"George Wallace and Black Power." A&E Television Networks, n.d. Video (VHS). 50 minutes. The History Channel, as part of its *20th Century with Mike Wallace* series, documents Alabama governor George Wallace's attempts to undermine the drive for desegregation (and the civil rights movement in general) in the South.

"Guns and God: The Sieges of Waco and Ruby Ridge." A&E Television Networks, 1999. Video (VHS). 50 minutes. Part of the History Channel program *20th Century with Mike Wallace*, this video examines Waco and Ruby Ridge in light of the fact that many extremists view these incidents as the primary examples of the manner in which federal authorities abuse their power to silence critics of the U.S. government. It includes interviews with government authorities, as well as a discussion of the congressional inquiries into both cases.

"Hate Across America." A&E Television Networks, 1999. Video (VHS). 50 minutes. The History Channel's *20th Century with Mike Wallace* traces the modern history of hate crimes from the Ku Klux Klan's murder of three civil rights activists in Mississippi in 1964 to the more polished, sophisticated, and computer-savvy image that white supremacist groups began to cultivate during the 1990s.

"Hunt for the Unabomber." A&E Television Networks, n.d. Video (VHS). 50 minutes. A&E's *American Justice* program follows the 17-year search for the Unabomber, which ended when Theodore Kaczynski's brother turned him in after recognizing his writing style in the published Unabomber Manifesto. It includes interviews with FBI profilers, the arresting officers, prosecutors, and friends of Kaczynski.

"The Ku Klux Klan." A&E Television Networks, 1999. Video (VHS). 50 minutes. The History Channel and its *20th Century with Mike Wallace* trace the development of the Ku Klux Klan from its beginnings in rural Tennessee after the Civil War, through it heyday during the 1920s, to its continued, albeit troubled, existence in modern America.

"McCarthy Reconsidered." A&E Television Networks, 1999. Video (VHS). 50 minutes. This video, part of the *20th Century with Mike Wallace* series uses information from CIA files and declassified Soviet documents to ask whether the apparent paranoia that led Joseph McCarthy to brand people as communists was not actually justified and whether the Wisconsin senator has been unfairly vilified by historians.

"Nazis in America." A&E Television Networks, 1999. Video (VHS). 50 minutes. History Channel's *20th Century with Mike Wallace* traces the origin of the American Nazi movement and explores the motivations of U.S. citizens who have voluntarily aligned themselves with the philosophies espoused by Adolf Hitler. It includes an interview with *The Turner Diaries* author and National Alliance leader William Pierce.

"The New Skinheads." A&E Television Networks, n.d. Video (VHS). 50 minutes. The A&E show *Investigative Reports* traces the development of the skinhead movement from its beginnings in England during the 1970s to its sophisticated networking with such hate groups as the Ku Klux Klan and Aryan Nations during the late 1990s. It shows how "new" skinheads have begun to grow their hair and hide their tattoos in an attempt to pass unnoticed in mainstream society, thus becoming more secretive and dangerous than before.

"Oklahoma City Bombing." A&E Television Networks, 1999. Video (VHS). 50 minutes. Part of the History Channel's *20th Century with Mike Wallace*, this video explores the events and circumstances surrounding the bombing of the Alfred P. Murrah Federal Building in Oklahoma City, including early rumors that Islamic terrorists were responsible, the manhunt for McVeigh, the heroic efforts of rescue workers, and the underground, antigovernment Far Right through which McVeigh moved during the years leading up to the bombing.

"The Rosenbergs." A&E Television Networks, n.d. Video (VHS). 50 minutes. A&E's *American Justice* program studies the background and aftermath of the 1953 executions of Julius and Ethel Rosenberg, who were accused of selling U.S. A-bomb secrets to the Soviet Union. It includes interviews with attorneys involved in the case. Among the highlights is a mock retrial conducted by the American Bar Association on the 40th anniversary of the Rosenberg's sentencing.

"Senator Joseph McCarthy: An American Inquisitor." A&E Television Networks, n.d. Video (VHS). 50 minutes. *Biography*, an A&E program, depicts Wisconsin senator Joseph McCarthy's rise to power, his leading role in launching the Red Scare with his claims that Soviet-backed communists had infiltrated the State Department, and his fall from power after the U.S. Army hearings.

"30 Frames a Second: The WTO in Seattle." Directed by Rustin Thompson. Oley, Penn.: White Noise Productions/Bullfrog Films, 2001. Photojournalist Thompson documents the civil unrest that erupted during the 1999 World Trade Organization (WTO) meeting in Seattle, Washington. Engaging images of clashes between protesters and police are accompanied by a voiceover narrative in which Thompson acknowledges his inability to remain subjective despite his journalistic intentions.

"Timothy McVeigh: Soldier of Terror." A&E Television Networks, n.d. Video (VHS). 50 minutes. The A&E cable show *Biography* traces McVeigh from his childhood in upstate New York, through his illustrious but short-lived career in the U.S. Army that eventually led to disillusionment with America, and finally to his fascination with the antigovernment far Right and the bombing of the Murrah Federal Building in Oklahoma City. It includes interviews with neighbors and childhood friends.

"Waco: Rules of Engagement." Directed by William Gazecki. Los Angeles: Fifth Estate Productions/Somford Entertainment, 1997. This is perhaps the most compelling of the numerous films and books that question the federal government's handling and explanations of the Waco standoff in 1993. The filmmakers use interviews, news footage, congressional testimony, and analysis of infrared video in an attempt to show that the standoff did not have to end in the deaths of 86 civilians.

CHAPTER 8

ORGANIZATIONS AND AGENCIES

This chapter provides contact information for organizations and agencies involved in fundamentalist and extremist causes. Among these are research institutes, civil liberties organizations, watchdog groups, activist groups, and fundamentalist and extremist organizations.

ACT Up
332 Bleecker Street
Suite G5
New York, NY 10014
URL: http://www.actupny.org
E-mail: actupny@panix.com
Phone: (212) 966-4873
ACT Up was founded in 1987 with the purpose of ending the AIDS crisis through the use of direct-action protests and demonstrations, lobbying techniques, and medical research. Its web site includes a research bibliography, as well as civil disobedience and demonstration manuals.

American-Arab Anti-
Discrimination Committee
4201 Connecticut Avenue, NW
Suite 500
Washington, D.C. 20008
URL: http://www.adc.org
E-mail: adc@adc.org
Phone: (202) 244-2990
Fax: (202) 244-3196
This organization publishes books and articles aimed at raising public awareness about discrimination and hate crimes against Arab Americans, as well as anti-Arab stereotyping in the media.

American Association
of Christian Schools
P.O. Box 1097
Independence, MO 64051
URL: http://www.aacs.org
E-mail: national@aacs.org
Phone: (816) 795-7709
Fax: (816) 252-6700
The association was founded in 1972 to focus on promoting and establishing Protestant Christian schools in America. It tracks current events and legislation that may affect the freedoms of such institutions.

American Center for Law and Justice
P.O. Box 64429
Virginia Beach, VA 23467
URL: http://www.aclj.org
Phone: (757) 226-2489
Fax: (757) 226-2836
In 1990 Pat Robertson established this center to provide legal assistance in cases involving the religious liberty of Christians. It publishes *Case Notes*, which reports on relevant court cases.

American Civil Liberties Union
132 West 43rd Street
New York, NY 10036
URL: http://www.aclu.org
E-mail: aclu@aclu.org
Phone: (212) 944-9800
Fax: (212) 869-9065
The ACLU provides legal advice and support for people whose civil rights guaranteed by the Constitution are endangered. The web site gives information about recent court cases relevant to civil liberties issues. The union publishes *ACLU Online* and the semiannual *Civil Liberties Alert.*

American Nazi Party
P.O. Box 503
Eastpointe, MI 48021
URL: http://www.american naziparty.com
E-mail: rocky88@prodigy.net
Phone: (734) 729-1702
The party promotes the ideology of National Socialism espoused by Adolf Hitler and publishes books by George Lincoln Rockwell, as well as its *Stormtrooper* magazine.

Animal Liberation Front
P.O. Box 950
Camarillo, CA 93011
URL: http://www.animal liberationfront.com
This animal rights group promotes vegetarianism while condemning vivisection, animal testing, wearing leather and furs, and hunting. It advocates the destruction of the property of those it claims engage in abuse or killing of animals. The web site includes the ALF's primer on planning actions, the organization's history, and articles on such topics as "101 Reasons to Be Vegetarian."

Anti-Defamation League
823 United Nations Plaza
New York, NY 10017
URL: http://www.adl.org
E-mail: webmaster@adl.org
Phone: (212) 490-2525
The ADL was founded in 1913 to fight anti-Semitism, promote democracy, and encourage benign relations among all religious faiths. Its web site includes a database of extremist groups and their leaders, diagrams of hate symbols, and links to state hate-crime laws. It publishes *ADL on the Frontline.*

Aryan Nations
P.O. Box 362
Hayden Lake, ID 83835
URL: http://www.aryan-nations.org

E-mail: aryannhq@aryan-nations.org
Phone: (208) 772-2408
Fax: (208) 762-2379
Despite losing its compound in a court settlement in 2001, Richard Butler's white supremacist group maintains a presence in Idaho. The web site's content is characterized by conspiracy theories and Christian Identity ideology.

Campus Crusade for Christ
100 Lake Hart Drive
Orlando, FL 32832
URL: http://www.campus
   crusade.com
Phone: (407) 826-2000
Since its founding as a college ministry in 1951 by Bill Bright, the CCC has expanded its evangelical reach to include high school students, military personnel, prisoners, and even politicians.

Center for Democracy
   and Technology
1634 I Street, NW
Suite 1100
Washington, D.C. 20006
URL: http://www.cdt.org
E-mail: webmaster@cdt.org
Phone: (202) 637-9800
Fax: (202) 637-0968
This civil liberties group works to "promote democratic values and constitutional liberties in the digital age."

Center for Democratic Renewal
P.O. Box 50469
Atlanta, GA 30302-0469

URL: http://www.thecdr.org
E-mail: cdr@igc.apc.org
Phone: (404) 221-0025
Fax: (404) 221-0045
Formerly known as the National Anti-Klan Network, this community-based coalition works to monitor and fight hate group and white supremacist activity. It publishes pamphlets, reports, information packets, books, and the bimonthly *Monitor* magazine.

Chalcedon Foundation
P.O. Box 158
Vallecito, CA 95251
URL: http://www.chalcedon.edu
Phone: (209) 736-4365
Rousas John Rushdoony founded this Christian reconstructionist organization in 1965 to impose strict biblical law on the world. It publishes the monthly *Chalcedon Report*.

Christian Coalition
499 South Capitol Street, SW
Suite 615
Washington, D.C. 20003
URL: http://www.cc.org
E-mail: coalition@cc.org
Phone: (202) 479-6900
Fax: (202) 479-4260
The Christian Coalition was founded in 1989 by Pat Robertson to organize fundamentalist Christians to support conservative legislation. Although the organization does not support candidates, it does publicize the voting records of politicians so members know where they stand on issues important to fundamentalists.

Communist Party USA
235 West 23rd Street
New York, NY 10011
URL: http://www.cpusa.org
E-mail: cpusa@cpusa.org
Phone: (212) 989-4994
Fax: (212) 229-1713
The militant activist party works to install a socialist system of government in the United States. It believes that the capitalist system has failed, causing suffering and injustice to millions around the world. The organization's youth arm is called the Young Communist League. The party publishes *People's Weekly World.*

Concerned Women for America
1015 15th Street, NW
Suite 1100
Washington, D.C. 20005
URL: http://www.cwfa.org
E-mail: mail@cwfa.org
Phone: (202) 488-7000
Fax: (202) 488-0806
Founded in the late 1970s by Beverly LaHaye to apply biblical principles to such core issues as the sanctity of human life, defense of the family, education, pornography, religious freedom, and national sovereignty, the group provides legal aid for parents who challenge public school policy.

Democratic Socialists of America
180 Varick Street
12th Floor
New York, NY 10014
URL: http://www.dsausa.org
E-mail: dsa@dsausa.org

Phone: (212) 727-8610
Fax: (212) 727-8616
The DSA claims to be the largest socialist organization in the United States, as well as the principal U.S. affiliate of the Socialist International. It works toward social change and the establishment of a strong socialist presence in American communities and politics. The organization's youth section is known as the Young Democratic Socialists. It publishes *Democratic Left* magazine.

Eagle Forum
P.O. Box 618
Alton, IL 62002
URL: http://www.eagleforum.org
E-mail: eagle@eagleforum.org
Phone: (618) 462-5415
Fax: (618) 462-8909
Founded by Phyllis Schlafly to fight abortion legislation and the Equal Rights Amendment, it is also concerned with family and education issues. It publishes the monthly *Phyllis Schlafly Report* and the *Education Reporter*. The web site provides a link to Schlafly's weekly call-in radio show.

Earth First!
URL: http://www.earthfirst.org
Earth First! Journal
P.O. Box 3023
Tucson, AZ 85702
URL: http://www.earthfirst
   journal.org
E-mail: collective@
   earthfirstjournal.org
Phone: (520) 620-6900

Fax: (413) 254-0057
Earth First! Media Center
P.O. Box 324
Redway, CA 95560
E-mail: efmc@asis.com
This radical environmental group was founded in 1981, and its tactics are reflected in the slogan "No Compromise in Defense of Mother Earth." Earth First!ers helped pioneer such direct-action tactics as tree spiking, tree sitting, human blockades, and the destruction of heavy equipment. Since the group maintains no central office, the *Earth First!* journal is the best source of information.

Earth Liberation Front
URL: http://www.earth
   liberationfront.com
E-mail: elfpress@tao.ca
Phone: (503) 478-0902
Although it has no central headquarters or identifiable leaders, the Earth Liberation Front does maintain a web site with press releases, how-to guides, and advice on what to do if the Federal Bureau of Investigation knocks on your door.

Electronic Frontier Foundation
454 Shotwell Street
San Francisco, CA 94110
URL: http://www.eff.org
E-mail: info@eff.org
Phone: (415) 436-9333
Fax: (415) 436-9993
Formed in 1990 to protect fundamental rights to free speech in electronic media, the EFF opposes legislation that it considers threatening to these rights and provides defense in civil liberties court cases. It publishes an online newsletter and Internet guidebooks.

Electronic Privacy Information
   Center
1718 Connecticut Avenue, NW
Suite 200
Washington, D.C. 20009
URL: http://www.epic.org
E-mail: info@epic.org
Phone: (202) 483-1140
Fax: (202) 483-1248
The center was established in 1994 to focus public attention on privacy, First Amendment, and constitutional issues relating to emerging electronic media and communication systems. It litigates civil liberties issues and publishes several books, including *Privacy Law Sourcebook, Consumer Law Sourcebook, and Technology and Privacy.*

Family Research Council
801 G Street, NW
Washington, D.C. 20001
URL: http://www.frc.org
Phone: (202) 393-2100
This research group is affiliated with James Dobson's Focus on the Family radio ministry, which promotes "traditional" family values by supporting relevant legislation and educating the public on such matters.

Focus on the Family
Colorado Springs, CO 80903
URL: http://www.family.org
Phone: (719) 531-5181
Fax: (719) 531-3424

197

Support organization for James Dobson's radio program of the same name that provides Bible-based guidance on marriage, parenting, and education.

Freedom From Religion Foundation
P.O. Box 750
Madison, WI 53701
URL: http://www.ffrf.org
E-mail: ffrf@mailbag.com
Phone: (608) 256-8900
The group was founded in 1978 to promote the constitutional principle of separation of church and state and to educate the public about the values of nontheists. It provides college scholarships for "free thinkers," litigates church-state separation issues, produces films and public service announcement for television, and publishes books and *Freethought Today* magazine.

Greenpeace USA
702 H Street, NW
Washington, D.C. 20001
URL: http://www.greenpeace usa.org
Phone: (800) 326-0959
The global environmental organization is dedicated to peaceful direct action with the aim of curbing global warming, genetic engineering, nuclear testing, whaling, and deforestation. It publishes fact sheets, brochures, and reports.

HateWatch
P.O. Box 380151
Cambridge, MA 02238-0151
URL: http://www.hatewatch.org
E-mail: info@hatewatch.org
Phone: (617) 876-3796
Founded in 1996, this web-based organization monitors hate-group activity on the Internet. The web site includes research articles and a number of links to other watchdog groups.

International Association for Counterterrorism and Security Professionals
URL: http://www.iacsp.com
E-mail: iacsp@erols.com
The association was founded in 1992 to educate people about terrorism with the aim of developing innovative and effective counterterrorism measures. It publishes *The Journal of Counterterrorism and Security International.*

Jewish Defense League
P.O. Box 480370
Los Angeles, CA 90048
URL: http://www.jdl.org
E-mail: jdl@jdl.org
Phone: (818) 980-8535
Fax: (781) 634-0338
This activist organization, chaired by Irv Rubin, was founded to fight anti-Semitism and monitor the neo-Nazi movement. It often uses direct-action tactics.

John Birch Society
P.O. Box 8040
Appleton, WI 54912
URL: http://www.jbs.org
Phone: (920) 749-3780
Fax: (920) 749-5062

Robert Welch founded the society in 1958 to oppose communism, totalitarianism, and federal regulation while promoting the family unit and a utopian Christian future for the world. Core issues include pulling the United States out of the United Nations, lowering taxes, reclaiming the Panama Canal, supporting local police, and fighting against the conspiracy they believe seeks to establish a one-government world. It publishes the *John Birch Society Bulletin* and *New American*.

Militia of Montana
P.O. Box 1486
Noxon, MT 59853
URL: http://www.militiaof
   montana.com
E-mail: militia@montana.com
Phone: (406) 847-2735
Fax: (406) 847-2246
This is one of the largest militias in the United States and the one after which many others are modeled. The web site includes a link to the "Militia of Montana Preparedness Catalog." It publishes the periodical *Taking Aim*.

National Alliance
P.O. Box 90
Hillsboro, WV 24946
URL: http://www.natall.com
E-mail: national@natvan.com
Phone: (304) 653-4600
The web site of William Pierce's white supremacist organization provides links to National Vanguard Books and Resistance Records, as well as Pierce's *American Dissident*

Voices radio program. It publishes *National Vanguard* and *Free Speech*.

National Coalition Against
   Censorship
275 Seventh Avenue
New York, NY 10001
URL: http://www.ncac.org
E-mail: ncac@ncac.org
Phone: (212) 807-6222
Fax: (212) 807-6245
This alliance of 50 national nonprofit organizations—including library, artistic, religious, educational, professional, labor, and civil liberties groups—is dedicated to fighting for freedom of thought and expression. It publishes flyers, essays, magazine article reprints, and the quarterly *Censorship News*.

National Gay and Lesbian
   Task Force
1700 Kalorama Road, NW
Washington, D.C. 20009
URL: http://www.ngltf.org
E-mail: ngltf@ngltf.org
Phone: (202) 332-6483
Fax: (202) 332-0207
Founded in 1973 to work for the civil rights of gay, lesbian, bisexual, and transgendered people and toward building a powerful political and social justice movement, the task force trains leaders, equips organizers, and mobilizes voters. It also publishes books and studies on AIDS, voting, and social discrimination.

National Legal Foundation
P.O. Box 64427
Virginia Beach, VA 23467

URL: http://nlf.net
E-mail: nlf@nlf.net
Phone: (757) 463-6133
Fax: (757) 463-6055
In 1985 Pat Robertson founded the organization to provide legal aid in the defense of religious freedom for Christians.

**National Right to Life
   Committee**
419 7th Street, NW
Suite 500
Washington, D.C. 20004
URL: http://www.nrlc.org
E-mail: nrlc@nrlc.org
Phone: (202) 626-8800
Founded in 1973 as part of the backlash against *Roe v. Wade* to fight against abortion, euthanasia, and infanticide, the committee publishes *National Right to Life News.*

**People for the American Way
   Foundation**
2000 M Street, NW
Suite 400
Washington, D.C. 20036
URL: http://www.pfaw.org
E-mail: pfaw@pfaw.org
Phone: (202) 467-4999
   or (800) 326-7329
People for the American Way was founded in 1980 by television producer Norman Lear to monitor what it calls the "undemocratic" activity of the religious Right, oppose censorship, and support reproductive rights. Other important issues include education and pluralism. It publishes a newsletter, *Right Wing Watch Online, Education*

Activist Online, and the annual *Attacks on the Freedom to Learn.*

**People for the Ethical
   Treatment of Animals**
501 Front Street
Norfolk, VA 23510
URL: http://www.peta.org
E-mail: info@peta-online.org
Phone: (757) 622-7382
Fax: (757) 622-0457
Founded in 1980 on the principle that "animals are not ours to eat, wear, experiment on, or use for entertainment," PETA's tactics range from direct action to advertising on billboards. It also works to educate the public and policy makers on animal rights issues and publishes the quarterly *Animal Times.*

Political Research Associates
1310 Broadway
Suite 201
Somerville, MA 02144
URL: http://www.publiceye.org/
   main.htm
E-mail: pra@igc.org
Phone: (617) 666-5300
Fax: (617) 666-6622
This organization monitors right-wing organizations, leaders, ideas, and activities in the United States. It provides speakers for special events, distributes activist resource kits, archives material, and publishes *Public Eye* (three issues per year).

Progressive Labor Party
150 West 28th Street
Room 301
New York, NY 10001

URL: http://www.plp.org
E-mail:plp@plp.org
Phone: (212) 255-3959
Fax: (212) 255-0685
Working toward the communist revolution, with the goal of abolishing nation-states and establishing one working class and a one-party world, the party publishes *Progressive Labor*, a journal of communist theory and practice, and *The Communist*, which focuses on politics.

Revolutionary Communist Party
P.O. Box 3486
Merchandise Mart
Chicago, IL 60654
URL: http://www.rwor.org
Phone: (773) 227-4066
Fax: (773) 227-4497
This Marxist-Leninist/Maoist group struggles against capitalism and globalization and publishes *Revolutionary Worker*.

Southern Poverty Law Center
400 Washington Avenue
Montgomery, AL 36104
URL: http://www.splcenter.org
Phone: (334) 956-8200
This nonprofit national organization fights hate, intolerance, and discrimination through education and litigation. Founder Morris Dees's legal successes against hate groups have made him one of the most despised men in the eyes of white supremacists. The web site includes hate symbols, a catalog of hate incidents, and geographically arranged lists of hate groups and

Patriot groups. It publishes the quarterly *Intelligence Report*.

Stormfront
P.O. Box 6637
West Palm Beach, FL 33405
URL: http://www.stormfront.org
E-mail: comments@stormfront.org
Phone: (561) 833-0030
Fax: (561) 820-0051
This "white nationalist resource page" was one of the first white supremacist sites to appear on the Internet during the mid-1990s. The texts in the online library deal with white nationalism, immigration, revisionism, National Socialism, and Judaism. The site includes a women's page and a kid's page.

Terrorism Research Center
URL: http://www.terrorism.com
E-mail: trc@terrorism.com
The center provides information on terrorism and information warfare. The web site features essays on current issues, as well as links to other documents, research, and resources concerned with terrorism.

White Aryan Resistance
P.O. Box 65
Fallbrook, CA 92088
URL: http://www.resist.com
E-mail: warmetzger@aol.com
Phone: (760) 723-8996
The web site of Tom Metzger's white supremacist organization explains WAR's position on such topics as women, race, homosexuals, abortions, the environment,

immigration, taxes, and lawmakers. The group publishes *WAR*.

Workers World Party
55 West 17th Street
New York, NY 10011
URL: http://www.workers.org

E-mail: wwp@workers.org
Phone: (212) 627-2994
Fax: (212) 675-7869

Through its web site and *Workers World* magazine, this organization hopes to install a socialist government in the United States.

PART III

APPENDICES

APPENDIX A

Tennessee v. John T. Scopes (1925)

Judge: John T. Raulston
Chief defense lawyers: Clarence Darrow, Arthur Garfield Hays, and Dudley Field Malone
Chief prosecutors: William Jennings Bryan, Ben G. McKenzie, and A. T. Stewart
[excerpts from trial transcripts]

TRIAL DAY 1

Potential juror J. P. Massingill, sworn in by the court, responds to questions by the court.

Q: Have you formed or expressed an opinion as to the guilt or innocence of the defendant in this case?
A: From rumors and newspapers—of course, I read. I don't know anything about the evidence.
Q: You haven't talked with any person who professed to know the facts?
A: No, sir.
Q: Now, Mr. Massingill, could you go into the jury box and wholly disregard any impression or opinion you have?
A: Yes, sir.
Q: And try the case wholly on the law and the evidence, rendering a fair and impartial verdict to both sides?
A: I think so. Yes, sir.
Court: He seems to be competent, gentlemen.

Defense lawyer Clarence Darrow next questions the potential juror and rejects him.

Q: What is your business?

A: I am a minister.

Q: Whereabouts?

A: I live in Rhea County.

Q: Where do you preach?

A: I preach over the county in the rural sections.

Q: You mean you haven't any regular church?

A: I have. I am pastoring four churches, have four appointments.

Q: Ever preach on evolution?

A: I don't think so, definitely; that is, on evolution alone.

Q: Did you ever preach on evolution?

A: Yes. I haven't as a subject, just taken that up in connection with other subjects. I have referred to it in discussing it.

Q: Against it or for it?

A: I am strictly for the Bible.

Q: I am talking about evolution. I am not talking about the Bible. Did you preach for or against evolution?

A: Is that a fair question, judge?

Court: Yes, answer the question.

A: Well, I preached against it, of course! (Applause).

Q: Why, "of course?"

Court: Let's have order.

Darrow: Your honor, I am going to ask to have anybody excluded that applauds.

Court: Yes, if you repeat that, ladies and gentlemen, you will be excluded. We cannot have applause. If you have any feeling in this case you must not express it in the courthouse, so don't repeat the applause. If you do, I will have to exclude you.

Q: You have a very firm conviction—a very strong opinion against evolution, haven't you?

A: Well, some points in evolution.

Q: Are you trying to get on this jury?

A: No, sir.

Q: Have you formed a strong conviction against evolution?

A: Well, I have.

Q: You think you would be a fair juror in this case?

A: Well, I can take the law and the evidence in the case, I think, and try a man right.

Q: I asked if you think you thought you could be a fair juror.

A: Yes, sir.

Q: You have heard that he is an evolutionist, haven't you?

A: Yes, sir, I have heard that.

Q: And in your opinion he has been teaching contrary to the Bible?

A. T. Stewart: If your honor please, I except to that. The question involved here will be whether or not—not, I apprehend if Mr. Scopes taught anything that is contrary to the Bible—that isn't the question. He has asked him whether or not he has prejudged the guilt of the defendant.

Court: He has a right to know that.

Stewart: The man has already stated to him that he had no opinion in the case.

Darrow: Do you think he would be a fair juror in the case?

Stewart: Yes, I do, if he says so.

Darrow: I don't.

Court: I think the lawyers have the right to get all the information they can on the subject, and I will treat both sides alike.

Court: Have you, in your mind now, Mr. Massingill, a fixed opinion that he has taught a theory contrary to the theory of the Bible as to the creation of man?

A: Yes, sir.

Court: Would that have any weight with you or any bearing with you in the trial of this case if you were selected as a juror?

A: I think I am fair and honest enough to lay aside things and give a man justice.

Court: You may proceed, gentlemen. He seems to be competent.

Darrow: You now have an opinion that evolution is contrary to the Bible and that my client has been teaching evolution; as you stand there now, that is your opinion?

A: From the information I have in regard to his teaching.

Q: That is your opinion now, isn't it, as you stand there now?

A: Sure it is.

Q: You could change it if you heard evidence enough to change it on?

A: Yes, sir.

Q: Otherwise you couldn't?

A: I have no right to; I don't think.

Darrow: I challenge for cause.

Court: Well, I want every juror to start in with an open mind. I will excuse you, Mr. Massingill.

Potential juror J. T. Leuty is sworn in and replies to questions asked by the court.

Q: Have you formed or expressed an opinion as to the guilt or innocence of this defendant?

A: No, sir.

Q: If chosen on the jury, could you go into the box without prejudice or bias either way, and try the case on the law and the evidence?

A: Yes, sir.
Court: He is a competent juror.

Ben G. McKenzie, lawyer for the prosecution, proceeds to question the potential juror.

Q: Mr. Leuty, you say you have been hearing about this case?
A: No, sir, just talk.
Q: When he was arrested?
A: Yes, sir.
Q: And, of course, everybody formed an opinion, and naturally would. That's right?
A: No, sir; I didn't hear any evidence in this case and didn't form any opinion at all.
Q: You didn't form any opinion from what you heard other people say?
A: No, sir.
Q: And haven't an opinion now?
A: No, sir.

Defense lawyer Clarence Darrow then questions the potential juror. During the process, the prosecution rejects him.

Q: Have you ever been a member of a church?
A: No, sir.
Q: How long have you lived here?
A: All my life.
Q: What is your business?
A: Well, I am a kind of a farmer now.
Q: Here in Dayton?
A: No, sir. I live in Rhea Springs.
Q: That is in this county?
A: Yes, sir.
Q: You have never studied evolution?
A: No, sir.
Q: Are you much of a reader?
A: I read some. I used to read a great deal.
Q: Books?
A: Yes, and magazines and newspapers. Used to read books.
Q: You used to read books. And you went to school here, I suppose, rather than where you live now?
A: I went to the public schools in Rhea County.
Q: Did you ever hear anybody talk about evolution?
A: Oh, well, I have heard it talked about when they got this question up.

Q: They never talked about it before down here, did they?
A: Well, they might in a general way, but people never paid much attention to it.
Q: You have not any prejudice against the doctrine or idea of evolution?
A: No, sir.
Q: You don't know what your neighbors think about this case?
A: I suppose some of them have thought about it.
Q: You wouldn't care what they thought if you were on this jury?
A: No, it wouldn't make any difference to me if I was on this jury.
Q: If you were on this jury it would not make any difference to you what your neighbors thought?
A: No, sir.
McKenzie: Challenge by the state.
Court: Mr. Leuty, we will excuse you.
Darrow: Have they got a right to do that?
Court: Perhaps you don't understand our practice. They examine a juror. They pass him to you, and you can examine him and say that you pass him back. Then they have the right to challenge him. They have a right to pass him back and then you take him or reject him. That is our practice.
Darrow: I thought they were trying to put something over on us.
Court: No. If they tried to I would not let them.
Darrow: Don't let them.

TRIAL DAY 2

Defense lawyer Clarence Darrow argues that Tennessee's antievolution law is unconstitutional.

Darrow: If today you can take a thing like evolution and make it a crime to teach it in the public school, tomorrow you can make it a crime to teach it in the private schools, and the next year you can make it a crime to teach it to the hustings or in the church. At the next session you may ban books and the newspapers. Soon you may set Catholic against Protestant and Protestant against Protestant, and try to foist your own religion upon the minds of men. If you can do one you can do the other. Ignorance and fanaticism is ever busy and needs feeding. Always it is feeding and gloating for more. Today it is the public school teachers, tomorrow the private. The next day the preachers and the lecturers, the magazines, the books, the newspapers. After a while, your honor, it is the setting of man against man and creed against creed until with flying banners and beating drums we are marching backward to the glorious ages of the sixteenth century when bigots lighted fagots to burn the men who dared to bring any intelligence and enlightenment and culture to the human mind.

TRIAL DAY 3

Before the regular session is opened, a debate over prayer occurs.

Court: Reverend Stribling, will you open with prayer?
Darrow: Your honor, I want to make an objection before the jury comes in.
Court: What is it, Mr. Darrow?
Darrow: I object to prayer, and I object to the jury being present when the court rules on the objection.
Stewart: What is it?
Court: He objects to the court being opened with prayer, especially in the presence of the jury.
Stewart: The jury is not here.
Court: No, I do not want to be unreasonable about anything, but I believe I have a right; I am responsible for the conduct of the court. It has been my custom since I have been a judge to have prayers in the courtroom when it was convenient, and I know of no reason why I should not follow up this custom, so I will overrule the objection.
Darrow: I understand from the court himself that he has sometimes opened the court with prayer and sometimes not, and we took no exceptions on the first day, but seeing this is persisted in every session, and the nature of this case being one where it is claimed by the state that there is a conflict between science and religion, above all other cases there should be no part taken outside of the evidence in this case and no attempt by means of prayer or in any other way to influence the deliberation and consideration of the jury of the facts in this case.
Court: Do you want to say anything?
McKenzie: That matter has been passed upon by our supreme court. Judge Shepherd took a case from the court, when the jury, after retiring to consider their verdict, at the suggestion of one of them to bow in prayer, asked divine guidance, afterwards delivering a verdict not excepted to, and afterwards taken to the supreme court: It was commendable to the jury to ask divine guidance.
Darrow: I do not object to the jury or anyone else praying in secret or in private, but I do object to the turning of this courtroom into a meeting house in the trial of this case. You have no right to do it.
Court: You have a right to put your exceptions on the record.
Stewart: In order that the record may show the state's position, the state makes no contention, as stated by counsel for the defense, that this is a conflict between science and religion insofar as the merits are concerned; it is a case involving the fact as to whether or not a school teacher has taught a doctrine prohibited by statute, and we, for the state, think it is

quite proper to open the court with prayer if the court sees fit to do it, and such an idea extended by the agnostic counsel for the defense is foreign to the thoughts and ideas of the people who do not know anything about infidelity and care less.

Hays: May I ask to enter an exception to the statement "agnostic counsel for the defense"?

Malone: I would like to reply to this remark of the attorney general. Whereas I respect my colleague Mr. Darrow's right to believe or not to believe as long as he is as honest in his unbelief as I am in my belief, as one of the members of counsel who is not an agnostic, I would like to state the objection from my point of view. Your honor has the discretion to have a prayer or not to have a prayer. There was no exception offered, and I can assure the court when we talked it over among ourselves as colleagues, there was no exception felt to the opening of these proceedings by prayer the first day, but I would like to ask your honor whether in all the trials over which your honor has presided, this court has had a clergyman every morning of every day of every trial to open the court with prayer? Our objection goes to the fact that we believe that this daily opening of the court with prayers, those prayers we have already heard, having been duly argumentative that they help to increase the atmosphere of hostility to our point of view, which already exists in this community by widespread propaganda.

Stewart: In reply to that, there is still no question involved in this lawsuit as to whether or not Scopes taught a doctrine prohibited by the statute, that is that man descended from a lower order of animals. So far as creating an atmosphere of hostility is concerned, I would advise Mr. Malone that this is a God-fearing country.

Malone: And it is no more God-fearing country than that from which I came.

Court: Gentlemen, do not turn this into an argument.

Darrow: I would like to reply to counsel, that this statute says no doctrine shall be taught which is contrary to the divine account contained in the Bible. So there is no question about the religious character of these proceedings.

Court: This court has no purpose except to find the truth and do justice to all the issues involved in this case. In answer to counsel for the defendant, as to my custom, I will say the several years I have been on the bench I have used my discretion in opening the court with prayer, at times when there was a minister present and it was convenient to do so; other times when there was no large assemblage of people and no minister present, I have not always followed this custom, but I think it is a matter wholly within the discretion of the court. I have instructed the ministers who have been invited to my rostrum to open the court with prayer, to make no reference to the issues involved in this case. I see nothing that might influence the court or jury as to the issues. I believe in prayer myself; I constantly invoke divine guidance myself, when I am on the bench and off the bench. I see no reason why I should not continue to do this.

TRIAL DAY 4

Defense lawyer Dudley Field Malone states the theory of the defense.

Malone: The purpose of the defense will be to set before you all available facts and information from every branch of science to aid you in forming an opinion of what evolution is, and of what value to progress and comfort is the theory of evolution, for you are the judged of the law and the facts, and the defense wishes to aid you in every way to intelligent opinion.

The defense denies that it is part of any movement of conspiracy on the part of scientists to destroy the authority of Christianity or the Bible. The defense denies that any such conspiracy exists except in the mind and purpose of the evangelical leader of the prosecution. The defense maintains that the book of Genesis is in part a hymn, in part an allegory and work of religious interpretations written by men who believe that the earth was flat and whose authority cannot be accepted to control the teachings of science in our schools.

The narrow purpose of the defense is to establish the innocence of the defendant Scopes. The broad purpose of the defense will be to prove that the Bible is a work of religious aspiration and rules of conduct which must be kept in the field of theology.

The defense maintains that there is no more justification for imposing the conflicting views of the Bible on courses of biology than there would be for imposing the views of biologists on courses of comparative religion. We maintain that science and religion embrace two separate and distinct fields of thought and learning.

We remember that Jesus said: "Render unto Caesar the things that are Caesar's and unto God the things that are God's."

Prosecuting attorney Ben G. McKenzie attacks the defense's theory.

McKenzie: This is wholly improper, argumentative. It is not a statement as to what the issues are. Your honor has already held that this act is constitutional, it being the law of the land, there is but one issue before this court and jury, and that is, did the defendant violate the statute. That statute interprets itself, and says that whenever a man teaches that man descended from a lower order of animals as contradistinguished from the record of the creation of man as given by the word of God, that he is guilty. Does the proof show that he did that, that is the only issue, if it please the honorable court, before this jury. My friend is talking about a theory of evolution that it took him two years to write, that speech (laughter). That is not proper, if your honor please, if it is proper, it would be like a couple of gentleman over in my country, where they were engaged and were trying a lawsuit before a justice of the peace, and they had a large number of witnesses. Finally one lawyer said, "let us have a conference," and they went out to confer, and they came back in and said, "if your honor please, the witnesses in this case, some of them are not very well, others are awfully ignorant, and we have just agreed among ourselves to dispense with the evidence and argue the case." That is what my good friend Malone wants to do. (Loud laughter and officer rapping for order.)

Howard Morgan, a student of John T. Scopes, testifies. Prosecutor A. T. Stewart first questions the witness.

Q: Your name is Howard Morgan?
A: Yes, sir.
Q: You are Mr. Luke Morgan's son?
A: Yes, sir.
Q: Your father is in the bank here, Dayton Bank and Trust company?
A: Yes, sir.
Q: How old are you?
A: Fourteen years.
Q: Did you attend school here at Dayton last year?
A: Yes, sir.
Q: What school?
A: High school.
Q: Central High School?
A: Yes, sir.
Q: Did you study anything under Professor Scopes?
A: Yes, sir.
Q: Did you study this book, *General Science*?
A: Yes, sir.
Q: Were you studying that book in April of this year, Howard?
A: Yes, sir.
Q: Did Professor Scopes teach it to you?
A: Yes, sir.
Q: When did you complete the book?
A: Latter part of April.
Q: When was school out?

A: First or second of May.

Q: You studied it then up to a week or so before school was out?

A: Yes, sir.

Q: Now, you say you were studying this book in April. How did Professor Scopes teach that book to you? I mean by that, did he ask you questions and you answered them, or did he give you lectures, or both? Just explain to the jury here now, these gentleman here in front of you, how he taught the books to you.

A: Well, sometimes he would ask us questions and then he would lecture to us on different subjects in the book.

Q: Sometimes he asked you questions and sometimes lectured to you on different subjects in the book?

A: Yes, sir.

Q: Did he ever undertake to teach you anything about evolution?

A: Yes, sir.

Q: Just state in your own words, Howard, what he taught you and when it was.

A: It was along about the second of April.

Q: Of this year?

A: Yes, sir, of this year. He said that the earth was once a hot molten mass too hot for plant or animal life to exist upon it. In the sea the earth cooled off; there was a little germ of one cell organism formed, and this organism kept evolving until it got to be a pretty good-sized animal, and then came on to be a land animal, and it kept on evolving, and from this was man. . . .

Q: I ask you further, Howard: How did he classify man with reference to other animals? What did he say about them?

A: Well, the book and he both classified man along with cats and dogs, cows, horses, monkeys, lions, horses, and all that.

Q: What did he say they were?

A: Mammals.

Q: Classified them along with dogs, cats, horses, monkeys, and cows?

A: Yes, sir.

Defense attorney Clarence Darrow cross-examines the witness.

Q: Let's see, your name is what?

A: Howard Morgan.

Q: Now, Howard, what do you mean by classify?

A: Well, it means classify these animals we mentioned, that men were just the same as them, in other words . . .

Q: He didn't say a cat was the same as a man?

A: No, sir. He said man had a reasoning power, that these animals did not.

Q: There is some doubt about that, but that is what he said, is it? (Laughter in the courtroom.)

Court: Order.
Stewart: With some men.
Darrow: A great many.
Q: Now, Howard, he said they were all mammals, didn't he?
A: Yes, sir.
Q: Did he tell you what a mammal was, or don't you remember?
A: Well, he just said these animals were mammals and man was a mammal.
Q: No, but did he tell you what distinguished mammals from other animals?
A: I don't remember.
Q: If he did, you have forgotten it? Didn't he say that mammals were those beings which suckled their young?
A: I don't remember about that.
Q: You don't remember?
A: No.
Q: Do you remember what he said that made any animal a mammal, what it was, or don't you remember?
A: I don't remember.
Q: But he said that all of them were mammals?
A: All what?
Q: Dogs and horses, monkeys, cows, man, whales, I cannot state all of them, but he said all of those were mammals?
A: Yes, sir, but I don't know about the whales; he said all those other ones. (Laughter in the courtroom.)
Court: Order.
Q: Well, did he tell you anything else that was wicked?
A: No, not that I remember of.
Q: Now, he said the earth was once a molten mass of liquid, didn't he?
A: Yes.
Q: By molten, you understand melted?
A: Yes, sir.
Q: After that, it got cooled enough and the soil came, that plants grew. Is that right?
A: Yes, sir. Yes, sir.
Q: And that the first life was in the sea? And that it developed into life on the land?
A: Yes, sir.
Q: And finally into the highest organism which is known to man?
A: Yes, sir.
Q: Now, that is about what he taught you? It has not hurt you any, has it?
A: No, sir.
Darrow: That's all.

TRIAL DAY 6

An argument ensues over whether the defense is using the trial for publicity reasons.

Stewart: It is a known fact that the defense considers this a campaign of education to get before the people their ideas of evolution and scientific principles. This case has the aspect of novelty and therefore has been sensationalized by the newspapers, and of course these gentlemen want to take advantage of the opportunity. I don't want to make any accusations that they are improperly taking advantage of it. They are lawyers, and they have these ideas, and it is an opportunity to begin a campaign of education for their ideas and theories of evolution and of scientific principles, and I take it that will not be disputed, and all I ask, if the court please, is that we not go beyond the pale of the law in making this investigation.

Malone: I just want to make this statement for the purposes of the record, that the defense is not engaged in a campaign of education, although the way the defense has handled the case has probably been of educational value. We represent no organization nor organizations for the purpose of education. Your honor knows that everything the court says not only goes out to the world through the newspapers but through the radio, and it is difficult for a court these days to exclude a jury from what is going on in the courtroom, because it would be difficult for a juror to go anywhere in the utmost privacy and not hear what's going on, so the rules would have to be changed to meet the advance of science. If the defense is representing anything, it is merely representing the attempt to meet the campaign of propaganda which has been begun by a distinguished member of the prosecution.

Judge John T. Raulston excludes expert testimony.

Raulston: This case is now before the court upon a motion by the attorney general to exclude from the consideration of the jury certain expert testimony offered by the defendant, the import of such testimony being an effort to explain the origin of man and life. The state insists that such evidence is wholly irrelevant, incompetent, and impertinent to the issues pending, and that it should be excluded. Upon the other hand, the defendant insists that this evidence is highly competent and relevant to the issues involved, and should be admitted. Now upon these issues as brought up, it becomes the duty of the court to determine the question of the admissibility of this expert testimony offered by the defendant. It is not within the province of the court under these issues to decide and determine which is true: the story of divine creation as taught in the Bible, or the story of the creation of man as taught by evolution. Let us now inquire what is the true interpretation of this statute. Did the legislature mean that before an accused could be convicted, the state must prove two things: First, that the accused taught a theory denying the story of divine creation as taught in the Bible; and second, that man descended from a lower order of animals. If the first must be specially proven, then we must have proof as to what the story of divine creation is and that a theory was taught denying that story. But if the second clause is explanatory of the first, and speaks into the act the intention of the legislature and the meaning of the first clause, it would be otherwise. In the act involved in the case at bar, if it is found consistent to interpret the latter clause as explanatory of the legislative intent as to the offense against, then why call experts? The ordinary, non-expert mind can comprehend the simple language, "descended from a lower order of animals." These are not ambiguous words or complex terms. But while discussing these words by way of parenthesis, I desire to suggest that I believe evolutionists should at least show man the consideration to substitute the world "ascend" for the word "descend." In the final analysis, this court, after a most earnest and careful consideration, has reached the conclusions that under the provisions of the act involved in this case, it is made unlawful thereby to teach in the public schools of the state of Tennessee the theory that man descended from a lower order of animals. If the court is correct in this, then the evidence of experts would shed no light on the issues. Therefore, the court is content to sustain the motion of the attorney general to exclude the expert testimony.

Defense lawyer Clarence Darrow is found in contempt of the court.

Darrow: We want to make statements here of what we expect to prove. I do not understand why every request of the state and every suggestion of the prosecution should meet with an endless waste of time, and a bare suggestion of anything that is perfectly competent on our part should be immediately overruled.
Court: I hope you do not mean to reflect upon the court?
Darrow: Well, your honor has the right to hope.
Court: I have the right to do something else, perhaps.
Darrow: All right, all right.
Court: The court has withheld any action until passion had time to subdue, and it could be arranged that the jury would be kept separate and apart from proceedings so as not to know of the matters concerning which the court is now about to speak. And these matters having been arranged, the court feels that it is now time for him to speak: Both the state and federal governments maintain courts, that those who cannot agree may have their difference properly adjudicated. If the courts are not kept above reproach,

their usefulness will be destroyed. He who would unlawfully and wrongfully show contempt for a court of justice sows the seeds of discord and breeds contempt for both the law and the courts, and thereby does an injustice both to the courts and good society. Men may become prominent, but they should never feel themselves superior to the law or justice. The criticism of individual conduct of a man who happens to be a judge may be of small consequence, but to criticize him while on the bench is unwarranted and shows disrespect for the official, and also shows disrespect for the state or the commonwealth in which the court is maintained. It is my policy to show the same courtesy to the lawyers of sister states that I show the lawyers of my own state, but I think this courtesy should be reciprocated; those to whom it is extended should at least be respectful to the court over which I preside. He who would hurl contempt into the records of my court insults and outrages the good people of one of the greatest states of the union—a state which, on account of its loyalty, has justly won for itself the title of the Volunteer State. It has been my policy on the bench to be cautious and to endeavor to avoid hastily and rashly rushing to conclusions. But in the face of what I consider an unjustified expression of contempt for this court and its decrees, made by Clarence Darrow on July 17, 1925, I feel that further forbearance would cease to be a virtue, and in an effort to protect the good name of my state, and to protect the dignity of the court over which I preside, I am constrained and impelled to call upon the said Darrow, to know what he has to say why he should not be dealt with for contempt. Therefore, I hereby order that instanter citation from this court be served upon the said Clarence Darrow, requiring him to appear in this court at 9 o'clock a.m., Tuesday, July 21, 1925, and make answer to this citation. I also direct that upon the serving of the said citation that he be required to make an execute a good and lawful bond for $5,000 for his appearance from day to day upon said citation and not depart the court without leave.

Darrow: What is the bond, your honor?
Court: $5,000.

At the next session of the court, defense lawyer Darrow apologizes for being in contempt of the court.

Stewart: Darrow has a statement that he wants to make at this time, and I think it is proper that your honor hear him, and I want to ask the court to hear the statement.
Court: All right, I will hear you, Colonel Darrow.
Darrow: Your honor, quite apart from any question of what is right or wrong in this matter which your honor mentioned and which I will discuss

in a moment—quite apart from that, and on my own account if nothing else was involved, I would feel that I ought to say what I am going to say. Of course, your honor will remember that whatever took place was hurried; one thing followed another, and the truth is, I did not know just how it looked until I read over the minutes as your honor did, and when I read them over I was sorry that I had said it. I have been practicing law for 47 years, and I have been pretty busy, and most of the time in court I have had many a case where I have had to do what I have been doing here—fighting the public opinion of the people, in the community where I was trying the case, even in my own town—and I never yet have in all my time had any criticism by the court for anything I have done in court. That is, I have tried to treat the court fairly and a little more than fairly because when I recognize the odds against me, I try to lean the other way the best I can, and I don't think any such occasion ever arose before in my practice. I am not saying this, your honor, to influence you, but to put myself right. I do think, however, your honor, that I went further than I should have done. So far as its having been premeditated or made for the purpose of insult to the court, I had not the slightest thought of that. One thing snapped out after another, as other lawyers have done in this case, not, however, where the judge was involved, and apologized for it afterwards, and so far as the people of Tennessee are concerned, your honor suggested that in your opinion—I don't know as I was ever in a community in my life where my religious ideas differed as widely from the great mass as I have found them since I have been in Tennessee. Yet I came here a perfect stranger, and I can say what I have said before, that I have not found upon anybody's part—any citizen here in this town or outside—the slightest discourtesy. I have been treated better, kindlier, and more hospitably than I fancied would have been the case in the North, and that is due largely to the ideas that southern people have, and they are, perhaps, more hospitable than we are up north. I am quite certain that the remark should not have been made and the court could not help taking notice of it, and I am sorry that I made it ever since I got time to read it, and I want to apologize to the court for it. (Applause.)

Court: Anyone else have anything to say? In behalf of Colonel Darrow in any way? (No response.)

If this little incident had been personal between Colonel Darrow and myself, it would have been passed by as unnoticed, but when a Judge speaks from the bench, his acts are not personal but are part of the machine that is part of the great state where he lives. I could not afford to pass those words by without notice, because to do so would not do justice to the great state for which I speak when I speak from the bench. I am proud of Tennessee. I think Tennessee is a great state. It has produced such men as the Jacksons, such as James K. Polk. My friends, and Colonel

Darrow, the man that I believe came into the world to save man from sin, the man that died on the cross that man might be redeemed, taught that it was godly to forgive, and were it not for the forgiving nature of himself, I would fear for man. The savior died on the cross pleading with God for the men who crucified Him. I believe in that Christ. I believe in these principles. I accept Colonel Darrow's apology. I am sure his remarks were not premeditated. I am sure that if he had time to have thought and deliberated, he would not have spoken those words. He spoke those words, perhaps, just at a moment when he felt that he had suffered perhaps one of the greatest disappointments of his life when the court had held against him. Taking that view of it, I feel that I am justified in speaking for the people of the great state that I represent when I speak as I do to say to him that we forgive him and we forgot it and we commend him to go back home and learn in his heart the words of the man who said, "If you thirst, come unto Me and I will give thee life." (Applause.)

TRIAL DAY 7

A "Read Your Bible" banner is removed from courthouse.

Darrow: Your honor, before you send for the jury, I think it my duty to make this motion. Off to the left of where the jury sits, a little bit and about ten feet in front of them is a large sign about ten feet long reading, "Read Your Bible," and a hand pointing to it. The word "Bible" is in large letters, perhaps a foot and a half long, and the printing . . .
Court: Hardly that long, I think.
Darrow: What is that?
Court: Hardly that long.
Darrow: Why, we will call it a foot. I move that it be removed.
Court: Yes.
McKenzie: If your honor please, why should it be removed? It is their defense and stated before the court that they do not deny the Bible, that they expected to introduce proof to make it harmonize. Why should we remove the sign cautioning the people to read the Word of God just to satisfy the others in the case?
Darrow: Let me say something. Your honor, I just want to make this suggestion. Mr. Bryan says that the Bible and evolution conflict. Well, I do not know; I am for evolution, anyway. We might agree to get up a sign of equal size on the other side and in the same position reading "Hunter's Biology" or "Read your evolution." This sign is not here for no purpose, and

Appendix A

it can have no effect but to influence this case, and I read the Bible myself—more or less—and it is pretty good reading in places. But this case has been made, a case where it is to be the Bible or evolution, and we have been informed by Mr. Bryan, who himself is a profound Bible student and has an essay every Sunday as to what it means. We have been informed that a Tennessee jury who are not especially educated are better judges of the Bible than all the scholars in the world, and when they see that sign, it means to them their construction of the Bible. It is pretty obvious; it is not fair, your honor, and we object to it.

Court: The issues in this case, as they have been finally determined by this court, is whether or not it is unlawful to teach that man descended from a lower order of animals. I do not understand that issue involved the Bible. If the Bible is involved, I believe in it and am always on its side, but it is not for me to decide in this case. If the presence of the sign irritates anyone, or if anyone thinks it might influence the jury in any way, I have no purpose except to give both sides a fair trial in this case. Feeling that way about it, I will let the sign come down. Let the jury be brought around.

Clarence Darrow cross-examines prosecuting attorney William Jennings Bryan.

Q: You have given considerable study to the Bible, haven't you, Mr. Bryan?
A: Yes, sir, I have tried to.
Q: Then you have made a general study of it?
A: Yes, I have; I have studied the Bible for about fifty years, or sometime more than that, but, of course, I have studied it more as I have become older than when I was but a boy.
Q: You claim that everything in the Bible should be literally interpreted?
A: I believe everything in the Bible should be accepted as it is given there: some of the Bible is given illustratively. For instance: "Ye are the salt of the earth." I would not insist that man was actually salt, or that he had flesh of salt, but it is used in the sense of salt as saving God's people.
Q: But when you read that Jonah swallowed the whale—or that the whale swallowed Jonah—excuse me please—how do you literally interpret that?
A: When I read that a big fish swallowed Jonah—it does not say whale.
Q: That is my recollection of it. A big fish, and I believe it, and I believe in a God who can make a whale and can make a man and make both what He pleases.
Q: Now, you say, the big fish swallowed Jonah, and he there remained how long—three days—and then he spewed him upon the land. You believe that the big fish was made to swallow Jonah?

A: I am not prepared to say that; the Bible merely says it was done.

Q: You don't know whether it was the ordinary run of fish, or made for that purpose?

A: You may guess; you evolutionists guess . . .

Q: You are not prepared to say whether that fish was made especially to swallow a man or not?

A: The Bible doesn't say, so I am not prepared to say.

Q: But do you believe He made them—that He made such a fish and that it was big enough to swallow Jonah?

A: Yes, sir. Let me add: One miracle is just as easy to believe as another.

Q: Just as hard?

A: It is hard to believe for you, but easy for me. A miracle is a thing performed beyond what man can perform. When you get within the realm of miracles; and it is just as easy to believe the miracle of Jonah as any other miracle in the Bible.

Q: Perfectly easy to believe that Jonah swallowed the whale?

A: If the Bible said so; the Bible doesn't make as extreme statements as evolutionists do . . .

Q: The Bible says Joshua commanded the sun to stand still for the purpose of lengthening the day, doesn't it, and you believe it.

A: I do.

Q: Do you believe at that time the entire sun went around the earth?

A: No, I believe that the earth goes around the sun.

Q: Do you believe that the men who wrote it thought that the day could be lengthened or that the sun could be stopped?

A: I don't know what they thought.

Q: You don't know?

A: I think they wrote the fact without expressing their own thoughts.

Q: Have you an opinion as to whether or not the men who wrote that thought?

Stewart: I want to object, your honor; it has gone beyond the pale of any issue that could possibly be injected into this lawsuit, except by imagination. I do not think the defendant has a right to conduct the examination any further and I ask your honor to exclude it.

Witness: It seems to me it would be too exacting to confine the defense to the facts; if they are not allowed to get away from the facts, what have they to deal with?

Court: Mr. Bryan is willing to be examined. Go ahead.

Darrow: I read that years ago. Can you answer my question directly? If the day was lengthened by stopping either the earth or the sun, it must have been the earth?

A: Well, I should say so.

Q: Now, Mr. Bryan, have you ever pondered what would have happened to the earth if it had stood still?

A: No.

Q: You have not?

A: No; the God I believe in could have taken care of that, Mr. Darrow.

Q: I see. Have you ever pondered what would naturally happen to the earth if it stood still suddenly?

A: No.

Q: Don't you know it would have been converted into molten mass of matter?

A: You testify to that when you get on the stand, I will give you a chance.

Q: Don't you believe it?

A: I would want to hear expert testimony on that.

Q: You have never investigated that subject?

A: I don't think I have ever had the question asked.

Q: Or ever thought of it?

A: I have been too busy on things that I thought were of more importance than that.

Q: You believe the story of the flood to be a literal interpretation?

A: Yes, sir.

Q: When was that Flood?

A: I would not attempt to fix the date. The date is fixed, as suggested this morning.

Q: About 4004 B.C.?

A: That has been the estimate of a man that is accepted today. I would not say it is accurate.

Q: That estimate is printed in the Bible?

A: Everybody knows, at least, I think most of the people know, that was the estimate given.

Q: But what do you think that the Bible, itself says? Don't you know how it was arrived at?

A: I never made a calculation.

Q: A calculation from what?

A: I could not say.

Q: From the generations of man?

A: I would not want to say that.

Q: What do you think?

A: I do not think about things I don't think about.

Q: Do you think about things you do think about?

A: Well, sometimes.

(Laughter in the courtroom.)

Policeman: Let us have order . . .

Fundamentalists and Extremists

Stewart: Your honor, he is perfectly able to take care of this, but we are attaining no evidence. This is not competent evidence.

Witness: These gentleman have not had much chance—they did not come here to try this case. They came here to try revealed religion. I am here to defend it and they can ask me any question they please.

Court: All right. (Applause from the courtroom.)

Darrow: Great applause from the bleachers.

Witness: From those whom you call "Yokels."

Darrow: I have never called them yokels.

Witness: That is the ignorance of Tennessee, the bigotry.

Darrow: You mean who are applauding you? (Applause.)

Witness: Those are the people whom you insult.

Darrow: You insult every man of science and learning in the world because he does not believe in your fool religion.

Court: I will not stand for that.

Darrow: For what he is doing?

Court: I am talking to both of you . . .

Q: Wait until you get to me. Do you know anything about how many people there were in Egypt 3,500 years ago, or how many people there were in China 5,000 years ago?

A: No.

Q: Have you ever tried to find out?

A: No, sir. You are the first man I ever heard of who has been interested in it. (Laughter.)

Q: Mr. Bryan, am I the first man you ever heard of who has been interested in the age of human societies and primitive man?

A: You are the first man I ever heard speak of the number of people at those different periods.

Q: Where have you lived all your life?

A: Not near you. (Laughter and applause.)

Q: Nor near anybody of learning?

A: Oh, don't assume you know it all.

Q: Do you know there are thousands of books in our libraries on all those subjects I have been asking you about?

A: I couldn't say, but I will take your word for it . . .

Q: Have you any idea how old the earth is?

A: No.

Q: The Book you have introduced in evidence tells you, doesn't it?

A: I don't think it does, Mr. Darrow.

Q: Let's see whether it does; is this the one?

A: That is the one, I think.

Q: It says B.C. 4004?

224

Appendix A

A: That is Bishop Usher's calculation.

Q: That is printed in the Bible you introduced?

A: Yes, sir . . .

Q: Would you say that the earth was only 4000 years old?

A: Oh, no; I think it is much older than that.

Q: How much?

A: I couldn't say.

Q: Do you say whether the Bible itself says it is older than that?

A: I don't think it is older or not.

Q: Do you think the earth was made in six days?

A: Not six days of twenty-four hours.

Q: Doesn't it say so?

A: No, sir . . .

Court: Are you about through, Mr. Darrow?

Darrow: I want to ask a few more questions about the creation.

Court: I know. We are going to adjourn when Mr. Bryan comes off the stand for the day. Be very brief, Mr. Darrow. Of course, I believe I will make myself clearer. Of course, it is incompetent testimony before the jury. The only reason I am allowing this to go in at all is that they may have it in the appellate court as showing what the affidavit would be.

Witness: The reason I am answering is not for the benefit of the superior court. It is to keep these gentleman from saying I was afraid to meet them and let them question me, and I want the Christian world to know that any atheist, agnostic, unbeliever, can question me anytime as to my belief in God, and I will answer him.

Darrow: I want to take an exception to this conduct of this witness. He may be very popular down here in the hills . . .

Witness: Your honor, they have not asked a question legally and the only reason they have asked any question is for the purpose, as the question about Jonah was asked, for a chance to give this agnostic an opportunity to criticize a believer in the word of God; and I answered the question in order to shut his mouth so that he cannot go out and tell his atheistic friends that I would not answer his questions. That is the only reason, no more reason in the world.

Malone: Your honor on this very subject, I would like to say that I would have asked Mr. Bryan—and I consider myself as good a Christian as he is—every question that Mr. Darrow has asked him for the purpose of bringing out whether or not there is to be taken in this court a literal interpretation of the Bible, or whether, obviously, as these questions indicate, if a general and literal construction cannot be put upon the parts of the Bible which have been covered by Mr. Darrow's questions. I hope for the last time no further attempt will be made by counsel on the other side of the case, or Mr. Bryan, to say the defense is concerned at all with Mr. Darrow's particular religious views or lack of religious views. We are here as lawyers with the same right to our views. I have the same right to mine as a Christian as Mr. Bryan has to his, and we do not intend to have this case charged by Mr. Darrow's agnosticism or Mr. Bryan's brand of Christianity. (A great applause.)

Darrow: Mr. Bryan, do you believe that the first woman was Eve?

A: Yes.

Q: Do you believe she was literally made out of Adam's rib?

A: I do.

Q: Did you ever discover where Cain got his wife?

A: No, sir; I leave the agnostics to hunt for her.

Q: You have never found out?

A: I have never tried to find.

Q: You have never tried to find?

A: No.

Q: The Bible says he got one, doesn't it? Were there other people on the earth at that time?

A: I cannot say.

Q: You cannot say. Did that ever enter your consideration?

A: Never bothered me.

Q: There were no others recorded, but Cain got a wife.

A: That is what the Bible says.

Q: Where she came from you do not know. All right. Does the statement, "The morning and the evening were the first day," and "The morning and the evening were the second day," mean anything to you?

A: I do not think it necessarily means a twenty-four-hour day.

Q: You do not?

A: No.

Q: What do you consider it to be?

A: I have not attempted to explain it. If you will take the second chapter— let me have the book. (Examining Bible.) The fourth verse of the second chapter says: "These are the generations of the heavens and of the earth, when they were created in the day that the Lord God made the earth and the heavens," the word "day" there in the very next chapter is used to describe a period. I do not see that there is any necessity for construing the words, "the evening and the morning," as meaning necessarily a twenty-four-hour day, "in the day when the Lord made the heaven and the earth."

Q: Then, when the Bible said, for instance, "and God called the firmament heaven. And the evening and the morning were the second day," that does not necessarily mean twenty-four hours?

A: I do not think it necessarily does.

Q: Do you think it does or does not?
A: I know a great many think so.
Q: What do you think?
A: I do not think it does.
Q: You think those were not literal days?
A: I do not think they were twenty-four-hour days.
Q: What do you think about it?
A: That is my opinion—I do not know that my opinion is better on that subject than those who think it does.
Q: You do not think that?
A: No. But I think it would be just as easy for the kind of God we believe in to make the earth in six days as in six years or in 6 million years or in 600 million years. I do not think it important whether we believe one or the other.
Q: Do you think those were literal days?
A: My impression is they were periods, but I would not attempt to argue as against anybody who wanted to believe in literal days.
Q: I will read it to you from the Bible: "And the Lord God said unto the serpent, because thou hast done this, thou art cursed above all cattle, and above every beast of the field; upon thy belly shalt thou go and dust shalt thou eat all the days of thy life." Do you think that is why the serpent is compelled to crawl upon its belly?
A: I believe that.
Q: Have you any idea how the snake went before that time?
A: No, sir.
Q: Do you know whether he walked on his tail or not?
A: No, sir. I have no way to know. (Laughter in audience.)
Q: Now, you refer to the cloud that was put in heaven after the flood, the rainbow. Do you believe in that?
A: Read it.
Q: All right, Mr. Bryan, I will read it for you.
Bryan: Your Honor, I think I can shorten this testimony. The only purpose Mr. Darrow has is to slur at the Bible, but I will answer his question. I will answer it all at once, and I have no objection in the world, I want the world to know that this man, who does not believe in a God, is trying to use a court in Tennessee . . .
Darrow: I object to that.
Bryan: (Continuing) to slur at it, and while it will require time, I am willing to take it.
Darrow: I object to your statement. I am exempting you on your fool ideas that no intelligent Christian on earth believes.
Court: Court is adjourned until 9 o'clock tomorrow morning.

TRIAL DAY 8

Darrow asks jury to return a verdict of "guilty."

Darrow: May I say a few words to the jury? Gentlemen of the jury, we are sorry to have not had a chance to say anything to you. We will do it some other time. Now, we came down to offer evidence in this case and the court has held under the law that the evidence we had is not admissible, so all we can do is to take an exception and carry it to a higher court to see whether the evidence is admissible or not. As far as this case stands before the jury, the court has told you very plainly that if you think my client taught that man descended from a lower order of animals, you will find him guilty, and you heard the testimony of the boys on that questions and heard read the books, and there is no dispute about the facts. Scopes did not go on the stand, because he could not deny the statements made by the boys. I do not know how you may feel, I am not especially interested in it, but this case and this law will never be decided until it gets to a higher court, and it cannot get to a higher court probably, very well, unless you bring in a verdict. So, I do not want any of you to think we are going to find any fault with you as to your verdict. I am frank to say, while we think it is wrong, and we ought to have been permitted to put in our evidence, the court felt otherwise, as he had a right to hold. We cannot argue to you gentlemen under the instructions given by the court—we cannot even explain to you that we think you should return a verdict of not guilty. We do not see how you could. We do not ask it. We think we will save our point and take it to the higher court and settle whether the law is good, and also whether he should have permitted the evidence. I guess that is plain enough.

VERDICT AND SENTENCING

Court: Mr. Foreman, will you tell us whether you have agreed on a verdict?
Foreman: Yes, sir, we have your honor.
Court: What do you find?
Foreman: We have found for the state, found the defendant guilty.
Court: Did you fix the fine?
Foreman: No, sir.
Court: You leave it to the court?
Foreman: Leave it to the court.
Court: Mr. Scopes, will you come around here, please, sir. (The defendant presents himself before the court.)

Appendix A

Court: Mr. Scopes, the jury has found you guilty under this indictment, charging you with having taught in the schools of Rhea county, in violation of what is commonly known as the anti-evolution statute, which makes it unlawful for any teacher to teach in any of the public schools of the state, supported in whole or in part by the public school funds of the state, any theory that denies the story of the divine creation of man, and teach instead thereof that man has descended from a lower order of animals. The jury have found you guilty. The statute make this an offense punishable by fine of not less than $100 nor more than $500. The court now fixes your fine at $100, and imposes that fine upon you.

Court: Oh—Have you anything to say, Mr. Scopes, as to why the court should not impose punishment upon you?

Defendant J. T. Scopes: Your honor, I feel that I have been convicted of violating an unjust statute. I will continue in the future, as I have in the past, to oppose this law in any way I can. Any other action would be in violation of my ideal of academic freedom—that is, to teach the truth as guaranteed in our constitution of personal and religious freedom. I think the fine is unjust.

Final remarks of the attorneys and Judge Raulston.

McKenzie: On behalf of Rhea county and Gen. Stewart, and on behalf of the prosecution, I desire to say to the gentlemen who have just made their statements, that we are delighted to have had you with us. We have learned to take a broader view of life since you came. You have brought to us your ideas—your views—and we have communicated to you as best we could, some of our views. As to whether or not we like those views, that is a matter that should not address itself to us at this time, but we do appreciate your views, and while much has been said and much has been written about the narrow-minded people of Tennessee we do not feel hard toward you for having said that, because that is your idea. We people here want to be more broad-minded than some have given us credit for, and we appreciate your coming and we have been greatly elevated, edified and educated by your presence. And should the time ever come when you are back near the garden spot of the world, we hope that you will stop and stay awhile with us here in order that we may chat about the days of the past, when the Scopes trial was tried in Dayton. (Applause.)

Court: Col. Bryan, I will hear you.

Bryan: I don't know that there is any special reason why I should add to what has been said, and yet the subject has been presented from so many viewpoints that I hope the court will pardon me if I mention a viewpoint that has not been referred to. Dayton is the center and the seat of this trial largely by circumstance. We are told that more words have been sent across the ocean by cable to Europe and Australia about this trial than has ever been sent by cable in regard to anything else happening in the United States. That isn't because the trial is held in Dayton. It isn't because a schoolteacher has been subjected to the danger of a fine $100 to $500, but I think illustrates how people can be drawn into prominence by attaching themselves to a great cause. Causes stir the world. It is because it goes deep. It is because it extends wide, and because it reaches into a future beyond the power of man to see. Here has been fought out a little case of little consequence as a case, but the world is interested because it raises an issue, and that issue will some day be settled right, whether it is settled on our side or the other side. It is going to be settled right. There can be no settlement of a great cause without discussion, and people will not discuss a cause until their attention is drawn to it, and the value of this trial is not in any incident of the trial, it is not because of anybody who is attached to it, either in an official way or as counsel on either side. Human beings are mighty small, your honor. We are apt to magnify the personal element and we sometimes become inflated with our importance, but the world little cares for man as an individual. He is born, he works, he dies, but causes go on forever, and we who participated in this case may congratulate ourselves that we have attached ourselves to a mighty issue.

Darrow: May I say a word?

Court: Colonel, be glad to hear from you.

Darrow: I want to say a word. I want to say in thorough sincerity that I appreciate the courtesy of the counsel on the other side from the beginning of this case, at least the Tennessee counsel, that I appreciated the hospitality of the citizens here. I shall go away with a feeling of respect and gratitude toward them for their courtesy and their liberality toward us persons; and that I appreciate the kind, and I think I may say, general treatment of this court, who might have sent me to jail, but did not. (Laughter in the courtroom.)

And on the side of the controversy between the court and myself I have already ruled that the court was right, so I do not need to go further.

Court: Thank you.

Darrow: But, I mean it.

Court: Yes.

Darrow: Of course, there is much that Mr. Bryan has said that is true. And nature—nature, I refer to does not choose any special setting for more events. I fancy that the place where the Magna Carta was wrested from the barons in England was a very small place, probably not as big as Dayton. But events come along as they come along. I think this case will be remembered because it is the first case of this sort since we stopped trying people in America for witchcraft because here we have done our best to turn back the tide that has sought to force itself upon this—upon this modern world, of testing every fact in science by a religious dictum. That is all I care to say.

Court: My fellow citizens, I recently read somewhere what I think was a definition of a great man, and that was this: That he possesses a passion to know the truth and have the courage to declare it in the face of all opposition. It is easy enough, my friends, to have a passion to find a truth, or to find a fact, rather, that coincides with our preconceived notions and ideas, but it sometimes takes courage to search diligently for a truth, that may destroy our preconceived notions and ideas. Now, my friends, the people in America are great people. We are great people. We are great in the South, and they are great in the North. We are great because we are willing to lay down our differences when we fight the battle out and be friends. And, let me tell you, there are two things in this world that are indestructible that man cannot destroy, or no force in the world can destroy.

One is truth. You may crush it to the earth but it will rise again. It is indestructible, and the causes of the law of God. Another thing indestructible in America and in Europe and everywhere else, is the word of God, that He has given to man, that man use it as a waybill to the other world. Indestructible, my friends, by any force because it is the world of the Man, of the forces that created the universe, and He has said in His word that "My word will not perish" but will live forever.

I am glad to have had these gentlemen with us. This little talk of mine comes from my heart, gentlemen. I have had some difficult problems to decide in this lawsuit, and I only pray to God that I have decided them right. If I have not, the higher courts will find the mistake. But if I failed to decide them right, it was for the want of legal learning, and legal attainment, and not for the want of a disposition to do everybody justice. We are glad to have you with us. (Applause.)

Hays: May I, as one of the counsel for the defense, ask your honor to allow me to send you the *Origin of Species and the Descent of Man*, by Charles Darwin? (Laughter.)

Court: Yes; yes. (Laughter and applause.)

Court: Has anyone else anything to say.

(No response.)

If not— . . .

APPENDIX B

BROWN V. BOARD OF EDUCATION, 347 U.S. 483 (1954)

[portions of ruling are omitted]

Justice Earl Warren delivered the opinion of the Court.

These cases come to us from the States of Kansas, South Carolina, Virginia, and Delaware. They are premised on different facts and different local conditions, but a common legal question justifies their consideration together in this consolidated opinion.

In each of the cases, minors of the Negro race, through their legal representatives, seek the aid of the courts in obtaining admission to the public schools of their community on a nonsegregated basis. In each instance, they had been denied admission to schools attended by white children under laws requiring or permitting segregation according to race.

This segregation was alleged to deprive the plaintiffs of the equal protection of the laws under the Fourteenth Amendment. In each of the cases other than the Delaware case, a three-judge federal district court denied relief to the plaintiffs on the so-called "separate but equal" doctrine announced by this Court in *Plessy v. Ferguson.* . . .

Under that doctrine, equality of treatment is accorded when the races are provided substantially equal facilities, even though these facilities be separate. In the Delaware case, the Supreme Court of Delaware adhered to that doctrine, but ordered that the plaintiffs be admitted to the white schools because of their superiority to the Negro schools.

The plaintiffs contend that segregated public schools are not "equal" and cannot be made "equal," and that hence they are deprived of the equal protection of the laws. Because of the obvious importance of the question presented, the Court took jurisdiction. Argument was heard in the 1952 Term, and reargument was heard this Term on certain questions propounded by the Court.

Appendix B

Reargument was largely devoted to the circumstances surrounding the adoption of the Fourteenth Amendment in 1868. It covered exhaustively consideration of the Amendment in Congress, ratification by the states, then-existing practices in racial segregation, and the views of proponents and opponents of the Amendment.

This discussion and our own investigation convince us that, although these sources cast some light, it is not enough to resolve the problem with which we are faced. At best, they are inconclusive. The most avid proponents of the post-War Amendments undoubtedly intended them to remove all legal distinctions among "all persons born or naturalized in the United States."

Their opponents, just as certainly, were antagonistic to both the letter and the spirit of the Amendments and wished them to have the most limited effect. What others in Congress and the state legislatures had in mind cannot be determined with any degree of certainty.

An additional reason for the inconclusive nature of the Amendment's history with respect to segregated schools is the status of public education at that time. In the South, the movement toward free common schools, supported by general taxation, had not yet taken hold. Education of white children was largely in the hands of private groups. Education of Negroes was almost nonexistent, and practically all of the race were illiterate. In fact, any education of Negroes was forbidden by law in some states. Today, in contrast, many Negroes have achieved outstanding success in the arts and sciences, as well as in the business and professional world. It is true that public school education at the time of the Amendment had advanced further in the North, but the effect of the Amendment on Northern States was generally ignored in the congressional debates. Even in the North, the conditions of public education did not approximate those existing today. The curriculum was usually rudimentary; ungraded schools were common in rural areas; the school term was but three months a year in many states, and compulsory school attendance was virtually unknown.

As a consequence, it is not surprising that there should be so little in the history of the Fourteenth Amendment relating to its intended effect on public education.

In approaching this problem, we cannot turn the clock back to 1868, when the Amendment was adopted, or even to 1896, when *Plessy v. Ferguson* was written. We must consider public education in the light of its full development and its present place in American life throughout the Nation. Only in this way can it be determined if segregation in public schools deprives these plaintiffs of the equal protection of the laws.

Today, education is perhaps the most important function of state and local governments. Compulsory school attendance laws and the great expenditures for education both demonstrate our recognition of the importance of education to our democratic society. It is required in the performance of our most basic public responsibilities, even service in the armed forces. It is the very foundation of good citizenship.

Today it is a principal instrument in awakening the child to cultural values, in preparing him for later professional training, and in helping him to adjust normally to his environment. In these days, it is doubtful that any child may reasonably be expected to succeed in life if he is denied the opportunity of an education. Such an opportunity, where the state has undertaken to provide it, is a right which must be made available to all on equal terms.

We come then to the question presented: Does segregation of children in public schools solely on the basis of race, even though the physical facilities and other "tangible" factors may be equal, deprive the children of the minority group of equal educational opportunities? We believe that it does.

In *Sweatt v. Painter* . . . in finding that a segregated law school for Negroes could not provide them equal educational opportunities, this Court relied in large part on "those qualities which are incapable of objective measurement but which make for greatness in a law school."

In *McLaurin v. Oklahoma State Regents* . . . the Court, in requiring that a Negro admitted to a white graduate school be treated like all other students, again resorted to intangible considerations: ". . . his ability to study, to engage in discussions and exchange views with other students, and, in general, to learn his profession."

Such considerations apply with added force to children in grade and high schools. To separate them from others of similar age and qualifications solely because of their race generates a feeling of inferiority as to their status in the community that may affect their hearts and minds in a way unlikely ever to be undone. The effect of this separation on their educational opportunities was well stated by a finding in the Kansas case by a court which nevertheless felt compelled to rule against the Negro plaintiffs:

Segregation of white and colored children in public schools has a detrimental effect upon the colored children. The impact is greater when it has the sanction of the law, for the policy of separating the races is usually interpreted as denoting the inferiority of the negro group. A sense of inferiority affects the motivation of a child to learn. Segregation with the sanction of law, therefore, has a tendency to [retard] the educational and mental development of negro children and to deprive them of some of the benefits they would receive in a racial[ly] integrated school system.

Whatever may have been the extent of psychological knowledge at the time of *Plessy v. Ferguson*, this finding is amply supported by modern authority. Any language in *Plessy v. Ferguson* contrary to this finding is rejected.

We conclude that, in the field of public education, the doctrine of "separate but equal" has no place. Separate educational facilities are inherently unequal. Therefore, we hold that the plaintiffs and others similarly situated for whom the actions have been brought are, by reason of the segregation complained of, deprived of the equal protection of the laws guaranteed by the Fourteenth Amendment. This disposition makes unnecessary any discussion whether such segregation also violates the Due Process Clause of the Fourteenth Amendment.

Because these are class actions, because of the wide applicability of this decision, and because of the great variety of local conditions, the formulation of decrees in these cases presents problems of considerable complexity. On reargument, the consideration of appropriate relief was necessarily subordinated to the primary question—the constitutionality of segregation in public education.

We have now announced that such segregation is a denial of the equal protection of the laws. In order that we may have the full assistance of the parties in formulating decrees, the cases will be restored to the docket, and the parties are requested to present further argument on Questions 4 and 5 previously propounded by the Court for the reargument this Term.

The Attorney General of the United States is again invited to participate. The Attorneys General of the states requiring or permitting segregation in public education will also be permitted to appear as *amici curiae* upon request to do so by September 15, 1954, and submission of briefs by October 1, 1954.

It is so ordered.

APPENDIX C

ROE V. WADE, 410 U.S. 113 (1973)

[portions of ruling are omitted]

Justice Harry A. Blackmun delivered the opinion of the Court.

. . . We forthwith acknowledge our awareness of the sensitive and emotional nature of the abortion controversy, of the vigorous opposing views, even among physicians, and of the deep and seemingly absolute convictions that the subject inspires. One's philosophy, one's experiences, one's exposure to the raw edges of human existence, one's religious training, one's attitudes toward life and family and their values, and the moral standards one establishes and seeks to observe, are all likely to influence and to color one's thinking and conclusions about abortion.

In addition, population growth, pollution, poverty, and racial overtones tend to complicate and not to simplify the problem.

Our task, of course, is to resolve the issue by constitutional measurement, free of emotion and of predilection. We seek earnestly to do this, and, because we do, we have inquired into, and in this opinion place some emphasis upon, medical and medical-legal history and what that history reveals about man's attitudes toward the abortion procedure over the centuries. We bear in mind, too, Mr. Justice Holmes' admonition in his now-vindicated dissent in *Lochner v. New York* . . .

> *[The Constitution] is made for people of fundamentally differing views, and the accident of our finding certain opinions natural and familiar or novel and even shocking ought not to conclude our judgment upon the question whether statutes embodying them conflict with the Constitution of the United States.*

The Texas statutes that concern us here . . . make it a crime to "procure an abortion," as therein defined, or to attempt one, except with respect to "an abortion procured or attempted by medical advice for the purpose of saving the life of the mother." Similar statutes are in existence in a majority of the States . . .

The principal thrust of appellant's attack on the Texas statutes is that they improperly invade a right, said to be possessed by the pregnant woman, to choose to terminate her pregnancy. Appellant would discover this right in the concept of personal "liberty" embodied in the Fourteenth Amendment's Due Process Clause; or in personal, marital, familial, and sexual privacy said to be protected by the Bill of Rights or its penumbras. . . . Before addressing this claim, we feel it desirable briefly to survey, in several aspects, the history of abortion, for such insight as that history may afford us, and then to examine the state purposes and interests behind the criminal abortion laws.

It perhaps is not generally appreciated that the restrictive criminal abortion laws in effect in a majority of States today are of relatively recent vintage. Those laws, generally proscribing abortion or its attempt at any time during pregnancy except when necessary to preserve the pregnant woman's life, are not of ancient or even of common law origin. Instead, they derive from statutory changes effected, for the most part, in the latter half of the 19th century . . .

It is thus apparent that, at common law, at the time of the adoption of our Constitution, and throughout the major portion of the 19th century, abortion was viewed with less disfavor than under most American statutes currently in effect. Phrasing it another way, a woman enjoyed a substantially broader right to terminate a pregnancy than she does in most States today. At least with respect to the early stage of pregnancy, and very possibly without such a limitation, the opportunity to make this choice was present in this country well into the 19th century. Even later, the law continued for some time to treat less punitively an abortion procured in early pregnancy . . .

Three reasons have been advanced to explain historically the enactment of criminal abortion laws in the 19th century and to justify their continued existence.

It has been argued occasionally that these laws were the product of a Victorian social concern to discourage illicit sexual conduct. Texas, however, does not advance this justification in the present case, and it appears that no court or commentator has taken the argument seriously . . .

A second reason is concerned with abortion as a medical procedure. When most criminal abortion laws were first enacted, the procedure was a hazardous one for the woman. This was particularly true prior to the development of antisepsis. . . . Abortion mortality was high. Even after 1900, and perhaps until as late as the development of antibiotics in the 1940s, standard modern techniques such as dilation and curettage were not nearly so safe as they are today. Thus it has been argued that a State's real concern in enacting a criminal abortion law was to protect the pregnant woman, that is, to restrain her from submitting to a procedure that placed her life in serious jeopardy.

Modern medical techniques have altered this situation. Appellants and various *amici* refer to medical data indicating that abortion in early pregnancy, that is, prior to the end of first trimester, although not without risk, is now relatively safe. Mortality rates for women undergoing early abortions, where the procedure is legal, appear to be as low or lower than the rates for normal childbirth. Consequently, any interest of the State in protecting the woman from an inherently hazardous procedure, except when it would be equally dangerous for her to forgo it, has largely disappeared. Of course, important state interests in the area of health and medical standards do remain. The State has a legitimate interest in seeing to it that abortion, like any other medical procedure, is performed under circumstances that insure maximum safety for the patient. . . . Moreover, the risk to the woman increases as her pregnancy continues. Thus the State retains a definite interest in protecting the woman's own health and safety when an abortion is proposed at a late stage of pregnancy.

The third reason is the State's interest—some phrase it in terms of duty—in protecting prenatal life. Some of the argument for this justification rests on the theory that a new human life is present from the moment of conception. The State's interest and general obligation to protect life then extends, it is argued, to prenatal life. Only when the life of the pregnant woman itself is at stake, balanced against the life she carries within her, should the interests of the embryo or fetus not prevail. Logically, of course, a legitimate state interest in this area need not stand or fall on acceptance of the belief that life begins at conception or at some other point prior to live birth. In assessing the State's interest, recognition may be given to the less rigid claim that as long as at least *potential* life is involved, the State may assert interests beyond the protection of the pregnant woman alone . . .

It is with these interests, and the weight to be attached to them, that this case is concerned.

The Constitution does not explicitly mention any right of privacy. In a line of decisions, however, going back perhaps as far as *Union Pacific R. Co. v. Botsford*, 141 U.S. 250, 251 (1891), the Court has recognized that a right of personal privacy, or a guarantee of certain areas or zones of privacy, does exist under the Constitution. In varying contexts, the Court or individual Justices have, indeed, found at least the roots of that right in the First Amendment; . . . in the Fourth and Fifth Amendments; . . . in the penumbras of the Bill of Rights; . . . in the Ninth Amendment; . . . or in the concept of liberty guaranteed by the first section of the Fourteenth Amendment. . . . These decisions make it clear that only personal rights that can be deemed "fundamental" or "implicit in the concept of ordered liberty" . . . are included in this guarantee of personal privacy. They also make it clear that the right has some extension to activities relating to marriage, procreation, contraception, family relationships, and child-rearing and education.

This right of privacy, whether it be founded in the Fourteenth Amendment's concept of personal liberty and restrictions upon state action, as we feel it is, or, as the District Court determined, in the Ninth Amendment's reservation of rights to the people, is broad enough to encompass a woman's decision whether or not to terminate her pregnancy. The detriment that the State would impose upon the pregnant woman by denying this choice altogether is apparent. Specific and direct harm medically diagnosable even in early pregnancy may be involved. Maternity, or additional offspring, may force upon the woman a distressful life and future. Psychological harm may be imminent. Mental and physical health may be taxed by child care. There is also the distress, for all concerned, associated with the unwanted child, and there is the problem of bringing a child into a family already unable, psychologically and otherwise, to care for it. In other cases, as in this one, the additional difficulties and continuing stigma of unwed motherhood may be involved. All these are factors the woman and her responsible physician necessarily will consider in consultation.

On the basis of elements such as these, appellant and some *amici* argue that the woman's right is absolute and that she is entitled to terminate her pregnancy at whatever time, in whatever way, and for whatever reason she alone chooses. With this we do not agree. Appellant's arguments that Texas either has no valid interest at all in regulating the abortion decision, or no interest strong enough to support any limitation upon the woman's sole determination, are unpersuasive. The Court's decisions recognizing a right of privacy also acknowledge that some state regulation in areas protected by that right is appropriate. As noted above, a State may properly assert important interests in safeguarding health, in maintaining medical standards, and in protecting potential life. At some point in pregnancy, these respective interests become sufficiently compelling to sustain regulation of the factors that govern the abortion decision. The privacy right involved, therefore, cannot be said to be absolute . . .

We, therefore, conclude that the right of personal privacy includes the abortion decision, but that this right is not unqualified, and must be considered against important state interests in regulation . . .

The appellee and certain *amici* argue that the fetus is a "person" within the language and meaning of the Fourteenth Amendment. In support of this, they outline at length and in detail the well known facts of fetal development. If this suggestion of personhood is established, the appellant's case, of course, collapses, for the fetus' right to life would then be guaranteed specifically by the Amendment. The appellant conceded as much on reargument. On the other hand, the appellee conceded on reargument that no case could be cited that holds that a fetus is a person within the meaning of the Fourteenth Amendment.

The Constitution does not define "person" in so many words. Section 1 of the Fourteenth Amendment contains three references to "person." The first, in defining "citizens," speaks of "persons born or naturalized in the United States." The word also appears both in the Due Process Clause and in the Equal Protection Clause. "Person" is used in other places in the Constitution. . . . But in nearly all these instances, the use of the word is such that it has application only post-natally. None indicates, with any assurance, that it has any possible pre-natal application . . .

Texas urges that, apart from the Fourteenth Amendment, life begins at conception and is present throughout pregnancy, and that, therefore, the State has a compelling interest in protecting that life from and after conception. We need not resolve the difficult question of when life begins. When those trained in the respective disciplines of medicine, philosophy, and theology are unable to arrive at any consensus, the judiciary, at this point in the development of man's knowledge, is not in a position to speculate as to the answer.

It should be sufficient to note briefly the wide divergence of thinking on this most sensitive and difficult question. There has always been strong support for the view that life does not begin until live birth. This was the belief of the Stoics. It appears to be the predominant, though not the unanimous, attitude of the Jewish faith. It may be taken to represent also the position of a large segment of the Protestant community, insofar as that can be ascertained; organized groups that have taken a formal position on the abortion issue have generally regarded abortion as a matter for the conscience of the individual and her family. As we have noted, the common law found greater significance in quickening. Physicians and their scientific colleagues have regarded that event with less interest and have tended to focus either upon conception, upon live birth, or upon the interim point at which the fetus becomes "viable," that is, potentially able to live outside the mother's womb, albeit with artificial aid. Viability is usually placed at about seven months (28 weeks) but may occur earlier, even at 24 weeks . . . Substantial problems for precise definition of this view are posed, however, by new embryological data that purport to indicate that conception is a "process" over time, rather than an event, and by new medical techniques such as menstrual extraction, the "morning-after" pill, implantation of embryos, artificial insemination, and even artificial wombs.

. . . We do not agree that, by adopting one theory of life, Texas may override the rights of the pregnant woman that are at stake. We repeat, however, that the State does have an important and legitimate interest in preserving and protecting the health of the pregnant woman, whether she be a resident of the State or a nonresident who seeks medical consultation and treatment there, and that it has still *another* important and legitimate interest in protecting the potentiality of human life. These interests are separate and distinct. Each grows in substantiality as the woman approaches term and, at a point during pregnancy, each becomes "compelling."

With respect to the State's important and legitimate interest in the health of the mother, the "compelling" point, in the light of present medical knowledge, is at approximately the end of the first trimester. This is so because of the now-established medical fact . . . that, until the end of the first trimester, mortality in abortion may be less than mortality in normal childbirth. It follows that, from and after this point, a State may regulate the abortion procedure to the extent that the regulation reasonably relates to the preservation and protection of maternal health. Examples of permissible state regulation in this area are requirements as to the qualifications of the person who is to perform the abortion; as to the licensure of that person; as to the facility in which the procedure is to be performed, that is, whether it must be a hospital or may be a clinic or some other place of less-than-hospital status; as to the licensing of the facility; and the like.

This means, on the other hand, that, for the period of pregnancy prior to this "compelling" point, the attending physician, in consultation with his patient, is free to determine, without regulation by the State, that, in his medical judgment, the patient's pregnancy should be terminated. If that decision is reached, the judgment may be effectuated by an abortion free of interference by the State . . .

With respect to the State's important and legitimate interest in potential life, the "compelling" point is at viability. This is so because the fetus then presumably has the capability of meaningful life outside the mother's womb. State regulation protective of fetal life after viability thus has both logical and biological justifications. If the State is interested in protecting fetal life after viability, it may go so far as to proscribe abortion during that period, except when it is necessary to preserve the life or health of the mother.

Measured against these standards, Texas, in restricting legal abortions to those "procured or attempted by medical advice for the purpose of saving the life of the mother," sweeps too broadly. The statute makes no distinction between abortions performed early in pregnancy and those performed later, and it limits to a single reason, "saving" the mother's life, the legal justification for the procedure. The statute, therefore, cannot survive the constitutional attack made upon it here . . .

Justice William H. Rehnquist filed a dissenting opinion.

. . . I would reach a conclusion opposite to that reached by the Court. I have difficulty in concluding, as the Court does, that the right of "privacy" is involved in this case. Texas, by the statute here challenged, bars the performance of a medical abortion by a licensed physician on a plaintiff such as Roe. A transaction resulting in an operation such as this is not "private" in the ordinary usage of that word. Nor is the "privacy" that the Court finds here even a distant relative of the freedom from searches and seizures protected by the Fourth Amendment to the Constitution, which the Court has referred to as embodying a right to privacy . . .

If the Court means by the term "privacy" no more than that the claim of a person to be free from unwanted state regulation of consensual transactions may be a form of "liberty" protected by the Fourteenth Amendment, there is no doubt that similar claims have been upheld in our earlier decisions on the basis of that liberty. I agree with the statement of Mr. Justice Stewart in his concurring opinion that the "liberty," against deprivation of which without due process the Fourteenth Amendment protects, embraces more than the rights found in the Bill of Rights. But that liberty is not guaranteed absolutely against deprivation, only against deprivation without due process of law. The test traditionally applied in the area of social and economic legislation is whether or not a law such as that challenged has a rational relation to a valid state objective. . . . But the Court's sweeping invalidation of any restrictions on abortion during the first trimester is impossible to justify under that standard, and the conscious weighing of competing factors that the Court's opinion apparently substitutes for the established test is far more appropriate to a legislative judgment than to a judicial one.

The Court eschews the history of the Fourteenth Amendment in its reliance on the "compelling state interest" test. . . . But the Court adds a new wrinkle to this test by transposing it from the legal considerations associated with the Equal Protection Clause of the Fourteenth Amendment to this case arising under the Due Process Clause of the Fourteenth Amendment. Unless I misapprehend the consequences of this transplanting of the "compelling state interest test," the Court's opinion will accomplish the seemingly impossible feat of leaving this area of the law more confused than it found it.

While the Court's opinion quotes from the dissent of Mr. Justice Holmes in *Lochner v. New York*, . . . the result it reaches is more closely attuned to the majority opinion of Mr. Justice Peckham in that case. As in *Lochner* and similar cases applying substantive due process standards to economic and social welfare legislation, the adoption of the compelling state interest standard will inevitably require this Court to examine the legislative policies and pass on the wisdom of these policies in the very process of deciding whether a particular state interest put forward may or may not be "compelling." The decision here to break pregnancy into three distinct terms and to outline the permissible restrictions the State may impose in each one, for example, partakes more of judicial legislation than it does of a determination of the intent of the drafters of the Fourteenth Amendment.

The fact that a majority of the States reflecting, after all, the majority sentiment in those States, have had restrictions on abortions for at least a century is a strong indication, it seems to me, that the asserted right to an abortion is not "so rooted in the traditions and conscience of our people as to be ranked as fundamental." . . . Even today, when society's views on abortion are changing, the very existence of the debate is evidence that the "right" to an abortion is not so universally accepted as the appellant would have us believe.

To reach its result, the Court necessarily has had to find within the scope of the Fourteenth Amendment a right that was apparently completely unknown to the drafters of the Amendment. As early as 1821, the first state law dealing directly with abortion was enacted by the Connecticut Legislature. . . . By the time of the adoption of the Fourteenth Amendment in 1868, there were at least 36 laws enacted by state or territorial legislatures limiting abortion. While many States have amended or updated their laws, 21 of the laws on the books in 1868 remain in effect today. Indeed, the Texas state struck down today was, as the majority notes, first enacted in 1857, and "has remained substantially unchanged to the present time." . . .

There apparently was no question concerning the validity of this provision or of any of the other state statutes when the Fourteenth Amendment was adopted. The only conclusion possible from this history is that the drafters did not intend to have the Fourteenth Amendment withdraw from the States the power to legislate with respect to this matter . . .

For all of the foregoing reasons, I respectfully dissent.

INDEX

Locators in **boldface** indicate main topics. Locators followed by *g* indicate glossary entries.

Index

arson 14, 32, 124
Animal Liberation
Front, use by 100
Earth Liberation
Front, use by 48,
104, 105
pro-life activists, use
by 15, 87
articles and papers
on extremism
179–189
on fundamentalism
150–159
Articles of Confederation
25
Aryan Congress 43, 97,
111
Aryan Nations **42–43**,
111, 116, 194–195
Aryan Congress and
97, 111
court cases involving
42–43, 100, 105,
111
Aryans 42, 124
assassination 120
by anarchists 27
by Islamic
fundamentalists
100
by neo-Nazis 32,
119
federal legislation
56, 57
Ashcroft, John 21
ATF. *See* Bureau of
Alcohol, Tobacco and
Firearms

B
Bakker, Jim 18, 99, **109**,
110, 114, 120
Bakker, Tammy Faye 18,
109, 114
Bakunin, Mikhail 26–27,
123

Baptist Church 123*g*
Bari, Judi 47, 107
Barrett, James 102
Bauer, Gary 20
Beach, Henry L. 44
Beam, Louis 40, 45, 100
Behold a Pale Horse
(Cooper) 46
Berg, Alan 43, 98, 116
Berger, Victor L. 28
Berry, Shawn Alan 40,
103
Bible 3–4, 8–10
apocalypse 123
bans on school Bible
reading 10, 76,
93
biblical books
Acts 125
Daniel 123
Genesis 3, 78
John 123
Mark 123
Revelation 123,
125
Thessalonians
123
and Darwinism 8,
63
and government
policy 16
and Higher
Criticism 3, 8,
125
inerrancy 8, 9, 64,
90, 125
interpretation 4
Mosaic law 126
and Puritanism 5
and racism 10, 42,
43, 101
sola scriptura 4
translations 4
Bible Balloon Project
31, 92, 115

bibliographic resources
143–191
bookstore catalogs
138
library catalogs
137–138
on extremism
160–191
on fundamentalism
143–160
periodical databases
138–139
Billings, Robert 16
bin Laden, Osama 22,
107
biographical listing
109–121
bioterrorism 106
Birth of a Nation, The
(Griffith) 29, 91
Black, Don 38, 39, 101
Black Bloc anarchists 50
Black Legion 30
Black Liberation Army
35
black nationalism 34
Black Panther Party
34–35, 36–37, 94, 95,
112, 117
Blanton, Thomas, Jr. 33,
105, 107
BLM. *See* Bureau of
Land Management
Blue Book (Welch) 120
Blue Eyed Devils, the 39
Bob Jones University 9,
116
Bolshevik Revolution 28
bombs
anarchists, use by
27, 90
abortion clinics, use
against 15, 98,
103

247

Index

Index

Index

Index

Index

Tribulation, the 8, 42, 126
Trochmann, John 45, 46, 101
Truman, Harry S. 10, 115, 120
Turner Diaries, The (Pierce) 41, 43, 98, 116, 117, 118
TWP. *See* Wildlands Project, The

U

UKA. *See* United Klans of America
Unabomber. *See* Kaczynski, Theodore
Unabomber Manifesto 102, 116
United Klans of America (UKA) 33, 40, 99
United Nations 44, 127
Uniting and Strengthening America by Providing Appropriate Tools Required to Intercept and Obstruct Terrorism Act of 2001. *See* USA PATRIOT Act of 2001
University of Southern California 113
USA PATRIOT Act of 2001 58
U.S. Klans 32
U.S. v. McWilliams 30–31, 92

V

veganism 48
Veneman, Ann 49
videos
on extremism 189–191
on fundamentalism 159–160
Vietnam War 34, 35, 94, 114, 115
Vigilantes of Christendom, The (Hoskins) 43
Viguerie, Richard 16
Voting Rights Act of 1965 33
vouchers, school 13

W

Waagner, Clayton Lee 15
Waco (Texas) standoff 45, 46, 101, 117
Wallace, George 118
Wallace v. Jaffree **82–83**
WAR. *See* White Aryan Resistance
Wardell, Dave 12
Washington for Jesus rally 102, 110
Washington Post 49, 102, 116
watchdog and antihate web sites 136
Watergate scandal 10, 115
Watson, Paul 47
Watts (Los Angeles) 38, 96
WCOTC. *See* World Church of the Creator
Weathermen 36, 95, 97
Weather Underground 36, 95, 97
Weaver, Randy 44–45, 101, 102, 117
Weaver, Sammy 44
Weaver, Vicky 44–45
web sites 131–137
academic sites 135–136
civil liberties sites 136
fundamentalist and extremist sites 137
government sites 135
watchdog and antihate sites 136
Webster v. Reproductive Health Services 82, **83–85**, 86, 100
Weiner, Lee 37
Welch, Robert 31, 93, 120–121
Westboro (Kansas) Baptist Church 13
Weyrich, Paul 16, 20, 97, 104, **121**
When Life Hurts, We Can Help (Army of God) 15
White Aryan Resistance (WAR) **40–41**, 100, 117, 201–202
Whitefield, George 7, 89
Whitehorn, Laura 98
White Man's Bible 41
white power music 39, 41
white separatism 42–43, 111, 113, 116, 127
white supremacy **38–43**, 98, 111, 124, 126, 127g. *See also* Christian Identity, Ku Klux Klan, Nazism, neo-Nazism, skinheads
white worship 41
White Youth Alliance 113
Whitney, Charlotte Anita 64–65

DATE DUE